education in the arts

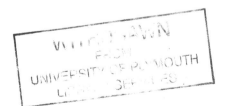

education in the arts

teaching and learning in the contemporary curriculum

Edited by Christine Sinclair, Neryl Jeanneret and John O'Toole

OXFORD
UNIVERSITY PRESS
AUSTRALIA & NEW ZEALAND

OXFORD
UNIVERSITY PRESS
AUSTRALIA & NEW ZEALAND

253 Normanby Road, South Melbourne, Victoria 3205, Australia

Oxford University Press is a department of the University of Oxford.
It furthers the University's objective of excellence in research,
scholarship, and education by publishing worldwide in

Oxford New York

Auckland Cape Town Dar es Salaam Hong Kong Karachi
Kuala Lumpur Madrid Melbourne Mexico City Nairobi
New Delhi Shanghai Taipei Toronto

With offices in

Argentina Austria Brazil Chile Czech Republic France Greece
Guatemala Hungary Italy Japan Poland Portugal Singapore
South Korea Switzerland Thailand Turkey Ukraine Vietnam

OXFORD is a trademark of Oxford University Press
in the UK and in certain other countries

National Library of Australia Cataloguing-in-Publication data

Sinclair, Christine.

Education in the arts: teaching and learning in the contemporary curriculum/
Christine Sinclair, Neryl Jeanneret, John O'Toole.

9780195560565 (pbk.)

Includes index.
Bibliography.

Arts—Study and teaching—Australia. Effective teaching.

Jeanneret, Neryl.
O'Toole, J. (John)

700.71

Edited by Edward Caruso
Cover design, text design and typeset by Kerry Cooke, eggplant communications
Cover images by Miflippo / Cora Reed / Dimitris Kolyris / Galina Barskaya / Pavel Losevsky / Tadija Savic
Proofread by Liz Filleul
Indexed by Jeanne Rudd
Printed in Hong Kong by Sheck Wah Tong Printing Press Ltd.

Contents

List of Figures

List of Tables

About the Authors

Jane Bird is currently a lecturer in drama education in Artistic and Creative Education at The University of Melbourne. She lectures in both undergraduate and postgraduate studies of Drama Education. Jane is the co-author of the VCE student textbook series *Acting Smart* for both Drama and Theatre Studies that are in their fifth edition. She has had ongoing relationships with the VCAA in various roles, from writer of curriculum documents and exam papers to performance examiner for Drama and Theatre Studies. Jane taught in a range of secondary schools, both government and independent, for over fifteen years. She is currently completing her Masters of Education at The University of Melbourne, focusing on the processes of constructing an ethnographic performance.

Robert Brown is a visual arts lecturer working in primary and early childhood education at the Melbourne Graduate School of Education. He also acts as project manager at The University of Melbourne's Early Learning Centre, Abbotsford, a research and demonstration centre that provides an arts-centred early childhood program for children aged 3–5 years. In 2007 Robert began a three-year role as Senior Research Associate in an ARC project investigating the practices of ArtPlay, a unique facility established by The City of Melbourne, which provides artist-led programs for children.

Jan Deans is a senior lecturer within the Graduate School of Education at The University of Melbourne and Director of the University's research and demonstration Early Learning Centre. During her career Jan has taught in early childhood, primary, tertiary, and special education settings. Her research interests include learning through dance, story as a vehicle for cross-cultural teaching and learning, quality assurance in early childhood, and arts-based teaching and learning. She has worked with Indigenous communities in Australia and with children and teachers in China, Singapore, and Japan, and has extensive experience as an early childhood consultant within the education and government sector.

Kate Donelan is one of Australia's leading drama educators. She is the head of drama within Artistic and Creative Education in the Melbourne Graduate School of Education. She has played an active role in arts curriculum and policy development in Australia, and has held leadership positions in peak arts education organisations, school councils, and theatre company boards. She was President of the National Association of Drama in Education and the Vice-President of IDEA (the International Drama/Theatre and Education Association). She was the recipient of the inaugural Drama Australia President's award for outstanding contribution to Australian drama education. She is currently undertaking two nationally funded research projects examining the social impact of the creative arts on marginalised young people in schools, community, and custodial settings. In 2007 she received the American Alliance for Theatre and Education Distinguished Dissertation award for her longitudinal ethnographic study of intercultural learning within a performing arts project in a multicultural school community. Her research and practice reflects a longstanding commitment to 'intercultural understanding' and the development of 'multicultural literacy' in Australian classrooms and drama workshops.

Kelly Freebody is a lecturer in drama and English education in the Faculty of Education and Social Work at The University of Sydney. Her teaching and research interests include educational drama, theatre, literacy, social justice, and qualitative research methods, particularly conversation analysis and membership categorisation analysis.

Wesley Imms is the head of visual art education in Artistic and Creative Education at the Melbourne Graduate School of Education, and has held leadership positions in peak art education organisations, including Australian Art Education and Art Education Victoria. His teaching experience includes many years in classrooms within Australia and overseas. His research and publications include national and international journal articles, as well as teacher support materials on a diverse array of topics that overlap visual art education and boys' education, information and communications technology (ICT) in classrooms, and teacher training. He is currently national vice-president of Art Education Australia.

Neryl Jeanneret is the head of music education in Artistic and Creative Education at the Melbourne Graduate School of Education, and has held leadership positions in peak music education organisations, including the Australian Society for Music Education and the International Society for Music Education's Policy Commission. She has a background in curriculum design for music classrooms, having served as an advisor to the New South Wales Department of Education and Board of Studies for many years. Her teaching experience includes music for early childhood, primary, and secondary pre-service teachers, as well as educational psychology, assessment, curriculum, sociology, and the psychology of music in undergraduate and postgraduate programs. She has lectured to pre-service teachers in Australia, Canada, and the United States, as well as presenting at both national and international forums. Her publications include national and international journal articles, as well as teacher support materials for the Australian Music Centre, Musica Viva, Opera Australia, the Sydney Symphony Orchestra, the NSW Board of Studies, and the NSW Department of Education and Training.

Pam Macintyre is a lecturer in the Bachelor of Education Primary Course, the Bachelor of Teaching and Master of Education courses, specialising in children's and young adult literature. She was the Victorian Judge for the Children's Book Council Awards in 1996 and 1997, a member of the Victorian Premier's Literary Awards Committee from 1994 to 1996, has been a judge for the Aurealis Awards, the Victorian Premier's Literary Awards, and the

Nestlé Write around Australia Competition. She is a member of the National Executive of the Children's Book Council of Australia, a member the Schools Programming Committee of the Melbourne Writers' Festival, and a member of the Australasian Children's Literature Association for Research (ACLAR). She regularly reviews children's and young adult books for the *Australian Book Review* and occasionally for the *Age*. She is the editor of the quarterly journal *Viewpoint*, on books for young adults.

John O'Toole is Professor of arts education in Artistic and Creative Education at the Melbourne Graduate School of Education. He also holds the Chair of Arts Education at The University of Melbourne. He was formerly Professor of Drama Education and Applied Theatre at Griffith University. He has taught drama and arts education for nearly forty years on all continents and to all ages, and has written many books on drama, besides being a community playwright and director. He was founder-member of the Queensland, Australian and international drama education associations (Drama Queensland, Drama Australia, and IDEA), and Director of Publications and 1996 Congress Co-Convenor for IDEA. In 2001 he received the American Alliance for Theater and Education Award for Lifetime Research.

Jo Raphael is lecturer in drama education in the Faculty of Arts and Education at Deakin University in Melbourne where she teaches in both graduate and undergraduate programs. She has a background in teaching in schools, and her research and consultancy work provides regular opportunities for her to spend time within primary and secondary school classrooms and in community arts contexts. Jo's recent research interests and publications have been in the areas of drama education, special needs, drama and learning across the curriculum and within cultural institutions, and reflective learning through digital technologies. As a committee member of Drama Victoria for many years, Jo has worked on a range of drama education initiatives including *The VINE*, a project involving local and international sharing of performance-making processes through blogs. Jo is also a member of the executive of Drama Australia, where she currently holds the position of Director of Projects.

Julia Reid is a performing arts teacher at Carlton North Primary School in Melbourne's inner north. Her eclectic career includes work in the children's book industry, writing funding policies for children's disability services, and as a private music mentor and therapist. In addition to teaching in school-based settings, she writes plays and musicals for children's theatre: writing, organising, and overseeing large-scale performance events. She also spent many years as artistic and musical director of the children's theatre ensemble, Julia and the Baby Grands.

Richard Sallis is a lecturer in drama education in Artistic and Creative Education at the Melbourne Graduate School of Education. He has taught drama in both primary and secondary schools. He is a former President, and the current Director of International Liaison, for Drama Australia, the national drama educators' association. He is a co-author of the *Acting Smart* textbooks for Year 12 drama studies, and has for many years been involved in curriculum writing for drama education in Australia. His research interests include gender, drama/theatre and innovative ethnographic methodology. He is a recipient of the Freda Cohen Award from The University of Melbourne for the most meritorious Masters thesis (Research) in education. He is currently completing a PhD focusing on boys and drama education.

Christine Sinclair is a senior lecturer in writing at Swinburne University. She teaches in the postgraduate writing program, with particular interests in writing for research and for the theatre. Prior to this she was a Research Fellow in Artistic and Creative Education at The University of Melbourne. She has been a lecturer in drama and arts education at the undergraduate and post-graduate level at a number of universities. In addition to pre-service teacher training at primary and secondary school level, Christine has convened courses in acting, directing, and theatre in the community. She is also a freelance community artist, working as a writer and director in many community settings. Her PhD research was based at a primary school and centred on the creation of a whole school festival of performance for children and the wider community.

Andrew Swainston completed a Bachelor of Education degree at Melbourne State College in 1983. In 2000 he completed a Masters degree (Music Education) at the Institute of Education, University of London. Andrew worked as a music teacher for 20 years in Australia and the United Kingdom. He was Head of Music for five years at Lilian Baylis School in North Lambeth, London. In recent years Andrew was Music Director and Arts Co-ordinator at Williamstown High School Middle Years campus. Since 2006 he has been a music education lecturer at The University of Melbourne, and is currently undertaking a PhD studying the experiences of music teachers in their first two years of teaching. He is a regular columnist for the national music education publication *Music in Action*, and was a member of the UK-based World Music big band Bassa Bassa from 1991 to 1994.

Marnee Watkins is a lecturer in visual arts education in Artistic and Creative Education at the Melbourne Graduate School of Education. She is currently engaged in doctoral research focused on art-rich picture books, thinking and inquiry in the primary classroom. Marnee has twenty-eight years' experience in Victoria and the Northern Territory as a specialist art and generalist classroom teacher in pre-primary, primary, and middle years, and as a lecturer to pre-service teachers on visual arts in primary education and on curriculum development. Marnee has been actively involved in teacher professional development and school and system-wide curriculum projects.

Sarah Young is a freelance arts educator and she works with children and adults in a variety of settings. Sarah's focus is to develop story-making through drama and dance, and she encourages teachers to explore these art forms to enhance the curriculum. Sarah works with young children and is in awe of their sense of wonder and imaginings. The children's voice is at the centre of her work, and she uses their stories and drawings to develop picture books with them. Her work with children includes The Song Room, The University of Melbourne's Early Learning Centre and her own group, Telling Tales. She lectures the early childhood students at the Melbourne Graduate School of Education, as well as at Swinburne TAFE and the Lady Gowrie Training Centre. She has also worked for many years writing and performing in the Melbourne Symphony Orchestra's concerts for the early years.

Preface

Welcome to *Education in the Arts: Teaching and Learning in the Contemporary Curriculum* in the contemporary curriculum. This is a book about the principles and practice that underpin teaching and learning in the arts. Just as many arts practices are collaborative, this book is a highly collaborative enterprise.

Beginning with a team of arts educators from the disciplines of music, drama, and visual arts, all working in Arts Education at The University of Melbourne, this book emerged out of a desire to create a collection of resources, privileging both theory and practice, for pre-service primary education students, beginning teachers, and teachers wanting to work in and through the arts in their classrooms. As a team of arts educators, we were all experienced as practitioners and academics across a range of arts disciplines, and in our work with pre-service primary education students we were frequently being reminded of the potential and the challenges of teaching the arts in primary school settings. One of the most significant challenges is the changing landscape of the curriculum as it unfolds in primary schools and in tertiary institutions charged with the training of primary teachers—especially, we think, as it relates to the arts.

With this in mind, we committed to writing a book that reflects a multiplicity of voices, experiences, and points of view: a book that attempts to identify and articulate some of the key underlying principles of arts education that inform our practice and pedagogy, with points of reference drawn from the work of philosophers, researchers, educators, artists, and young people; and drawn from a range of artistic and theoretical disciplines. We have also expanded our writing team to include colleagues from other settings, pre-schools, schools, and universities whose experiences in other disciplines (dance, multimedia, literature) would complement our own.

As important as it was to identify and articulate principles, our work with education students has taught us of the importance of learning through practice. In this book, we balance the exploration of principles with examples of illuminating practice, a collection of case studies, each undertaken by one or a number of our writing team, in collaboration with classroom teachers, pre-service education students, and children (ages ranging from four to thirteen). As a further illustration of practice, we asked each of our case study writers to provide a brief exemplar to follow the case study—writers responded in a variety of ways, choosing to provide lesson plans, unit outlines, policy documents, and pathways to further references. These exemplars are to be read as 'open documents', possible applications of the implicit learning embedded in the case studies. We encourage student readers to develop their own 'illustrations of practice', drawing inspiration and guidance from both the case studies and the principles that inform and support the practice and which are articulated in Part One of the book. With this in mind, we have also included a number of 'activities for students', which provide signposts to other ways of thinking about and drawing on the experiences and understandings described in the case studies.

In putting the book together, we have been mindful that readers will come to it with a variety of needs and interests. Readers who are pre-service education students may be studying a specific discipline, and may therefore go to the case study sections first, only later referring back to the theoretical underpinnings discussed in the first six chapters. We have deliberately constructed the book to accommodate multiple entry points and have provided cross-references and a list of key terms to assist readers approaching the book in a non-linear way, possibly over the duration of a three- or four-year course.

When writing the chapters in Part One, where the key principles are first introduced and explored, we aimed to maintain links to practice and to possible applications of principles. Similarly, when writing the case studies and exemplars, we hoped to draw attention to the theoretical underpinnings informing our understanding. While we have diverse views and practices as arts educators, we share a belief in the importance of a strong grounding in theoretical principles informing practice, and an immersion in practice to further inform and extend our understanding of principles. We hope that this book captures something of this dialectic and invites our readers into furthering the dialogue between theory and practice in their schools, classrooms, and arts studios.

Chris Sinclair
Neryl Jeanneret
John O'Toole

Acknowledgments

The editorial team would like to thank the dedicated team of writers who so generously joined us in this enterprise, and took the time out of their commitments to families, students, and daily life, to open the windows on to the landscapes of practice in their various disciplines; and to share their understandings and wisdom regarding the principles that inform their practice.

We would also like to thank the pre-service education students from The University of Melbourne who participated in the case studies and kept us 'on track' with their honesty and insights; the teachers and school students who provided the voices of inspiration and challenge; and the schools who welcomed us into their communities of learning:

- Carlton North Primary School, Brunswick North West Primary School, Haileybury College, Williamstown Secondary College, St Mary's P.S. Ascotvale, Haileybury College Junior School, Carey Grammar, Plenty Parklands P.S., Footscray P.S.
- The University of Melbourne Early Learning Centre
- Musica Viva in Schools
- ArtPlay
- Students from the University of Melbourne Graduate School of Education
- Integrated Arts 2006
- Arts Option 3/4 (Drama) 2006
- Drama Semester 2 2007
- Music, Bachelor of Teaching Cycle 3, 2007
- Arts Option 4 (Visual Arts) ArtBlast 2006, 2007
- Celia Anderson
- Pip Bell
- Jeanette Jennings
- Robby Nason
- Victoria Ryle, Louise Saxton, Sarah Young and Suzana Zaper

How This Book Works

In the arts, just as in education and learning, theory and practice work hand in hand. This book combines a number of important purposes to provide readers with:

- basic understanding of the place of the arts in society and in schools
- an introduction to the basic principles of each art form and how to teach it
- vivid pictures of how the arts actually work in real primary classroom situations
- exemplars of lessons and units for you to try out in your own classroom, and although we can't teach you artistic skills through a book, perhaps most important of all, we hope to provide you with the confidence for you to bring the arts into your classroom and understand what they are doing for your students.

Part One comprises six chapters that cover the key generic principles that are common to all the arts in society and in schools. Of these, the first three explain the importance and relevance of the arts. Chapter 1 explains in detail the very close relationship between the arts and play in childhood, and shows how both are crucial not only to the development of creativity, but to learning in general. A key factor in the arts is their role in motivating and engaging young people in learning. Chapter 2 goes on from this to map the many roles that the arts play in human development and in personal, intellectual, and social growth. The words 'art' and 'culture' are often used almost synonymously, and Chapter 3 traces the role and importance of the arts within some of Australia's cultural and multicultural settings.

Chapters 4 to 6 start to relate the arts more specifically to schools and classrooms. Chapter 4 looks from the point of view of the orthodox school curriculum at the perhaps surprisingly significant role the arts play in teaching and learning what schools often call 'the basics', and broadens this into an investigation of the multiple literacies that young people need to equip them for the twenty-first century. Chapter 5 looks at classrooms from an artistic perspective, to get to grips with the aesthetic components—the particular artistic demands of properly teaching the arts. This moves into a discussion of what is often overlooked, especially in teacher education: that all teaching is itself an art form, where as teachers we are not only responsible for creating an aesthetic and harmonious environment for learning, but are ourselves public performers, taking part in a performative and deeply dramatic dialogue with our students. In Chapter 6 a current teacher up to her neck in a real school situation takes a reflective look at the background theory and principles informing her teaching.

Part Two comprises four chapters looking in depth at the individual art forms in schools. They are all structured in exactly the same way, with a number of distinct components. Each chapter opens with a section outlining the essential basic principles that need to be addressed in teaching in the particular art form. The bulk of the chapter comprises two case studies of the art form in action in the schools. All of these are real case studies, specially carried out for this book. Some of them entail just a teacher and primary students in their everyday setting; some describe work taking place with visiting student teachers or artists; some involve more than one class. They are not examples of perfect practice, but vivid examples of how the arts do work in the classroom. Here it must be remembered that this book cannot be comprehensive: after reading Part One the multiple functions and possibilities of the arts in schools will be very clear; moreover, even with the limited number of art forms identified in the arts syllabuses, there are more than we can effectively cover in this book, particularly those concerned with new media and screen technologies. Accordingly, we have tried to choose rich examples that demonstrate some important principles referred to in the chapter introduction, and which are practicable in some form for most teachers to be able to integrate. Each of the case studies therefore concludes with a practical exemplar, extrapolated from the case study and based on the topic and material, of a unit of work that can be immediately and simply implemented in the classroom. Each chapter then has a brief conclusion drawing together the commonalities and distinguishing features of the two case studies.

In Chapter 7 Drama is the art form. One case study portrays a unit of process drama based on a picture book, showing how through role-play and process drama students do not just act out, but engage as a group in exploring a powerful and complex text to investigate its deep implications. The other describes a piece of participatory theatre-in-education that student teachers designed for two classes of students in an unfamiliar location; however, in this case the exemplar has redesigned the drama for a single teacher to use in his or her own classroom. In Chapter 8 Music is the art form. One case study examines the across-curriculum potential of bringing multicultural music and a professional group of musicians into the school. The other portrays the music component of an arts unit that involves both Indigenous music, musicians and culture, and music technology. Chapter 9 is about Visual Arts. One case study takes a close look at the practice of a visual arts specialist teacher as she prepares her classes throughout the school for a visual arts exhibition on a common theme. The other describes what happens when a group of university students invade a school to work in a range of arts media with the students throughout all the grades for a whole day. Chapter 10 brings together the most embodied of art forms (Dance) and one of the least embodied (Computer Technology) to show the common principles at work in both. The first case study looks at dance in an early childhood setting, and how children can both learn to express their thoughts and feelings through dance, and learn to understand and use their bodies, gesture, and movement for expression and communication. The second shows how young people can articulate and reflect on, and therefore transform, their artistic experience (in this case drama and movement) through the structured use of weblogs.

Part Three extends the implementation of each of the arts in schools, first across the whole key learning area (KLA), and then right across the curriculum. Chapters 11 and 12 have the same shape as the chapters in Part Two: two case studies, with practical exemplars, topped and tailed by exposition and analysis of the guiding principles. Chapter 11 deals with integrating the arts, showing how, carefully structured, they can augment and add value to each other. One case study shows how a combination of music and drama can teach and create insights into the work of a visual artist. The other chronicles the sustained work in a range of art forms and art media—including drama, music, visual arts, and film—of a large group of teacher education students working with a whole year group to create a themed multi-arts festival. Chapter 12 broadens the scope of the arts to demonstrate some of their uses right across the curriculum. Both case studies simultaneously demonstrate further uses of integrated arts. One case study is focused on early childhood acquisition of language, through an intensive immersion in an arts-centred curriculum. The other looks at how the arts can provide the basis for rich tasks to address a learning context in Study of Society and the Environment (SOSE). The final chapter takes the form of a holistic and impressionistic reflection on the nature and effects of arts education, through a collage of the words and thoughts of the participants—teachers, school students, tertiary students, lecturers, parents, and even principals—culled from the case studies.

In this book, a large group of very experienced practitioners, with many years of practice, and also of teaching education students and teachers in-service as well as primary students, are pooling our knowledge and a little of our practice. We are a close team, who often work together across our art forms, and we have written this book as a team. Every arts classroom and context is unique, and so each chapter represents the particular views and practice of the chapter author or authors; but we all subscribe to the whole book.

The Arts and Creativity: A Manifesto for Schools

John O'Toole

We believe that the arts are so important that they should be at the centre of the primary school curriculum. In a few lucky and precious schools, they are, and the research shows that those children are deeply advantaged in their education.[1] In most schools they are a long way from that, often shouldered to the edge of the nest and sometimes out altogether by the 'owners', traditional and modern, of the Western curriculum: *language* and *literacy, maths* and *numeracy*, *science* and *social sciences*—all important and necessary, but not more so. Is literacy more basic than the ability to make sense of yourself and your environment, which is what the arts do especially for young children? Or to communicate culturally, symbolically and publicly, which is what they do for everybody? This is why we say that the arts are central to the curriculum.

They should also be central, because they naturally address one of the most pressing demands of the twenty-first century: creativity—the ability to foresee needs and problems, and respond imaginatively, innovatively, and flexibly to them. Schools and schooling systems today *are* mostly very aware of the potential role of the arts in the alchemy necessary to find the new philosopher's stone of creativity. All across Australia, and from Singapore to China, from Colombia to Senegal, education systems that once would have been uninterested in, or actively hostile to, any education that deflected from the production of effective engineers, scientists, businesspeople, and trained workforces, are turning to the arts, sometimes nervously, and sometimes, as in Australia, quite enthusiastically. During the writing of this book, the federal and state governments have put out a momentous joint National Statement on Education and the Arts,[2] which is quite unequivocal about the link between the arts and creativity, and about the commitment of all governments to fostering both.

> This new National Education and the Arts Statement aims … to foster a culture of creativity and innovation in Australia's school systems in partnership with creative individuals and organisations. The statement has been developed following extensive consultation with representatives within the arts and education sectors—both government and independent.
>
> Schools that value creativity lead the way in cultivating the well-informed and active citizens our future demands: where individuals are able to generate fresh ideas,

communicate effectively, take calculated risks and imaginative leaps, adapt easily to change and work cooperatively …

An education rich in creative arts maximises opportunities for learners to engage with innovative thinkers and leaders, and to experience the arts both as audience members and as artists. Such an education is vital to students' success as individuals and as members of society, emphasising not only creativity and innovation, but also the values of broad cultural understanding and social harmony that the arts can engender. As Ministers charged with education and nurturing the cultural life of the nation, we are committed to working together to support young Australians to realise their full creative potential.

This commitment is already reflected in government schooling policy documents throughout Australia, such as the *Victorian Essential Learning Standards* (Victorian Curriculum and Assessment Authority [VCAA, Melbourne] 2005–07). Queensland has brought the Departments of Education and the Arts together under one minister. All states now follow the 1994 National Curriculum Guidelines at least to the extent that they include the arts as one of the KLAs, or its equivalent, and have developed curricula and syllabuses in the arts from preschool to tertiary entrance.

Schools are taking up the challenge, though changing syllabuses and timetables, as well as the expectations of parents, takes time. Teachers too, are rising to the opportunities that the arts offer for the students and for their own teaching; after all, the arts are fun, and they are motivating, as we shall see. Of course, many teachers have limited experience of the arts, and even more limited training in arts education and pedagogy. Many teacher education students currently receive very brief introductions to the arts or arts education, let alone enough to make up the deficits in their (your) own schooling. Very few teachers are experienced and skilled across the very wide, diverse, and complex area that we call 'the arts'. That is a major reason for this book.

What are the arts, how do they work, and do they belong together?

The first thing to make clear is what we mean in this book by the word 'arts'—a diverse and complex grouping, yes, but not as wide, vague, or confusing as usages sometimes imply. Our education systems and schools are only just recovering from the mid-twentieth-century 'dualistic' view of the whole world of knowledge as divided into what CP Snow (1959) sardonically called 'two cultures': *Arts* (sometimes with the word 'humanities' attached) and *Sciences* (sometimes with the word 'natural' attached). Our university has a faculty called 'College of the Arts' and an 'Arts' Faculty that do almost entirely different things. The first faculty teaches the *creative and performing* arts of *dance, drama, film and media, music* and *visual arts*, and that is exactly what we are talking about in this book. The second teaches history, economics, sociology, languages, gender studies, and such like. The confusion is easily resolved in the adjective: the first, like this book, teaches *artistic* arts. The second does not (not primarily, anyway). And talking of adjectives, we will be using a synonym of the word 'artistic' a lot in this book: *aesthetic*. As the word aesthetic is sometimes also used in different ways that artists dispute among themselves, we will define it here for our purposes: we are using it across all our art forms, to denote any formal shaping at any level of the resources of the body and other expressive media to create an ordered fusion of emotional, sensory, and cognitive stimuli ... or when simpler terminology will suffice, just think 'artistic'!

In all Australian state and national education systems, *dance, drama, film and media, music* and *visual arts* have now come together as a KLA, which has parity with all other areas of the curriculum, at least theoretically. These of course are not all the creative arts. Sadly, *poetry* and other *creative writing*, which are self-evidently creative arts, are embedded elsewhere; and there is no room at all for culturally specific art forms taught in other countries' arts programs, like *hairstyling* and *floral art* in Senegal, or *stiltwalking* in Barbados (Bamford 2006, p. 51). Nevertheless, we've already come a long way: music and visual arts have long been part of Australian curricula, though usually not very important parts—till now certainly not 'key learning'. Drama, media arts, and dance have at various times crashed their way in from the co-curricular margins, or piggybacked on other subjects like English (drama and media) or Physical Education (dance).

What brings them together is everything that is embedded in that word *aesthetic*, and we shall be exploring the commonalities in more detail in Chapter 1. Of course, there are massive differences, too, which sometimes make for really difficult dilemmas in school situations, where making time for the arts at all is a struggle, and let's face it, all the arts are very time-consuming. Do we choose to teach music, visual arts, drama or dance, in the one hour a week allocated to the arts on our school timetable? Do we give the students a little bit of each, or try and integrate the art forms in some way? Do we spend our energies encouraging the artistically talented, or try and bring out the artist in everyone?

The arts not only share some very crucial commonalities, which makes it appropriate to group them together and think of them, as in this book, as a 'set' of subjects in schools, but they also share a very important common approach in our Australian schools. Most adults do know and think of the arts in common, that they are all ways for individuals and groups to experience the world sensually; express this experience personally, emotionally, and culturally; and communicate that expression to others publicly; and that will do perfectly well for starters. They can be taught for at least three different purposes, however. These are:

- Traditionally in the Western curriculum—and this is still the dominant mode in many other countries, for instance in Europe—students are primarily taught to *appreciate* the arts. This is a legacy of the Renaissance 'heritage arts' tradition that sees the arts as being among the pinnacles of expression of a culture, and artists as special beings with exceptional talent, skills, and training who provide the cultural product that permanently crystallises and represents the culture.

- Schools have another major function, of course, which is to prepare people for their working careers, sorting them out to make sure they are fitted for their jobs and professions (and that includes the arts industry), and that there are approximately the right number of each to fill those jobs. In some places this is what happens to the arts, where the first stage is identifying people with particular artistic talent and 'potential', and then training those people in the skills that will hopefully see them gainfully employed in the artistic professions. Overwhelmingly, this means increasing specialisation in those areas of arts where there are jobs: in the performing arts with *performance skills* (dancers, actors, musicians) and in the visual arts with *design skills*.
- In Australia, many remnants of both of these approaches can be found. However, all our arts syllabuses have taken a different starting point and approach. Perhaps in keeping with our egalitarian origins, together with our belief that there is more to education than job-incubation, we start from the premise that every child has the capacity and the need to express and communicate through the arts, as well as to respond to them; not every child will become famous, or a professional artist, but all should have access, and that in any case the practice of the arts is essential for their proper appreciation.

For this reason, our syllabuses have all basically followed contemporary arts education philosophers, by starting with the question: what do we *do* when we engage in the arts? On the surface, the answer might seem to be 'totally different things: paint, sing, dance, use cameras, work computers, and so on'. However, especially as young children, we all *express* our ideas about the world, our personal and social feelings, and our identity through the sensory and symbolic forms that are the arts, in order to *communicate* to other people. In other words we (1) *make*, compose, or create art-works, and we (2) *appreciate* and *respond to* other people's art works. In visual arts (and written literature), this is often all that is needed, as the artist makes an artefact using relatively permanent media such as paint or crayons or tactile materials (or print) that can be immediately communicated to and appreciated by the receiver. In all the performing arts, including filmmaking, there is another, intermediary component in the communication, involving (3) *presentation* to the receiver, or performance. What is created by the artist is made manifest first through the dancers', actors' or musicians' bodies, voices, or instruments (and the performers are often, or usually, other people), and then also often through a production stage also involving other people. This intermediary function then includes *interpretation, production,* and *performance.*

There is a fairly bewildering number of more or less synonymous terms, used with slight differences throughout Australian arts syllabuses, for these three—or sometimes only two— functions of making (forming, composing), presenting (performing, interpreting, presenting), and responding (appreciating, appraising) that are in effect common to what people do when they engage in any of the arts. In similar form, all three are more or less compulsory parts of arts syllabuses throughout Australia, with a very few errant exceptions, such as Victorian Senior

Music, which at the time of writing very sadly does not include composing for assessment. Chapter 5 gives more detail to help you through the different terminologies.

Key references

Bamford, Anne (2006) *The Wow Factor: Global Research Compendium of the Impact of Arts Education*, Waxmann, New York.

Snow, C.P. (1959) *The Two Cultures*, Rede Lecture, Senate House, Cambridge.

Victorian Essential Learning Standards 2005–2007 (2007) Victorian Curriculum and Assessment Authority, Melbourne.

Notes

1   Find out about the FACE school in Montreal, the Port Phillip Specialist School in Melbourne, or read: Deasy, R. (ed.) (2002), *Critical Links*, Washington DC: Arts Education Partnership; Bamford, A. (2006). *The WOW Factor: Global Compendium of Arts Education Research*, Waxmann, New York.

2   Ministerial Council on Education, Training and Youth Affairs (Federal) and Cultural Ministers' Council (all state governments) September 2007, *National Statement on Education and the Arts*, Department of Communication, Information Technology and the Arts, Canberra.

PART ONE

Key Principles

Art, Creativity, and Motivation

John O'Toole

In this chapter John O'Toole argues for the primacy of the arts in the curriculum, and constructs a play–art dialectic through which to explore the notion of a 'common aesthetic' and to examine the role of motivation in learning through the arts.

Art and play, learning, and creativity

In the introductory sections, we made several claims that the arts are, or should be, central to the primary school curriculum, because they help young people to make sense of the world, to communicate in diverse ways with other people, and to be creative. That's just the start of it—we are now going to explore these and make some even more ambitious claims that we would like you to think about.

The arts are so central because they provide both a basis for the whole curriculum, and a potential pedagogy (which arts educators have now turned into very real and workable classroom practices). Think about it: the arts are all about how we perceive the world through the senses, and sort into order and harmony the welter of stimuli from outside us and within us, to create meaningful reality. We make sense through our senses, and meaning.

- Through the eyes—*the visual arts*—the child constructs shape into order and spatial understanding, light and darkness, chromatic harmony and dissonance, symmetry, perspective and distance.
- Through touch—*the plastic arts*—the child understands and learns to manage texture and temperature, hardness and resilience, liquid and solid.
- Through the ears—*music*—the child hears and discriminates sounds, harmonies and dissonances, rhythms and sequences, tones and timbres.
- Through the body—*dance and movement*—the child discovers his or her kinaesthetic power, what the body can do in space, contrasts of stillness, slowness and speed, and all the types of movement the body is capable of.
- Through the body, too, and through language and the voice—*theatre and drama*—the child learns about relationships and about how we communicate, how every movement and gesture gives signals, how every sound we utter has a complexity of signals that relate to the movement and gesture, and how the words we choose and the way we articulate them provide us with our richest communication tool, live conversation, which is still the way we construct and conduct most of our social existence.
- All this sense-making would not be complete unless we could place it in time and space, and find cause and effect—*storytelling*—shaping for ourselves the ongoing personal narrative and shaping with others the social narratives of our lives.
- In addition, there are the technologies that provide a torrent of alternative media for all the above artistic inputs into the senses: the old ones—*print-based art and literature*; the twentieth-century ones—*video, taped sound, film*; and the new ones—*digital photography and film, computers and the internet, mp3 and bluetooth, and mobile phone technology*.

The job of the primary teacher is thus to help the children make sense and meaning, and to learn to manage their personal and social reality.

In earlier, though not more primitive, education systems, this reconstruction of sensual data into an ordered, balanced, and harmonious understanding of the self (a child's personal identity and place in the world); and of the demands, rights, and responsibilities of operating as a complex social being (social skills and the wisdom of the tribe) were taught primarily through the arts (painting, storytelling, dance theatre) and through play. In play, the child instinctively engages artistically to discover the science and the mystery of living. This flows naturally into life skills and capabilities essential in contemporary society. Far from taking valuable time from the direct inculcation of 'basic skills', a weight of research, not all of it new, affirms that music- and visual-arts-rich schooling actually increase mathematical capability, by around 6 per cent, it seems; drama-rich schooling, perhaps predictably, increases the forgotten basic, oracy, and also enhances literacy by as much, some studies suggest, as 24 per cent.[1]

Myth-busting

All this should make it quite mystifying why our 'modern' schooling system is as it is. However, of course, it is that way because of the structures and assumptions that we all pass on from our own schooling. Before they go to school, children have already learned lots and lots, from their entirely amateur parents and family and friends, who are usually unhelped by any 'professional' educators. Let's consider how young children learn: they learn through the senses and with their brains, bodies, and emotions all working together. They learn by exploring and testing, trial and error, by taking risks—learning by getting it wrong first, so they can get it right next time. They learn imaginatively through creative leaps and humour, playing with juxtaposition. They learn from everybody around, including peers and playmates, television, the people they see and meet, their surroundings; through copying and social interaction, discovering the external world together; through the worlds of social relationships and personal feeling and expression. They scaffold new learning on what they already know. Above all, they learn through *play* and the artistry of play—musical, linguistic, visual and design, dance, and dramatic play.

At around five years of age or so, we take them and pitch them for about half their waking life into a new game called school. Here, we leave play outside in the playground; a schoolroom is a place for something else, so we discourage 'playing around'. We focus on cognition and ban the emotions ('no tears', 'stop laughing'). We restrict or ban movement and the body. We severely restrict language and social interaction, and especially their endless questions ('stop talking and listen to me'). We replace their normal surroundings with a single room with specialised equipment and closed doors called 'the classroom', and their playmates, television, and the people round them with a small number of grown-up strangers called 'the teacher'. Here, exploring and playing with knowledge is replaced by something called *the* curriculum. This is special knowledge that the teachers have, so the questions are now asked by the teacher, and they are not real questions because the teacher already knows the answers—the right answers. Trial-and-error is replaced with those right answers. The questions and the excitement of risk and failure without penalty are replaced with penalties for failure and we learn not to take imaginative or intellectual risks, and especially not to make jokes. Curriculum knowledge is delivered as 'new' not scaffolded.

Among the other things we traditionally leave behind at the classroom door are: *play* and *art*. Play is seen as the province of the playground, or the fill-in time between matters of more importance. Art, somewhat more uneasily, is so often relegated to the margins and the co-curriculum.

The connections between play and art, and between both of them and learning, are fundamental. Both play and art are serious business—the business of the human imagination, defining reality through new possible realities, models of human experience, new angles and perspectives, creating order from chaos and also disturbing order to imagine new orders, finding harmonies and previously unheard melodies. By the time they come to school, children are already very good at play, and developing highly sophisticated artistic skills.

Long ago in the first half of the twentieth century the visual artists were the first to perceive the sophisticated aesthetic of very young children's play—their management of form and space combined with the boldness and freedom of discovery—and very grown-up artists like Picasso, Klee, and Miro were among the host of elite artists humble enough to acknowledge the debt they owed to the art of ordinary children and learn from it for their own art. Over a hundred years ago in education, John Dewey[2] was urging exactly the same thing. From him there is a line of theorists and educators demonstrating and proving that children's art and learning are inextricably linked, from Herbert Read and Louis Arnaud Reid to Elliot Eisner and John Matthews in visual arts; Keith Swanwick and Bennett Reimer in music; Johan Huizinga to Peter Slade and Dorothy Heathcote in dance and drama; and across all the arts Maxine Greene, Malcolm Ross, Peter Abbs, David Best, Ken Robinson, Shirley Brice Heath,[3] and hundreds more … and not forgetting the thousands of teachers who have not read those worthies, but who have discovered and implement this playful aesthetic instinctively.

Figure 1.1 shows how I think play and art work together, in the lives of both children and adults.

> Both play and art are about IF.
> Play starts from the dimension of curiosity (read from the left)
> and asks the question 'What if …'
> Art finishes with the dimension of control (read from the right)
> and creates the statement 'As if …'.

Figure 1.2 shows some of the characteristics of those dimensions.

Figure 1.1   Dialectic of play and art (a)

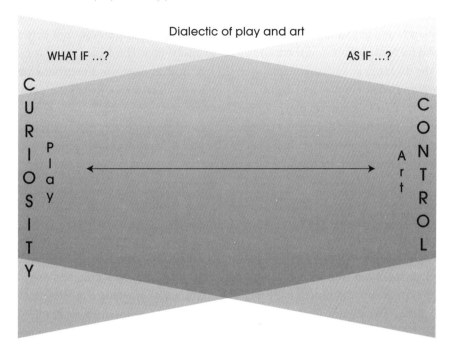

Figure 1.2   Dialectic of play and art (b)

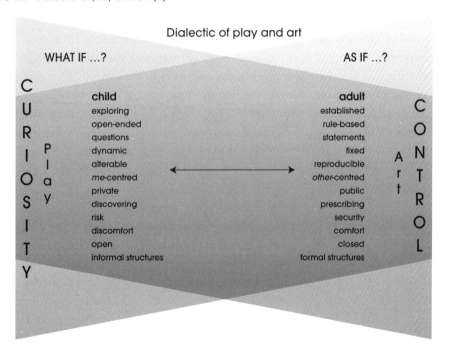

John O'Toole

Of course, none of these pairs of concepts are binary opposites, as they look on this two-dimensional diagram, but just at the opposite ends of an interplaying continuum, where players and artists find their own places, moving along the continuum between the more playful forms of art and the more artful forms of play. Hard-core art is at the right side of the diagram, and hard-core play is at the left. Both ends of the dimensions are open, as there is an element of play and negotiability in nearly all artworks, just as there is a strong component of art in nearly all play.

We will have quite a lot more to say about this, and the importance of arts education in this area, when we look at 'multi-literacies' in Chapter 4, because aesthetic literacy is one of the most important, but unrecognised, capacities that we can develop for real life.

Arts and creativity

The marginalisation of both play and arts in schools is not an accident, historically. The schooling system that we have rather unkindly described above was designed originally to produce a compliant and functionally literate and numerate workforce for the nineteenth-century industrial societies, and has been sustained, basically in the same way. The knowledge demands have over the years become exponentially higher. As the industrial society has mutated during the twentieth century into the information and electronic society, this has meant a much greater demand for literacy, numeracy, and scientific understanding. Among these increased demands, however, there has never until now been a mainstream demand for creativity. Quite the reverse: creativity means doing things differently, and, deliberately or accidentally, is to be discouraged in an age of industrial and scientific orthodoxy.

Creativity is of course core business both of play and the arts, which are often historically labelled 'the *creative* arts'. This was originally to distinguish them explicitly in the dualistic sciences v. humanities curriculum from the 'uncreative' arts like language arts, history, home economics, and typing. After being a very unfashionable word through most of the science- and logic-driven twentieth century, 'creativity' is currently experiencing a spectacular recovery. Now it is a highly desirable attribute in education and in the workplace, as we hurtle into a new millennium characterised by constant and imminent change, by the need for constant innovation and adjustment to the contingencies of chaos theory and fuzzy logic. This comes from the top end of town, from companies like IBM and Apple; from government reports such as the *All Our Futures: Creativity, Culture and Education* (NACCCE 1999); and from current commentaries, advice, and writings (for example, Robinson 2005; Florida, 2002, 2005a, 2005b).

Definitions of creativity have been changing too, becoming more and more diverse and less and less linear (from logical and behaviouristic definitions like 'solving problems' and 'five steps to creative solutions for products' to far more lateral and provisional (and playful) definitions like 'using imagination to generate possibilities'—which is used in the *Victorian Essential Learning Standards* (Victorian Curriculum and Assessment Authority [VCAA]).[4]

Given what we have said about creativity being the core business of the arts, it might seem surprising that a lot of the top end talk about creativity focuses on science and industry, on corporate invention, with the arts sometimes barely mentioned, and schools mentioned even less. We should not be surprised at either of these, since as we have already explained, for so many of those adults newly discovering that creativity is important, their own schooling in the arts was deficient or marginal, and their play was devalued as trivial. They are discovering what we have always known, and how to think and work as we have always thought and worked, and they need to be reminded of this.

Motivation

There is a burgeoning debate and literature on motivation in schools—helping students to engage with what is happening in classrooms. A quick library check immediately identified eighty books specifically on this topic, over twenty of which were published in the last two years. Furthermore, four of those included the word 'creativity' in the title. What is rarely acknowledged in the learned discussion is that you rarely have to work hard to motivate students to do what they are already interested in and do naturally. Returning to our unkind description of schooling, you can easily see that what we did when we removed children from their natural home learning environment to put them in schools was also remove the natural motivators, namely play and the arts. If you look at schools, and perhaps your own schooling, you will see a number of commonly observable features of whatever arts are happening in the school:

• arts classes are often extremely popular—(though not always—they tend to be either the most or the least popular classes)
• arts teachers ditto—and for the same reasons, which we will come to
• the reasons that students give for enjoying the arts include that arts are 'different', that they are 'active', and that they allow the students to 'express ourselves' and 'do things we want to do' (for example, Haseman 1990)
• in schools and in the wider community, the arts are often turned to as a kind of therapy, as a way of dealing with anti-social, disturbed, or dysfunctional students and groups, who—surprise, surprise—respond to 'doses' of the arts (for example, Flood et al. 1997). Cynics note that at least they keep the students out of mischief—and arts cynics note that in some very academically driven secondary schools, arts elective classes get to be the hospital wards of the school
• the arts are often most valued in working with the least 'academic' students, because they give those students the opportunity both to express themselves and achieve in 'other ways' (for example, Clegg 1972).

In other words, bringing the arts into both your curriculum and your pedagogy is just returning to using the natural motivators of learning, the natural ways of engaging young people by playfully and artfully bringing together the worlds outside (the physical and social worlds) with the world inside (the personal world).

Why then do not all teachers use the arts all the time as motivators, quite apart from the other advantages we have alluded to? And why do students not always respond with unbridled enthusiasm to any mention or introduction of the arts? This downside can be summed up as a sequence of three words: *devaluation, ignorance,* and *fear*. Some of our readers will be victims of this—which is part of the reason for this book. Because the arts have been so often *devalued* and marginalised in traditional schooling, only a small proportion of children grow up having had sustained and substantial education in the arts, particularly across the range (compared with having had a minimum of six and up to twelve years of continuous schooling in Maths, English, Science, and Studies of Society). Most teachers only receive a brief introduction to the arts in their pre-service training, sometimes not even that. This is compounded by those gaps in the pre-service students' own education, so that when they graduate, many teachers are still basically *ignorant* of the importance or the relevance of the arts to their students. Even many of the lucky ones who are aware of their importance, or are excited by their potential, feel they do not have the necessary basic skills themselves, let alone the pedagogy, and so they are too *fearful* to take the risk. And some of those who do come out with confidence and skills to do the job find themselves in schools where there is little understanding, support, or resources, and it is much easier *not* to teach the arts.

Let's continue this grim picture for a minute, and look at it from the students' perspective. Some teachers do try or are dragooned into teaching the arts, armed with insufficient understanding, skills, and pedagogy. As you probably know, and will see in these pages, teaching the arts is not simple, not plain sailing—especially, as we will be constantly reinforcing, arts teachers (like any good teachers) should take part themselves in the learning, not just stand outside and give information and instructions. Teaching:

- music demands some specialist knowledge, and at least a willingness to try musical activities with children
- visual arts demands visual acuity, design sense, and some control of a pencil (or mouse)
- drama demands an understanding of how to frame a situation so as to provide protection and permission, as well as dramatic tension and action, and managing groups in role and performance
- movement and dance demands knowledge of how the body works and what its capacities and tolerances are at different ages
- media demands some technical and critical understanding of those media.

The common thing they all need more than anything else is the understanding and ability to *know where the students are at, and start there*. To start too high, or expect too much, is a recipe for fear and demoralisation; to start too low is a recipe for boredom and contempt.

It is not all so bleak, but we are painting this picture so that you will be both robust and realistic about what you can achieve. Just remember that these are the exceptions.

The vast majority of children and young people look forward to the arts, are strongly and consistently motivated by them, and love to encounter them in school. To teach the arts takes some minimal training and resources, and it takes experience. You will find the first two in this book, and we hope this will give you the confidence to start, and constantly grow in your own way as you gain that experience.

Activities for students

Discussion: learning and play

Recall and share a story of learning that you experienced before formal schooling.

Writing task: school portrait

Create a 250-word pen portrait that reflects a dominant philosophy from your own schooling. Reflect on the place of the arts and creativity in your portrait. (Share and discuss.)

Key references

Abbs, P. (1987) *Living Powers: The Arts in Education*, Falmer, London.

Bamford, A. (2006) *The WOW Factor: Global Compendium of Arts Education research*, Waxmann, New York.

Best, D. (1992) *The Rationality of Feeling: Understanding the Arts in Education*, Falmer, London.

Clegg, A. (1972) *About our Schools*, Oxford, Blackwell.

Eisner, E. (1976) *The Arts, Human Development, and Education*, McCutchan, Berkeley.

Flood, J., Brice Heath, S. & Lapp, D. (1997) *Handbook of Research on Teaching Literacy through the Communicative and Visual Arts*, Prentice Hall, London.

Florida, R. (2002) *The Rise of the Creative Class and How it's Transforming Work, Leisure, Community and Everyday Life*, Basic Books, New York.

Florida, R. (2005a) *The Flight of the Creative Class*, HarperBusiness, New York.

Florida, R. (2005b) *Cities and the Creative Class*, Routledge, New York.

Haseman, B. (1990) 'Working Out!: A Survey of Drama in Queensland Secondary Schools', *NADIE Journal*, vol. 14, no. 2, 34–41.

Heathcote, D. & Bolton, G. (1995) *Drama for Learning: Dorothy Heathcote's Mantle of the Expert Approach to Education*, Heinemann, Portsmouth NH.

Huizinga, J. (1970) *Homo Ludens: A Study of the Play Element in Culture*, Temple, London.

Matthews, J. (1999) *The Art of Childhood and Adolescence: The Construction of Meaning*, Falmer, London.

Reimer, B. (1989) *A Philosophy of Music Education* (2nd edn), Prentice-Hall, New Jersey.

John O'Toole

Robinson, K. (1999) *All Our Futures: Creativity, Culture and Education: The Report of the NACCCE Committee*, National Advisory Committee on Creative and Cultural Education, London.

Robinson, K. (2005) 'Do Schools Kill Creativity?', lecture recorded online, Technology, Ideas, Design: Ideas Worth Spreading, retrieved 24 April 2008 from http://www.ted.com/index.php/talks/view/id/66.

Notes

1   See inter alia:

Bamford, A. (2006) *The WOW Factor: Global Research Compendium of the Impact of Arts Education*, Waxmann, New York.

Deasy, R. (2002) *Critical Links: Learning in the Arts and Student Academic and Social Development*, Arts Education Partnerships, Washington.

Gardner, H. & Perkins, D. (1989) *Art, Mind, and Education:Research from Project Zero*, University of Illinois, Urbane.

Clegg, A. (1972) *The Changing Primary School—its Problems and Priorities*, Chatto & Windus, London.

2   Dewey, J. (1934) *Art as Experience*, Minton, Balch, New York.

3   Read, H. (1964) *Art and Education*, Cheshire, Melbourne.

Reid, L. (1969) *Meaning in the Arts,*: Allen and Unwin, London.

Eisner, E. (1976) *The Arts, Human Development, and Education*, McCutchan, Berkeley.

Matthews, J. (1999) *The Art of Childhood and Adolescence: The Construction of Meaning*, Falmer, London.

Swanwick, K. (1988) *Music, Mind, and Education*, Routledge, London.

Reimer, B. (2003) *A Philosophy of Music Education: Advancing the Vision*, Prentice Hall, New Jersey.

Huizinga, J. (1970) *Homo Ludens: A Study of the Play Element in Culture*, Temple, London.

Slade, P. (1956) *Child Drama*, Cassell, London.

Heathcote, D. & Bolton, G. (1995) *Drama for Learning: Dorothy Heathcote's Mantle of the Expert Approach to Education*, Heinemann, Portsmouth NH.

Greene, M. (1995) *Releasing the Imagination: Essays on Education, the Arts, and Social Change*, Jossey-Bass, San Francisco.

Ross, M. (1983) *The Arts, a Way of Knowing*, Pergamon, Oxford.

Abbs, P. (1987) *Living Powers: the Arts in Education,* Falmer, London.

Best, D. (1992) *The Rationality of Feeling: Understanding the Arts in Education*, Falmer, London.

Robinson, K. (2001) *Out of Our Minds: Learning to be Creative*, John Wiley, New York.

Flood, J., Brice Heath, S., & Lapp, D. (1997) *Handbook of Research on Teaching Literacy through the Communicative and Visual Arts*, Prentice Hall, London.

4   For a much more detailed analysis of the changing definitions of creativity and how they impact on current curricula, see Jeanneret, N. & Forrest, D. (in press), 'Policy and Music Education: A "New" Culture of "Creativity"?', in C.C. Leung, R.L.C. Yip & T. Imada (eds) *Music Education Policy and Implementation: International Perspectives*, Hirosaki University Press, Japan.

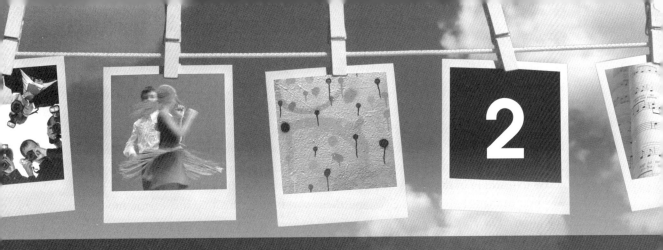

Learning in the Arts

Neryl Jeanneret

In this chapter, Neryl Jeanneret builds on a number of key ideas about cognition and learning, including the awareness, frequently articulated by teachers, that young children often understand more than they are able to verbalise. Neryl goes on to identify some key principles of cognitive, social, and skill development scaffolded by learning in different art forms, while drawing attention to some of the leading figures in this field.

As we have already explained, the arts are a central force in human existence and everyone should have sufficient and equal opportunities to participate in them throughout their lives. We believe that education is about creating equal opportunities for children to develop to their fullest potential, and the arts can play a very powerful role in realising that potential. This equity of opportunity to develop potential is most importantly about *access*. To deny access to learning in the arts is to deny access to what Bennett Reimer refers to as 'a basic way that humans know themselves and their world; they (the arts) are a basic mode of cognition' (1989, p. 11).

What can and do children learn in the arts? In this section we will explore some of the more generic outcomes of learning in the arts (see Figure 2.1), rather than the specifics of each art form that will be covered elsewhere. It must be remembered, however, that each art form is unique and what is experienced and learned in one art form cannot be duplicated through another. Every student should have experience in drama, music, visual arts, dance, literary, and technology-based arts programs that present a developmental sequence in line with the particular discipline's knowledge base. To merely 'dabble' in one or two of the arts

Figure 2.1   Importance of the arts in the primary curriculum

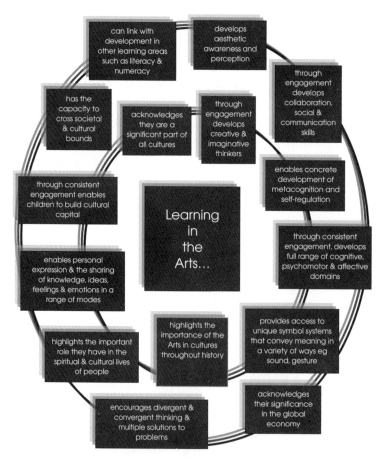

is like 'dabbling' in language or numeracy. That is not to say that you can't also integrate the arts, both together and with other learning areas that we will explore in later chapters.

From Figure 2.1, you can see that learning in the arts provides access to unique symbol systems that convey meaning in a variety of ways. Learning in the arts also enables personal expression and the sharing of knowledge, ideas, feelings, and emotions in a range of modes. Learning how to represent what we have experienced, know, think, and feel is a primary goal of education. Educators have to bear in mind that some aspects of human experience are simply better expressed through some modes than through others. Elliot Eisner has made the important point that if it were possible to convey everything that humans wanted to convey with one or two forms of representation, the others would be redundant. The arts wouldn't exist if verbal exchanges satisfied all our communication needs.

One factor that makes the arts unique is their capacity to communicate information and feelings through means other than language, either written or spoken. They use a range of unique symbol systems, as do language and mathematics. A number of philosophers and arts educators have considered how the arts convey meaning through these non-verbal means. Louis Arnaud Reid concluded that, 'I conceive of feeling as cognitive as well as affective, as always having content or an object. Even when we cannot possibly say what we feel, we are feeling a quality of something, though unnameable' (1986, pp. 5–6). Michael Polanyi (1976) reinforces this point that we are not always able to express our thoughts verbally with his famous statement 'we can know more than we can tell' (1967 p. 4). There are other ways of knowing and telling besides verbal language, and the arts are as powerful as any other form of human discourse. Teachers have known for many years that young children often understand more than they are able to verbalise; for instance, very young children (and adults) reconstructing traumatic experiences in drawing has long been used in therapy and counselling. The arts use visual, aural, verbal, and non-verbal forms of communication, and when students participate in the arts, they are involved in using both non-verbal *and* verbal forms of communication. They are using sound, movement, gesture, marks, form, and image to express their ideas, thoughts, and feelings, and children often show a preference for a particular medium. But how will they find their preference without having experienced the range of options the arts offer? And how will they fully embrace multi-literacy without the arts?

Learning in the arts develops creative and imaginative thinkers, as well as encouraging divergent and convergent thinking and multiple solutions to problems. Learning in the arts also enables concrete development of metacognition and self-regulation, and through consistent engagement it develops a full range of cognitive, psychomotor, and affective domains.

While we acknowledge that all areas of the curriculum have the potential to develop an imaginative and creative intellect in children, the potential of the arts in this development has often been neglected. It seems that many people do not associate the arts with 'thinking', and are unaware that

> the arts are not so much a result of inspiration and innate talent as they are a person's capacities for creative thinking and imagining, problem solving, creative judgment and a host of other mental processes. The arts represent forms of cognition every bit as potent

as the verbal and logical/mathematical forms of cognition that have been the traditional focus of public education (Cooper-Solomon 1995, p. 29).

The arts are able to teach divergent *and* convergent thinking, and encourage children to produce different, rather than similar solutions, because the solutions to artistic problems are multiple. The arts have the ability to provide an alternative to the true–false, memorise-that, name-this approach to learning that concerns some of the world's most distinguished educators (and arts advocates) such as Elliott Eisner (1982, 2002) and Ken Robinson (2001). Divergent reasoning is far more the case of the real world, where there are often many ways to address a problem and we need both kinds of reasoning to function effectively in both our social and work lives. As Chapman says, the arts are 'the very subjects where ambiguity, uncertainty, struggles of conscience, and independent thinking are as unavoidable as they are in life beyond schools' (2001, p. 23).

The arts have the capacity to involve children as active participants in their own learning. When we present children with artistic problems we are asking them to reflect on their own reactions and engage in critical thinking, analysis, and evaluation, rather than presenting them with what they should think. Children tend to stay on task, exploring and experimenting with solutions, when they are given the independence to do so. With facilitation and scaffolding from teachers, they begin to be metacognitive and self-regulative about their approach to tasks. The encouragement to think independently is the basis for creativity (Fowler 1994), which has been explored in the introduction and in Chapter 1. In his music advocacy speech at the 1996 Grammy Awards, Richard Dreyfuss reflected the beginnings of much of the current thinking in business, industry, and politics: 'It is from that creativity and imagination that the solutions to our political and social problems will come. We need that Well Rounded Mind, now. Without it, we simply make more difficult the problems we face' (Dreyfuss 1996).

Figure 2.2   Learning in the arts involves ...

Learning in the arts highlights the important role they have in the spiritual and cultural lives of people. It highlights the importance of the arts in cultures throughout history, having the capacity to cross societal and cultural bounds, and acknowledging a significant part of all cultures. The learning area of the arts provides children with unique and multiple ways of exploring, forming, expressing, and understanding their own and, importantly, others' ideas and feelings. The arts are one of the main ways that humanity identifies itself, both as individuals and as a culture. You would be well aware, for example, of the power of music in various peer cultures and how the music, dress, films, and so forth provide a sense of identity for many children, and especially adolescents. The arts are also important in providing a sense of community and the broader sense of culture related to ethnic origins. The arts convey the spirit, the beliefs, the social mores, as well as the traditions and the contemporary ideas of the people who created them. The exposure of children to the arts in a variety of cultures can have a powerful impact on the way in which they think about those cultures and can equip them with inter- and intra-cultural understanding. In Chapter 8, you will read about the compelling effects of an Aboriginal musician and storyteller working with young people. In this case, the arts go beyond being multicultural. By inviting cross-cultural communication, they become trans-cultural because they encourage children to consider the ideas and feelings expressed in cultures different from their own and to be tolerant of those differences. Charles Fowler (1994) takes this idea even further when he suggests that the arts have the capacity to teach us about empathy and thus increase our capacity for compassion and humanness. In summary, learning in the arts provides children with the skills and knowledge necessary to understand how the arts reflect and depict the diversity of our world, its cultures, traditions, and belief systems, and to develop an understanding of cultural change and differences.

Learning in the arts, through consistent engagement, enables children to build cultural capital and develops collaboration, social and communication skills. When studying the sociology of education, you may have encountered Pierre Bourdieu's writings about the way in which educational institutions can be responsible for reproducing social inequalities. The theory is complex and in it he refers to what he calls 'cultural capital', the possession of which brings power and status to the individual. More simply, cultural capital includes any advantages that might provide an individual with a higher status in society and can include forms of knowledge, skills, and education. One interpretation of Bourdieu's work sees parents providing their children with the attitudes and knowledge that can make the educational system one in which they are comfortable and a place where they can succeed. As we mentioned earlier, we believe there is a responsibility for teachers to provide their students with access to a range of the arts in a range of cultures simply because it may be these children's only opportunity for this experience given the range of home environments. These arts experiences can provide children with access to this 'cultural capital' that many would not otherwise have.

Another element of Bourdieu's theory focuses on communication through language as being a further source of social distinction and inequality. Experiences in the arts, as noted, provide alternate modes of expression and communication for children. Children's early

Neryl Jeanneret

communication involves a variety of modes including movement, music, role-play, and visual and plastic arts, which are independent of language. Johnson (2007) suggests that the arts can be an important factor in the development of language and literacy because 'early expression in the arts bolsters the child's experiences of successful communication, thereby fostering further communicative development' (p. 316). The development of communication, collaboration, and social skills are all fostered by the arts in that many activities involve groups working together towards a common goal.

Learning in the arts can link with development in other learning areas such as literacy and numeracy, and we will be looking in detail at this in Chapter 4. There has been much written about connections between the arts and development in other learning areas, and many of the studies mentioned in that chapter have attempted to find causal links to 'academic' achievement. While these studies are frequently well meaning, the results, whether positive or negative, can misleadingly place the arts in a different category from 'essential scholarship', which is often mistakenly assumed to be primarily the province of language and mathematics. The arts are every bit as scholarly and rigorous as any other learning area, but they are the only learning area that needs to be justified as part of the curriculum because they might, for example, improve abilities in Mathematics (see Smith 2001). Let us come from the perspective of the British aesthetician and critic Herbert Read who said in 1943, 'In the end I do not distinguish science and art, except as methods, and I believe that the opposition created between them in the past has been due to a limited view of both activities. Art is the representation, science the explanation of the same reality'. Let us think more in terms of how the arts might complement other learning areas while retaining their distinction. Consider the proposition that the arts 'leave room for and celebrate different ways into the same topic' (Davis 2005). Rather than ending with an arts activity as something of an add-on to a topic of study, consider ways in which the arts might begin the topic. Think of ways you can bring concepts from other learning areas into your arts lessons. A simple example is that creating and recounting stories clearly enhances literacy skills. Asking children to organise classroom instruments into groups according to whether they are wood, metal or skin, or the method by which they're played, involves skills of classification. This book provides countless examples of this kind of thinking, starting with the arts rather than finishing with (or without) them.

The two most influential educational psychologists of the twentieth century, Jean Piaget and Lev Vygotsky, arrived at their theories about children's mental and symbolic development through scrupulous study of young children, including the most detailed study of their play and their art (for example, Piaget 1962, and Vygotsky 1971). Both of these great psychologists realised that play and art are equally crucial to human development, and that art has its own developmental stages. There have been a number of suggestions about how children progress through levels of artistic development, but most of these have focused on the visual arts (see the work of Lowenfeld, whose book *Creative and Mental Growth* (1947) has gone through seven editions and is regarded as the single most influential textbook in art education during the latter half of the twentieth century). In 1980, Wolf and Gardner proposed four major stages of artistic development that correspond to Piaget's stages of cognitive development: (1) the child as direct communicator; (2) the child as symbol user; (3) the youth as craftsman; and (4) the youth as critic and full participant in the artistic process. Table 2.1 illustrates the first three of these stages, and it can be helpful when you consider it beside other models of development such as that of Piaget and Vygotsky.

Table 2.1 Artistic development (Wolf & Gardner 1980)

1 Birth to 18–24 months	• The child as a director/communicator is gaining practical knowledge from acting on the world. • During this time, the child learns to communicate, to trust others and gain an awareness that the world consists of stable objects about which one can communicate. • The role of the educator is to be responsive to the child's needs and communications.
2 From 18–24 months to 5–7 years	• The child is a symbol user. • During this time the child's artistic work is in the creation and 'reading' of artistic symbols gained by discovery through play. • The challenge for education is to respect the children's spontaneity, originality, and individuality while they move from their own idiosyncratic forms of representation to those dictated by society. It is a time to cherish and nurture the child's individual expression.
3 From 5–7 to 11–13 years	• The youth is a craftsperson—one who stands back from his or her work and perceives it in a more objective sense, often in terms of societal standards. • The child in this stage is more subject to peer influences and is moving from childhood to young adulthood. • The challenge of education is to help the child combine artistic craftsmanship and criticism with self-expression without being paralysed by feelings of inadequacy.

This section only touches the surface of what learning in the arts can be in the classroom, but we hope it will generate reflection, discussion, and further reading in the area.

Activities for students

Whole class activity: brainstorm

1   Consider the proposition that the arts 'leave room for and celebrate different ways into the same topic' (Davis 2005).

2   Look at a sample of a primary school science curriculum. Brainstorm ways that the arts could be used to introduce five different key topics.

Neryl Jeanneret

Small group task: follow-up

Select one of the topics from the group brainstorm, and develop an introductory lesson outline to illustrate how the arts activity and science curriculum intersect.

Written task (individual): language and literacy development

Consider one of the early childhood case studies from Part Two or Three of this book. Identify and discuss ways in which communication, collaborative, and social skills are fostered through the arts practice in the case study.

Major assignment: artistic development

With appropriate permissions, observe a young child (up to 8 years old) at play. Record observations. Identify examples of artistic development in the observation—based on Table 2.1. Articulate your conclusions regarding the arts and learning in early childhood.

Key references

Chapman, L. (2001) 'Can the Arts Win Hearts and Minds?' *Arts Education Policy Review,* 102(5), 21–3.

Cooper-Solomon, D. (1995) 'The Arts are Essential', *School Arts,* 94(6), 29.

Davis, J.H. (2005) 'Redefining Ratso Rizzo: Learning from the Arts about Process and Reflection', *Phi Delta Kappan,* 87, 11–17.

Dreyfuss, R. (1996) Speech at the 38th Annual Grammy Awards, 29 February 1996.

Eisner, E. (1982) *Cognition and Curriculum: A Basis for Deciding What to Teach,* Longman, New York.

Eisner, E. (2002) *The Educational Imagination: On the Design and Evaluation of School Programs,* Prentice Hall, New Jersey.

Fowler, C. (1994) 'Strong Arts, Strong Schools', *Educational Leadership,* 52(3).

Harker, R. (ed.) (1990) *Education and Cultural Capital,* Macmillan Press, London.

Johnson, H.L. (2007) 'Aesthetic Experience and Early Language and Literacy Development', *Early Child Development and Care,* 177(3).

Lowenfeld, V. (1947) *Creative and Mental Growth,* Macmillan, New York.

Piaget, J. (1962) *Play, Dreams and Imitation in Childhood,* Routledge & Kegan Paul, London.

Polanyi, M. (1967) *The Tacit Dimension,* Anchor Books, New York.

Read, H. (1943) *Education Through Art,* Faber and Faber, London.

Reid, L.A. (1986) '"Art" and the Arts', in M. Ross (ed.), *Assessment in the Arts,* Pergamon Press, Oxford.

Reimer, B. (1989) *A Philosophy of Music Education* (2nd edn), Prentice-Hall, New Jersey.

Robinson, K. (2001) *Out of Our Minds: Learning to be Creative,* Capstone Books, Oxford.

Smith, R.A. (2001) 'The Harvard REAP Study: Inherent "Versus" Instrumental Values', *Arts Education Policy Review*, 102(5).

Vygotsky, L. (1971) *The Psychology of Art*, MIT Press, Boston.

Wolf, D. & Gardner, H. (1980) 'Beyond Playing or Polishing: A Development View of Artistry', in J. Houseman (ed.), *Arts and the Schools* (pp. 47–77), McGraw-Hill, New York.

3

Arts Education as Intercultural and Social Dialogue

Kate Donelan

In this chapter Kate Donelan canvasses the complex issues associated with achieving intercultural understanding—questions of language, cultural sensitivities, and appropriation and the theoretical frameworks and arts practices that can cast light on the rocky and changing terrain inhabited by new generation 'global citizens'.

Successive waves of migration have created modern Australia—one of the most ethnically and linguistically diverse countries in the world. As a teacher in the twenty-first century, you will be working in school communities with people from different cultural, linguistic, social, and religious backgrounds. Your classroom may include children who are Indigenous, those who are descended from European or Asian settlers in the nineteenth or twentieth centuries, as well as those who are first-generation migrants, refugees, or asylum seekers who have recently fled war-torn countries. The impact of migration, displacement, travel, greater mobility, and globalisation will inevitably impact on the life experiences of the children you teach. In the context of an increasingly interconnected world the school curriculum needs to prepare students for becoming tolerant and aware local and global citizens. In this chapter I discuss the important role of the arts in cross-cultural education—in building children's capacity to understand the world from many different perspectives.

Before exploring the arts curriculum as a place for developing intercultural 'literacy' it is important to explain the use of some key concepts. Contemporary cultural theorists have helped us understand that people's 'identity' is not a fixed, static, and essential state, but a dynamic process that evolves throughout one's life. Within Australia the concept of 'cultural diversity' is defined broadly to include differences based on race, ethnicity, language, religion, value and belief systems, disability, class, sexuality, gender, age, and educational background. Within the field of education, 'intercultural' refers to one's experience of other groups and of other conventions, beliefs, values, and behaviours—of being between cultures. 'Intercultural' is often the preferred term for the relationship between cultures, indicating cultural interactions based on mutual respect (Fennes and Hapgood 1997). Many educators argue that an effective 'intercultural education' prepares young people for living in complex, democratic, pluralistic societies (Castles 1995).

Arts educators have long recognised the power of the arts to open up cross-cultural communication and intercultural understanding. Arts activities in the classroom enable students to imagine, engage with, interpret, and express a range of cultural experiences and perspectives—those that are familiar as well as those that are new and challenging. The symbolic and metaphoric languages of the arts open up pathways for young people to encounter and explore different cultural perspectives. Throughout the years of primary and middle school, students need regular opportunities to create, make, and share their ideas and experiences through the arts, as well as to engage with narratives, images, music, dance, stories, and performances that communicate different cultural responses to the world.

The arts play a vital role in intercultural learning as they provide the means for children to connect imaginatively with the lived experiences of people in different kinds of societies past and present. Drama, for example, provides young people with opportunities to stand in other people's shoes, to empathise with the worldviews of people with a range of life experiences, and to practise and develop more effective and sensitive communication within and across cultures. The arts curriculum can increase students' knowledge of and respect for different cultural expressions; participation in visual and performing arts activities can build students' awareness of various arts 'languages' and conventions,

Kate Donelan

and provide rich opportunities for exploring and engaging with new and evolving arts practices. A multicultural arts curriculum enables young people to create, explore, invent, interpret, and perform a diverse range of personal, social, and cultural stories and ideas. In this way the arts classroom becomes a safe, participatory space where students re-imagine themselves and expand their sense of people's lived experiences in diverse communities within an interconnected world.

Recent education literature emphasises the important role of the arts in developing multicultural literacy and intercultural understanding. Nicholson believes that in an increasingly globalised society, teachers need to consider how their curriculum in schools might 'reflect the dynamic cultural landscapes in which young people live' (2000, p. 160). The arts can introduce students to new ways of feeling and thinking through providing them with experiences of a range of cultural forms and artistic practices. My own research shows that performing arts and drama experiences can be a powerful way of developing embodied intercultural understanding, cultural knowledge, and respect for differences (Donelan 2002). For Saldaña, the arts curriculum can be the foundation of a 'multi-ethnic education' as it builds young people's 'knowledge about and respect for the traditions, history, values, languages, art forms, and literature of various ethnic groups' (1995, p. xii). The work of many primary and middle school teachers demonstrates that encouraging an active exploration of different values and traditions through multicultural arts programs can promote understanding across and among cultures.

Given the diversity of contemporary societies, and the increasing interaction between people from different regions of the world, schools are important places for developing cross-cultural understanding. Schools reflect the values and beliefs of their communities, and the social and cultural environment that surrounds them. Within an Australian context the arts curriculum needs to allow for a plurality of voices, for young people to express and communicate many different stories and ways of interpreting contemporary society through the visual and performing arts. Many arts educators in Australia acknowledge the diverse social and cultural communities in which they work and the need for their pedagogy to be inclusive and to promote respect for different ways of viewing the world. For example, *The Drama Australia Equity and Diversity Policy* (2004, p. 3) argues that drama educators need to 'engage with issues of identity, equity and diversity within their daily practices' and I can't imagine it would be any different for the other arts. The Australia Council's multicultural arts policy, *Arts in a Multicultural Australia* (2000), is underpinned by a commitment to 'building bridges, encouraging dialogues, creating and accepting opportunities' (p. 10). It broadens the definition of multicultural arts practice beyond a community and ethnic context to reflect a sense of the complexities of cultural identity and exchange within Australia and globally. The Australia Council's *National Education and the Arts Strategy* suggests that arts educators should provide opportunities for young people to 'explore and contribute to a plurality of ideas and practices reflective of the culturally diverse nature of Australian society' (2004, p. 9).

Many arts teachers see the task of building cross-cultural understanding as an integral part of their work with students. Within arts programs, and especially drama, racism, human rights and social justice are issues that are often directly addressed. Grady argues that rather than addressing cultural difference as a topic in the curriculum, arts educators should adopt difference as a practice so that their pedagogical and artistic choices are informed by a critical awareness of themselves and the context of the work. She calls on classroom teachers to critically examine their belief systems and their assumptions about cultural 'others', including the students they teach (Grady 2000).

The arts within the primary and middle school curriculum offers young people opportunities to build connections with other people's stories and experiences, and to imagine, enact, and experience the world from different perspectives. Drama has the capacity to emphasise a collaborative and participatory teaching approach that fosters dialogue among different voices, traditions, and ethnic backgrounds. Within a context of US multicultural classrooms, Manley and O'Neill write about the use of drama and arts-based programs to explore African-American history, heritage, and its relationship to their students' diverse cultural experiences (1997). Oral and written literature offers a context for the exploration of cultural themes and issues through arts-based practice. Through exploring the values embedded in culturally diverse stories young people can expand their emotional, intellectual, and creative perspectives. In response to the ethnic diversity of contemporary UK classrooms, Winston (1998) draws on traditional stories from a variety of cultural sources as pre-texts for drama that would apply equally well to other art forms. As an Australian drama educator, Simons uses stories to connect her students 'in metaphor to people around the world, in the past and in the future, helping us to explore what it means to be human' (Simons 2000, p. 25).

Intercultural awareness and communication is fostered when young people experience a participatory culture of shared storytelling through various media in their classroom. In a forum-like and creative learning environment students can refashion stories to their own meanings, 'influenced by the mobile and diverse culture, which they are both making and living' (Rosen 1999, p. 349). Using the collaborative, interactive processes of the arts, students can create and play with alternative versions of stories, communicating familiar and different values and standpoints through a variety of symbol systems. They can explore how particular narratives have been transformed and adapted to different contexts and for different audiences and purposes. Through representing their interpretations of a story and by embodying its characters and situations, students can gain access, from the inside, to the world of the story and its cultural reference points.

Young people who are introduced to different oral storytelling conventions can develop an understanding of how intercultural meaning is carried both in the form and content of a story, and in the communicative style of the storyteller. In my research on students' intercultural learning, I focused on a group of Australian students in a performing arts project led by an African artist. The students were introduced to Kenyan music, oracy, and storytelling traditions. With the guidance of their African teaching artist, they explored Kenyan storytelling conventions and call and response songs, and explored traditional African children's stories. As part of the project students developed their own version of an African narrative, the *Tortoise Story*, and adapted it to express contemporary issues through participatory storytelling, singing, percussion sounds, and dance. In this project the Kenyan teacher-artist was a cultural guide, introducing the students to unfamiliar arts conventions, explaining cultural references and encouraging the young people to actively explore and adapt Kenyan stories to create and communicate their own meanings.

Through arts activities students can construct images of imagined experiences, and can reinterpret their own and others' lives and attitudes. The arts can generate powerful learning about complex human behaviour because, although they draw from the social and cultural world, they work metaphorically; that is, they represent rather than replicate reality. Fleming (1998) argues that teachers can use the conventions of an art form to 'destabilise and challenge normal ways in which the world is seen and experienced' (p. 160). Arts elements and conventions can be used to create distance, defamiliarise taken-for-granted behaviour and customs, and provide alternative perspectives that are essential for building students' cultural awareness. The arts can affirm people's cultural identity and shared experiences, but they also provide the means for people to distance themselves from their own cultural backgrounds and start to see themselves in new ways. Arts experiences in the classroom invite a sharing and reflective analysis of different human values and cultural perspectives.

Anne Marshall, Australian Indigenous educator, relates the importance of the arts in children's education to the concept of 'songlines', which she defines as 'the close connectedness of people, events, social and religious beliefs, environment and movement through the land: a mapping of identity and country through the visual and performing arts'. She analyses 'the rich performance textures' of traditional Indigenous ceremonies with their mixtures of expressive media and symbolic forms. Simultaneous layers of meaning are explored through 'synaesthesia', which is 'the engagement and blending of all the senses in the acts of both creating and interpreting meaning'. She regards synaesthesia as the basis of all learning through the arts (2004, p. 56).

From Marshall's perspective Australian arts educators should teach all their students 'in the Aboriginal way'—to implement a curriculum based on 'multi-layered storytelling' involving all the senses in the acts of both creating and interpreting meaning. She advocates students building and performing stories that incorporate oral, visual, and auditory narratives, as well as 'body narratives, smell and taste narratives and landscape narratives'. In order to explore the 'being in the world' of Australian Aboriginal people, she suggests teachers draw on two different types of Indigenous narratives—those related to 'culture pre-invasion and its survival', and culture after European contact. She explains how, through performative storytelling, teachers can use contemporary narratives and fables to teach religious and spiritual concepts, ethics, law, and social structures. Students engage in the act of storytelling by 'linking knowledge, intellect, emotions, physicality and experience in the body'. Marshall believes the concept of 'songlines' can be applied broadly and that, in a sense, all people can be considered to be 'indigenous' to the places where they live. She urges teachers to assist Australian young people of diverse cultural backgrounds to reinterpret their own 'history narratives, songlines, dreaming stories and/or experiences of the world' (Marshall 2004, pp. 57–65).

In the context of a dangerously changed world, many educators have called for a renewed emphasis on the qualities that are central to the arts—empathic imagination and creativity. The tragic events in New York in 2001 highlighted the need for schools to adopt a humanising curriculum, to focus on ways to develop compassion, empathy, tolerance, interpersonal skills, and respect for difference (Neelands 2002, p. 8). By using arts experiences to imagine and discover new aspects of themselves, students can move beyond a restricted, socially and culturally defined sense of self and challenge their stereotyped images of other people.

The arts in the school curriculum offers rich opportunities for young people to explore different social and cultural experiences, to create, adapt, and perform intercultural narratives and build what Trinh (1989, p. 123) calls a 'vividly felt insight into the life of other people'. After participating in a drama project for the first time, Vi, a Hong Kong Australian girl from a multicultural school, commented: 'Theatre is like a place where you can visit any world you want or any character you want'. Some of her classmates were recent refugees with limited English, some had travelled with their families from rural and remote Australia in search of better life opportunities, and others were children of first- and second-generation migrants born in the inner city. These students all participated actively and collaboratively in a creative arts project where they researched, improvised, wrote, illustrated, and performed songs and stories about their parents' and grandparents' lives and their own emerging identities within contemporary Australian society.

An arts-rich curriculum enables the diverse young people we teach to build new understandings of their own and others' social and cultural worlds.

Activities for students

Workshop: write, draw, perform

Storytelling. Begin, as a whole group, sharing a traditional story—each student to bring a story of cultural significance to share with the whole group. Select one story to explore further. In small groups, explore interpretations of the story, through discussion, enactment, and retelling. Choose a medium of arts-based expression/representation for your group to 'retell' the story (drama, visual arts, plastic arts, multimedia, music). Share and discuss.

Kate Donelan

Key references

Australia Council (2000) *Arts in a Multicultural Australia (AMA)*, Australia Council, Sydney.

Australia Council (2004) *National Education and the Arts Strategy*, Australia Council, Sydney.

Castles, S. (1995) 'Introduction', paper presented at the Global Cultural Diversity Conference, Sydney.

Donelan, K. (2002) 'Embodied Practices: Ethnography and Intercultural Drama in the Classroom', *NJ (Drama Australia Journal)*, 26(2), 35–46.

Drama Australia (2004) *Equity and Diversity Guidelines*, retrieved 22 September 2007 from http://www.dramaaustralia.org.au/guidelines.html.

Fennes, H. & Hapgood, K. (1997) *Intercultural Learning in the Classroom*, Cassell, London.

Fleming, M. (1998) 'Cultural Awareness and Dramatic Art Forms', in M. Byram & M. Fleming (eds), *Language Learning in Intercultural Perspective* (pp. 147–57), Cambridge University Press, Cambridge.

Grady, S. (2000) *Drama and Diversity*, Heinemann, Portsmouth, NH.

Manley, A. & O'Neill, C. (eds) (1997) *Dreamseekers*, Heinemann, Portsmouth, NH.

Marshall, A. (2004) 'Singing Your Own Songlines: Approaches to Indigenous Drama', in M. Mooney & J. Nichols (eds), *Drama Journeys: Inside Drama Learning* (pp. 55–76), Sydney Currency Press, Sydney.

Neelands, J. (2002) '11/09 The space in our hearts', *Summer 2002*, 4–10.

Nicholson, H. (ed.) (2000) *Teaching Drama*, Continuum, London and New York.

Rosen, H. (1999) 'Narrative in Intercultural Education', *European Journal of Intercultural Studies*, 10(3), 343–53.

Saldaña, J. (1995) *Drama of Color*, Heinemann, Portsmouth, NH.

Simons, J. (2000) 'Walking in Another Person's Shoes: Storytelling and Role-play', in Nicholson, H. (ed.), *Teaching Drama* (16–25). Continuum, London and New York.

Trinh, T.M. (1989) *Woman, Native, Other: Writing Postcoloniality and Feminism*, Indiana University Press, Bloomington.

Winston, J. (1998) *Drama, Narrative and Moral Education: Exploring Traditional Tales in the Primary Years*, Falmer Press, London.

Multi-literacies and the Arts

John O'Toole

In this chapter John O'Toole provides a contemporary view of a very familiar topic in education: literacy. John harnesses the powerful arguments currently being mounted for a reconceptualising of literacy education to encompass a range of 'literacies', verbal and otherwise. The idea that schools educate for multi-literacies, and that the arts scaffold the development of these literacies, provides a cornerstone for this chapter and indeed for the principles articulated in this book. The multi-literacies discussed are oracy (speaking and listening), literacy (reading and writing), visual literacy (reading and interpreting visual symbols), mathematical literacy, technological literacy, critical, social, aesthetic and functional literacy in each of the art forms.

Back to the basics

Teaching the arts, you are teaching some very important knowledge, understandings, and skills in their own right, but you are also teaching much more than the arts themselves. You are, as we have mentioned in chapters 1 and 2, also teaching both literacy and numeracy. Research both old (Clegg 1980) and new (Bamford 2006) tells us that an arts-rich environment actually improves literacy and numeracy results, so by taking time to do the arts in your classroom you are not depriving the children of their literacy and numeracy teaching, but are seriously value-adding to it. Back in the 1960s, Alec Clegg, a UK Regional Director of Education, noticed that a group of schools with children from very impoverished backgrounds, who were being given arts-rich teaching, were consistently outscoring much more privileged schools in the 11-Plus examination, which tested only maths, mental arithmetic, comprehension, written grammar, and IQ. Since then various studies, none of them in themselves conclusive but all authoritative (for example, Gardner et al. 1989, Deasy 2002, Bamford 2006, and Wagner 1998), have explored this further to suggest that certain art forms develop and reinforce particular aspects of literacy and numeracy. Of course, we have to be cautious when claiming that any single intervention such as increasing arts provision in schools increases skills as complex as reading and mathematics—especially as there are many charlatans out there ready to seize on quick-fix and attractive notions, particularly for their own advantage. The 'Mozart Effect' (a speculation that might indeed have a grain of validity, that listening to music, especially Mozart apparently, temporarily increases temporal-spatial intelligence) has spawned quite an industry of shonky books and schemes claiming to improve intelligence, literacy, numeracy, bad behaviour, dim rats, and plant growth, as well as cure cancer.[1] On the other hand, there are increasing numbers of more cautious experiments that show positive results, such as the two hundred studies of the effect of drama on language scrutinised by Ann Podlozny (2000), or Martin Gardiner's carefully controlled 1996 study over two years, which indicated very strongly that regular and sustained teaching in visual arts and music improved standardised test results in reading (bringing low-performing students up to equality with their peers) and maths (putting them ahead).

In recent years, the term 'multi-literacies', coined in 1996 by a group of distinguished Australian, US, and UK educators who called themselves 'The New London Group' after their initial meeting venue, has become popular, and is much more helpful than 'the basics' or 'the three Rs'—only one of which is an R, incidentally—to define what is essential for young people to learn in schools:

> the authors' twin goals for literacy learning: creating access to the evolving language of
> work, power, and community, and fostering the critical engagement necessary for them
> to design their social futures and achieve success through fulfilling employment (Cazden
> et al. 1996, p. 1).

These goals signal much more than just textual literacy and numeracy. The influential human development psychologist Michael Csikszentmihalyi has written that

> Literacy presupposes the existence of a shared symbol system that mediates information
> between the individual's mind and external events (1990, p. 119)

and that means not just writing, but all the symbol systems, linguistic and otherwise, that
mediate meaning, each with their own literacy demands.

Suppose we start to address what these statements imply by looking at orthodox
literacy, as it is still usually interpreted in schools. *Reading and writing* have been and still
are enormously important, since ancient hieroglyphs turned into alphabets and ideographs,
and especially since the invention of the printing press. However, they are sandwiched
between two other equally, if not more important literacies: *oracy* and *computer literacy*.
For all the thousands of years before those scratches on tablets and papyrus, and still today
for 90 per cent of our lives, humans have depended on the most important and forgotten
basic of all: oracy, the ability to make live communication (which actually includes
verbal, vocal, and non-verbal language). And the importance in our lives of the computer
and internet, and all the connected technologies of mobile phones, iPods, PDAs and so on
is self-evident.

Oracy (speaking and listening ability)

We take for granted in our language and English syllabuses that schools develop oracy. The
Victorian Essential Learning Standards (VELS) Introduction to English states:

> The English domain is centred on the conscious and deliberate study of language in the
> variety of texts and contexts in which it is spoken, read, viewed and written. It is concerned
> with a wide range of written and spoken texts in print and electronic forms including
> literary texts such as novels, short stories, poetry, plays and non-fiction; film and other
> multimodal texts; media texts; information, commercial and workplace texts; everyday
> texts; and personal writing.

This is interesting in several ways. 'Spoken' is the first word in the list of how language
is manifested, suggesting that it is of primary importance. The next sentence, however,
though ambiguous, appears to be dealing almost entirely with print and electronic texts.
And traditionally in schools, far more curriculum time is given to those than to the spoken
word—if we remember that when in school, the teacher controls the oral language, and
for a lot of the time the students are doing not-talking activities. This becomes even
more the norm as the students get older, and more and more activities and assessments
are written. The UK National Oracy Project (Scott 1991, pp. A81–3) reported that prior
to coming to school, children overwhelmingly think of themselves as good talkers and
communicators—parents do not as a rule inhibit their children's language, and it's natural
to be proud and encouraging of each step, so parents instinctively 'scaffold' their child's
understanding of, and through language, by taking the child's ideas seriously, thinking
through what the child is trying to communicate, allowing the child to move ahead when

John O'Toole

ready, and supporting the child when she or he seems to need help. Then they go to school. By 7 or 8 years of age, after we trained communicators have taken over, children believe the following: talking stops you working; talking is not work; if you are allowed to talk the work is not important; teachers let you talk as long as you do it quietly. They have worked out for themselves the low status of talk in school. And of course, as students work their way up the year levels, there is progressively less time for talk and live interaction in the classroom, except from and through the teacher. And if this does not sufficiently indicate the low importance given to oracy in comparison to written literacy, then compare the number of standardised and other regular tests in oracy with those in literacy—none, did I hear you say?

All this goes to show that such oracy as adults have comes mainly from out-of-school life, by osmosis. Is it enough? How confident are you in speaking without notes to any gathering of any size and keeping their interest and attention? How sure are you when people are talking to you about personal or professional matters that you are accurately and perceptively reading the sub-texts, the unspoken signals that show how people are really feeling, their sincerity, their ironies? Could you learn a Shakespeare play or a book from a scripture by heart in a few days, as people were able to without strain only a few hundred years ago (before we learned to rely on writings instead of memory)?

There *is* strong evidence (Parsons et al. 1984, Wagner 1998, and Podlozny 2000) that the arts in schools do have significant positive effect on oracy—all the arts, but particularly drama, of course. In 1984 in Tasmania, the first major Australian study, *Drama, Language and Learning* showed that students' language significantly improved in kind, quality, and depth with significant use of drama in the classroom. Not only does drama give students permission and opportunity to talk a lot, but it demands practice in speaking like others, people within and beyond their experience, experimenting with and developing a range of registers from outside the classroom, new vocabulary, new gestural signals. Drama demands listening to tone and observing non-verbal signals (paralanguage) so as to read and respond to sub-texts accurately and effectively. Drama is in fact, the only way in which the teacher can normally introduce contexts for practising spoken language from outside the classroom and from outside the children's direct experience—and it is as simple as saying 'let's pretend that we are …'. Other arts have their importance in developing rather than inhibiting oracy too. Storytelling and story-making are vital in children's learning, and not only must teachers be good storytellers, but we also need to be alive to the opportunities to develop students' ability to tell a good story well. Dance and movement help students to understand, interpret, and manage the expressive elements of movement and the body, and to learn a broader and better coordinated range of gestural language. Music helps to tune the ear to the rhythms and cadences of language, to the subtleties of tonality, to the distinctive patterns of accent. And in the primary school all the arts, including visual arts and particularly film and television work, are invariably opportunities for collaborative endeavour in practical, embodied activities that demand discussion and decision-making, and they all help to provide natural and challenging speaking and listening tasks.

Literacy (reading and writing)

Going right back to the beginning of literacy, learning to read and write is all done through the eyes and ears, with the major help of visual arts, music, and storytelling. There are many competing and hotly contested theories about the best and most reliable way to teach children to read and write (alphabet, whole words, phonics, and so on). If we look at *any* of them, right through from historic ABC primers to today's animated computer schemes, we can see immediately that they all entail responding to and learning to manage aesthetically designed visual symbols, using aural cues of rhyme and rhythm and often melody too, and telling and acting out stories to provide contexts for meaningful word recognition. So, willy-nilly, anybody involved in reading and writing is involved in the arts, and the more artistic understanding and control the teacher has, the better able we are to recognise each child's need, and fine-tune the scheme or materials we are working with. Later on, creative storytelling and drama give wonderful opportunities for contextualised, motivated writing in any genre, particularly process drama: 'Let's write to the giant, to ask him to stop stealing our sheep'.

Mathematical literacy and numeracy

There has been a great deal of speculation that music has much in common with mathematics, and, as we have already noted, a growing amount of research to suggest that music improves maths, and vice versa, with similar research in the relationship between intensive visual arts teaching (and dance too) and improvement in spatial awareness, geometry, and so on. While none of this is conclusive, there is no evidence whatever to support the reverse notion, which many teachers and principals seem to fear: that increasing the time spent on the arts in schools will damage or hinder mathematical skills any more than literacy. This is based on a very simplistic notion indeed (or usually an unthought through assumption) that time spent on the arts is time out of maths. Far from it: much of your other academic reading, as well as the classrooms you have been in or worked in, will have shown you how complex and non-linear learning is, and how much understanding comes through learning in context—in meaningful tasks that embody a range and multiplicity of skills and knowledge at the same time. And the arts provide learning in a context that is highly motivated, too. In a unit on the Industrial Revolution, the students might study the relationships between the mechanics of the body and machines through music and dance sequences; through drama, as toy designers and factory workers they might study steam engines—science—so they can invent new mechanical toys; then make scale drawings and models of them—geometry; work out an economic price for them according to whether they will be sold to the children of the rich or the poor—more maths; create vivid advertisements for their products—visual arts—and write instructions for their use—more literacy practice. And they are getting historically literate, too.[2]

Technological literacy

It's a brave (and probably young) teacher that thinks she or he will be able to teach much about technological literacy to the digital natives that make up most of the class … at least without considerable help. Once more the arts can provide a platform, since children and young people already spend a great deal of time expressing themselves and discovering their identities in cyberspace, as well as enjoying themselves, doing activities full of design and intricate narratives and problem-solving. The sophisticated software available for creating, interpreting, and appreciating music and visual arts, and the many sites available for developing imaginative narratives and dramatic situations, continue to provide the high motivation that computer interactivity offers, and will broaden and deepen the range and intellectual challenge of the technology, while providing transferable skills for other uses of it. Some of the scholars of the internet have recognised this, explicitly in the case of writers like Brenda Laurel (1993) and Jenny Leach (2001), and instinctively by others like James Gee (2005) and Marc Prensky (2007). To give the students the power to create and compose through the web and other multimedia platforms, and to engage in multi-player narratives involving imagination and collaborative problem-solving, have another important function, too. Much of what the students encounter on the web is intently and deliberately manipulative, and of a very high order of aesthetic design (we will have more to say on this below). We need to give them the critical and skilful tools to understand, see through, and manage for themselves the virtual environments that confront them. The best way to develop *critical* understanding is to provide access to the creative tools that the professional designers and manipulators themselves use.

… and lots of other literacies

As you have just read, and no doubt come across in your language studies and reading, *critical literacy* is one of the most highly valued capabilities in contemporary education—literacy capable of critiquing not just written texts, but those texts generated in real-time (oral, embodied, and kinaesthetic texts); and on camera, computers, mobile phones, and other contemporary technology (screen, audio, computer, and other virtual texts). The notion of critical literacy actually depends on the ability to read behind the words, or whatever other units of meaning are presented (such as images, sounds, gestures, and actions) to discover the unspoken sub-texts—the attitudes, the political and philosophical ideologies, the world-view, the power relations and the emotions that give rise to every utterance, and shape it, but remain implicit or hidden from obvious view.

This demands an understanding of people and the relationships between them and society, and each other; in other words, *social literacies*. There are some very important social literacies, which all schools would see as an important part of our duty to foster, which are strongly developed through the arts, especially the performing arts, because they demand very sophisticated attention to and management of social and interpersonal contexts.

- One of the most important of these is *self-presentational literacy*, more commonly known as self-confidence in public. The performing arts are among those prime contexts where presenting ourselves as effectively as possible to audiences of strangers is part of the basic skills. Haseman in 1990 (collecting statistics only on drama) confirmed what every secondary performing arts teacher knows from talking to parents, students, and even principals—that encouraging self-confidence in public is one of the strongest, if not *the* strongest, motivation for students electing to take arts subjects.

- Another important social literacy is *interpersonal literacy*, the ability to work effectively in groups. Quite apart from the fact that human beings live almost entirely in social groups, more and more, the world of adult employment, once obsessed by individual competitive achievement, is recognising that teamwork and social communication skills are vital to any enterprise. Responding to this in the 1990s, the Queensland Board of Senior Secondary School Studies discovered to its alarm that the only senior-level assessment that actually consistently encourages ensemble work and increased social literacy (as opposed to inhibiting them) is found in the arts and again physical education. Naturally, because for the performing arts collaborative, complex, and precise ensemble work is vital … and has been since children learned naturally how to play together without fighting; for instance, in their dramatic play, especially when unsupervised or unwatched by adults, they can collaboratively preserve the illusion, and generate spontaneous and agreed fictional narratives for up to three hours without breaking roles (Dunn 2002). Visual arts, especially in the primary school, also play their part, because overwhelmingly they involve shared expression, creation, and response to the purposeful tasks of art making.

- Drama and storytelling, and visual arts too, are central to the effective development of *empathic literacy*, the ability to step into another person's shoes and change one's point of view, both emotionally and intellectually, to understand and manage human relationships, and how they are shaped by power and status relationships.

For all of these, and the many other literacies embedded in the term multi-literacies, all we have said above applies, as by this time you will realise, and probably be ahead of us in anticipating. For instance, returning to the Industrial Revolution example, through all the multiple art making embedded within the dramatic frame, the students were also acquiring an active and personalised understanding of the impact that this historical period had on our contemporary society and so, what we can learn from it today (which is both *historical literacy* and the best reason for studying history). We will leave you to cast through the rest of the curriculum domains yourselves, to fill in the opportunities that the arts offer, because we have one more extremely important set of literacies—*aesthetic literacy*, and *functional literacy in each of the art forms.*

John O'Toole

Aesthetic literacies

If you go back to Figure 1.2, there is, you may notice, a very large area of common ground in the middle, the territory of neither hard-core artists nor players, which we may express as in Figure 4.1:

Figure 4.1   Dialectic of play and art (c)

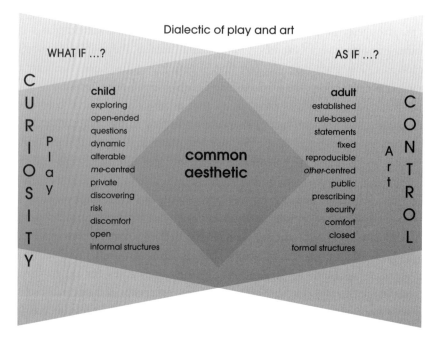

The phrase 'common ground' is doubly significant, as this is the territory of not just artists and players, but everybody, the social and personal places where our lives intersect with:

- the aesthetic of everyday life (the emotional and cognitive understanding of how we design, perform, storytell, and sing our lives)
- the playfulness of everyday life (the pleasure, the humour, the ironic subversion of our observation and wit and social intercourse).

In other words, there is a common aesthetic dimension that frames almost every aspect of contemporary life. We are not devaluing the word aesthetic by making it so broad as to be meaningless, or merely a simile for 'beautiful' or 'nice'. We are actually referring to the formal shaping of media to create a fusion of emotional, sensory, and cognitive impact in our lives: from visits to art spaces like theatres, cinemas, concerts, and galleries, to the pleasure we take in sketching, gardening, and decorating our homes. From everything on the internet, to the meticulous design of posters, billboards, and TV adverts, and to the performance art of the whole promotion industry aimed at grabbing both our conscious and our subliminal attention. From the music and dance we hear and make at parties, on iPods, in karaoke bars, to the muzak that insinuates itself into our subliminal minds in lifts and supermarkets, and the chants that lift us in religious and spiritual contexts, and the marches that equally inspire us into battle and slaughter. From the hours we watch television fictions, to the way we perform to each other the stories of our day and the strange encounters that happened to us. And then there's all the aesthetic of sport and many other of our pastimes, and the festivals, and so on. We are getting to live, it is said, in a 'hyperaesthetic reality' that we struggle to come to terms with (Lunenfeld 1996).

You'll no doubt have had very differing approval responses to this list of examples. Some of them you may very likely have shuddered at, like the subliminal ads, the supermarket muzak, and the military marches. This makes another overwhelming case for the arts in education—nobody could call that list unrelated to our real life, and unless we help to give young people the tools to understand, to manage for themselves, and to critique the forms and media of this ubiquitous and pervasive artistry, our young people will be unable to make their own ethical decisions, or wrest the power of art from the hands of those who do manipulate it for their own selfish ends. In other words, we need to give the students the holistic understanding to make sense of the good and bad artistry in the real and virtual worlds we are all part of. We must also give them far greater access to the skills of these arts, the technical and aesthetic skills, for them to have agency in these worlds.

Functional literacy in art form

And last, but by no means least, we should look at what each of the art forms offers our students in terms of necessary skills for life. Let's look first at the art most neglected in our schools: *dance*. Dance develops physical and kinaesthetic coordination, a sense of rhythm and flow of movement, helps young people to learn to use their bodies expressively and confidently, and develops highly important understanding of how bodies move in and occupy space, singly and in synchronisation. Of course, it also teaches people to dance, a social accomplishment whose lack is always sorely felt—and though social dance styles and genres change according to fashion and cultural factors, the control of motor coordination, tacit understanding of dance (body knowledge), and skill quickly to learn new dance forms is admired and prized—and at the moment, the province of a lucky few.

Everybody responds to *music*, at a very deep and often unconscious level. Musical memory is one of the most persistent parts of memory. However, think about how rarely in any social gathering we hear *Happy Birthday to You* actually sung tunefully, or any other song sung in harmony, and with a knowledge of all the words. As with dance, mainstream Australian culture has to some extent lost touch with the deeply ingrained musical skill training of a society that sings and dances, which has given every child growing up in many traditional monocultures the tacit knowledge of singing tunefully and harmoniously;

knowing all the words of many 'standards'; quickly able to pick up a tune and the lyrics of a new song; and dancing together in step and in complex rhythms. Contrary to what many musically demoralised Australians believe about themselves, almost nobody is tone deaf, though many have never been sufficiently helped to discriminate, or helped to hold a note and sing it confidently in public. Music is also a social attribute that is very culturally constrained, from a very young age, and people tend to respond easily to the narrow genres with which they are most familiar, through their family, their social group, and their peers and their media influences—which are then reinforced through the immediate access that contemporary technology gives to those genres. Effective music education can help to restore the confidence and develop the skills that the traditional child and adult take for granted; and broaden the understanding and appreciation of new and different genres and styles of music. And how valuable—and valued—in society it is to be able to create music and play an instrument competently.

Similarly, we are constantly called upon in life to create and respond to *visual images*—from sketching an idea or the explanation of a visual or physical image on the back of an envelope, to more complex designs for redesigning our house interior or creating our own Christmas card; from working out our appropriate dress for any occasion on a limited wardrobe and budget, to rearranging the furniture and what is on the walls of the home or office, or responding to a request about the design of a poster advertisement. All the former demand some skill with pencil, brush, or mouse; all the latter take discrimination and the ability to orient objects in space in terms of shape, colour, balance, and functionality; all of them demand spatial awareness, a sense of perspective and the confidence that we are able to carry out the task effectively. And this is before we start on the plastic arts, and having the ability and skill to shape aesthetically plastic, wood, metal, pastry, or concrete.

We have already touched on the functional literacies which are the province of *drama* and *storytelling*: the ability to keep an audience spellbound (or at the very least to get them to see us and hear us and keep their attention); the ability to arrest people's attention, too, and speak colourfully and dramatically with sincerity and articulately about what is important or vivid to us; to appear in public and know that we won't embarrass our audience or ourselves, but find an appropriate way of engaging them, whoever they are; to tell and perform bedtime stories to our children; to produce a public performative event that maximises its impact. Then there is that priceless ability of empathy, and understanding how human relationships work: to be able to stand in other people's shoes, role-play them and see the world through their eyes (and see ourselves through their eyes too) and see them as not 'other' but 'like me'.

And, finally, *all* of those basic functional literacies are the building blocks for each person to begin to fulfil their own potential, both as an artist and as an arts-lover. Just as you must understand and master the alphabet, before you can write anything, learn to stay afloat and propel yourself before you can swim anywhere, so before you can be an artist (a painter, sculptor, singer, musician, dancer, actor, playwright, storyteller, film-maker, multimedia maker) you must have the basic skills of the art form.

Activities for students

Assignment: solo or duo. Conduct your own case study—A day in a school

Spend one whole day in a school, including lunch and recess, before or after school. *Observation*: Identify all the different 'literacies' in evidence during the day—using the categories presented in the preceding chapter. *Analysis*: Consider the following questions: How are these literacies 'framed'—by which contexts, cultural, social, educational? How are these literacies 'scaffolded' in the classroom (if at all)? *Discuss*: From your observations choose an example of a literacy at work—consider the child or children's competency in that literacy, with a focus on the role of the teacher, the scaffolding of the skill acquisition, and the use of the arts (actual or possible).

Key references

Bamford, A. (2006) *The WOW Factor: Global Compendium of Arts Education Research*, Waxmann, New York.

Cazden, C. et al. (1996) 'A Pedagogy of Multi-literacies: Designing Social Futures', *Harvard Educational Review*, 66(1), 1–30.

Clegg, A. (1980) *About our Schools*, Oxford, Blackwell.

Csikszentmihalyi, M. (1990) 'Literacy and Intrinsic Motivation', *Daedalus*, 119(2), 119.

Deasy, R. (2002) *Critical Links: Learning in the Arts and Student Academic and Social Development*, Arts Education Partnerships, Washington.

Dunn, J. (2002) *Imagined Worlds in Play*, unpublished PhD thesis, Griffith University, Brisbane.

Gardiner, F., Fox, A., Knowles, F. & Jeffrey, D. (1996) 'Learning Improved by Arts Training', *Nature*, 381, 284.

Gardner, H. & Perkins, D. (1989) *Art, Mind, and Education: Research from Project Zero*, Urbana University of Illinois.

Gee, J. (2005) *Why Video Games are Good for Your Soul: Pleasure and Learning*, Common Ground, Altona.

Haseman, (1990) 'Working Out!: A Survey of Drama in Queensland Secondary Schools', *NADIE Journal*, vol. 14, no. 2, 34–41.

Laurel, B. (1993) *Computers as Theatre*, Addison-Wesley, Reading, MA.

Leach, J. (2001) 'A Hundred Possibilities: Creativity, Community and ICT', in A. Craft, R. Jeffrey, & M. Liebling (eds), *Creativity in Education*, Continuum, New York.

Lunenfeld, P. (1996) 'Theorizing in Real Time: Hyperaesthetics for the Technoculture', *After-Image* (Jan.–Feb.), retrieved 24 April 2008 from http://findarticles.com/p/articles/mi_m2479/is_n4_v23/ai_18339993.

John O'Toole

Parsons, B., Schaffner, M., Little, G., & Felton, H. (1984) *Drama, Language and Learning: NADIE Paper No 1*, National Association for Drama in Education, Hobart.

Podlozny, A. (2000) 'Strengthening Verbal Skills through the Use of Classroom Drama: A Clear Link', *Journal of Aesthetic Education*, 34(3/4), 239–75.

Prensky, M. (2007) *Games and Simulations in Online Learning: Research and Development Frameworks*, Information Science Publishers, Hershey PA.

Scott, K., in J. Johnson (Project Director) (1991) 'What Children Think About Talk', in *Talk and Learning 5–16: In-service Pack on Oracy for Teachers*, The Open University, Milton Keynes, UK.

VCAA (2007) *Victorian Essential Learning Standards: English*, retrieved 6 November 2007 from http://vels.vcaa.vic.edu.au/essential/discipline/english/index.html.

Wagner, B.-J. (1998) *Educational Drama and Language Arts: What the Research Shows*, Heinemann, Portsmouth, NH.

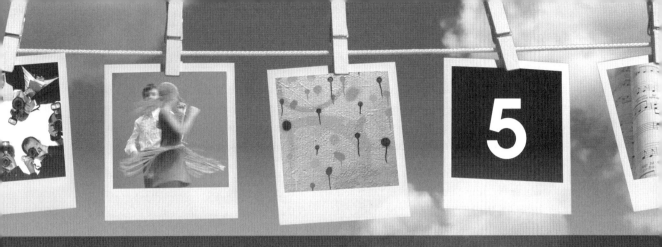

Teaching for the Aesthetic, Teaching as Aesthetic

Chris Sinclair

In this chapter, Chris Sinclair discusses some of the ways that the notion of the 'aesthetic' is understood and practised in school settings. She presents it as one of the essential but potentially problematic principles in arts education, and then signposts some of the ways that teachers of the arts might approach the scaffolding of aesthetic experiences and aesthetic learning for their students. The chapter concludes with a closer look at the aesthetics of teaching and proposes (and is not the first to do so) that there is artistry in the act of teaching.

> I think the arts is a thing that you have to make in your own world and do it in your own way. Art is a place you can go but I suppose you can't go deeper unless you do what you haven't done before. I tried bull riding and it is one of the best things I have done in my life and rugby—that is great. I haven't tried bungee jumping and I reckon if I tried that it would be great. They also change people—almost like an artist.
>
> (Patrick, Year 7) (Barrett and Smigiel 2003)

Before tackling the question of what it might mean to 'teach for the aesthetic' it is useful to pause for a moment to consider how children regard the arts generally, and more particularly, their role as arts-makers or art critics. A recent Australian study looked at how children understand and experience the arts in their daily lives. It revealed:

> that Australian children do see the arts as part of their daily lives, and that they understand and enjoy their participation in these activities. The difference appears to lie in the ways in which the arts are defined by (rather than for) these children, and the nature of their participation in arts activities (Barrett & Smigiel 2003).

This study, including the quote from Patrick, Year 7, reminds us, first, that it is easy to make assumptions about how children will engage with various aspects of their educational experiences and that these assumptions may not coincide with young people's perceptions at all, and second, that if you want to understand what children think about something, it can be very instructive to ask them!

The children referred to in the above study did not make a distinction between the arts as something one watches or looks at, or something one does oneself. They drew attention to experiences in which they could immerse themselves fully; that were enjoyable; that appealed to some sense of pattern or order. While there has been a long debate in the arts world about the relative merits and significance of 'high art' found in art galleries, theatres, and concert halls, versus populist art forms, like rock concerts, graffiti, raves, and *Neighbours*, the children in the study did not demonstrate concern about categorising their art experiences to fit with these pre-existing frameworks. Their judgments were very much driven by how participating or viewing the arts (based on their definition) made them feel. Perhaps many of them shared Michel Foucault's view of the person and their life as a work of art:

> What strikes me is the fact that in our society, art has become something which is related only to objects and not to individuals and /or to life—that art is something specialised and done by experts who are artists. But couldn't everyone's life become a work of art? (Foucault cited in McLean 1996, p. 18).

Definitions of the aesthetic in teaching

This is a very useful place to begin to consider what is meant by 'aesthetics' as we are using it in this book, and by the term aesthetic education. Aesthetics has a long history as a branch of philosophy. It was a term taken from the Greek, meaning 'sense perception'. In the eighteenth century, Baumgarten attempted to create a systematic study of the senses and articulated an understanding echoing Plato and Artistotle. He regarded 'aesthetic experience as sensuous knowledge … not purely and exclusively a state or condition of the senses, but a way in which, through our senses, we come to know the world more fully'(Bredin &

Santoro-Brienza 2000, pp. 3–4). While Baumgarten provided a framework for the study of fine arts as a branch of philosophy, there is a useful bridge between his definition of 'aesthetic experience as sensuous knowledge' and the ways in which concepts relating to 'the aesthetic'—aesthetic knowing, aesthetic engagement, and aesthetic education—are discussed in contemporary arts education.

For example, Csikszentmihalyi describes the aesthetic experience as: 'a state of mind where experiences are more clear and focused than everyday life' (cited in McLean 1996, p. 13). In Peter Abbs' work on aesthetic education, he has addressed many facets of the question of just how the aesthetic is factored into arts education, what it might 'look like' and how student understanding of the arts is informed by an aesthetic engagement with the arts. He suggests that there is such an entity as an 'aesthetic intelligence':

> The aesthetic denotes a mode of response inherent in human life which operates through the senses and the feelings and constitutes a form of intelligence comparable to, though different from, other forms of intelligence such as the mode of logical deduction (Abbs 1989, p. 4).

These descriptions/definitions highlight key qualities of the aesthetic as it might pertain to arts education. Words such as the *senses, feelings,* and *emotions* are emphasised, and in much of the writing about the aesthetics in arts education the key principle is that this is linked to an engagement *in* and *through* the arts rather than an abstract notion of knowing *about* the arts. It should be noted, however, that young people engaging in and through the arts can do so as arts-makers or as audience or spectators (the latter sometimes referred to here as 'percipients').

This book argues the case for the inclusion of the arts in the primary school. Understanding the role of the aesthetic within arts education is critical to the development of this argument. Philosophers, educational psychologists and learning theorists, arts educators and practitioners have all identified the place of aesthetics, aesthetic engagement, or aesthetic knowing as significant, not just for learning about the arts, but as a powerful component of a broad education. There is something distinctive about how and why children engage with the arts that enriches the education of the child in its broadest terms, beyond the cognitive acquisition of facts, which contributes to the development of creativity and imagination, and an understanding of the world. Drama educator Helen Nicholson proposes that aesthetics also provide a framework through which we can 'explain how and why art matters, to find words to describe the special powers with which the arts can illuminate, move and excite' (Nicholson 1999, p. 81).

Habermas suggests that the aesthetic experience goes beyond 'judgements of taste' to a possibility of intervention in 'cognitive procedures and normative expectations'—in other words, by disrupting expectations and existing understandings, an aesthetic experience can contribute to how one learns something new (Habermas, in McLean 1996, p. 16). Music educator Bennett Reimer offers a further development of this argument:

Opportunities to employ feeling in these cognitive operations [such as making dis-
criminations, events, classifying, abstracting, integrating, comprehending, anticipating,
synthesising and forming gestalts] and the experience of the expansion of the self such
engagements afford, are at the core of the value of the arts and of aesthetic education
(Reimer 1992, p. 39).

It's important to note that part of any discussion about aesthetics in the arts and in
education is that it can be used to promote certain values (what is 'good' art, and what isn't
art at all, for example) and that it is a culturally specific concept. In the twenty-first century,
with education (and the arts) situated in a postmodern relativist paradigm, it's necessary to
acknowledge how a concept such as aesthetics can be appropriated for political and cultural
ends. Helen Nicholson addresses this issue in a discussion about *aesthetics* and *difference* in
a drama classroom, and proposes that:

one of the problems of identifying the values of the aesthetic is that, whilst it appears
to signify a kind of functionlessness, it is, as Terry Eagleton (1990:3–4) points out, a
remarkably versatile concept. At different periods in history the aesthetic has been used to
authenticate a range of values (Nicholson 1999, p. 82).

However, in contemporary arts education practice Nicholson argues, there is a push
for a more pluralistic concept of the aesthetic, contingent on *history and location* (1999, p.
86). For the primary arts teacher, this means that one's own history, and the culture and
experiences that the children bring, and the specific community context that the teacher is
located in, all frame and help define the aesthetics of arts practice in that particular school
or educational setting. For example, the way that children understand, interpret, and make
art will be informed by a very different 'cultural tool kit' if they come from an Indigenous
background; are recently arrived from the Horn of Africa; live in a diverse multicultural
community; or have grown up in rural Australia with limited opportunities to engage
with formal arts practices. Nicholson's position reminds us of the possibilities present in
these diverse contexts: that a more pluralistic approach to the aesthetic in arts teaching
and learning enables the teacher to address questions of diversity, equity, and difference
through the arts practice that students engage in and with.

Teaching for the aesthetic: scaffolding aesthetic learning in and through the arts

There are a number of dimensions for the teacher to consider in order to teach *for* the
aesthetic. In one of his *Ten Propositions of Arts Education*, Peter Abbs maintains that to learn
about the arts, one must learn through the arts:

Proposition Nine … the arts must be taught through the aesthetic mode (Abbs 1994,
pp. 47–8).

Fundamental to this process, according to Abbs, is the act of connecting the present artistic practice with its heritage, with the 'aesthetic field' of artistic works that inform the practice. While many contemporary arts practitioners and educators take issue with this, suggesting that there are other relevant contexts besides the traditional 'aesthetic heritage' that ties current practice to the past, for Abbs this aesthetic heritage is much more than a set of historical artistic references. Visual artist Rod Taylor describes his understanding of Abbs' work in this way:

> The aesthetic field enables the arts as practised by children to be reconnected to the wider world of the arts as practised by others, both now and through time. As opposed to a view of art as constituting a series of artefacts or art objects, Abbs uses 'field' metaphorically to suggest 'a highly complex web of energy linking the artist to the audience, and both artist and audience to all inherited culture as now an active, now a latent shaping force'. Within this web of energy, 'the parts are seen in relationship, in a state of reciprocal flow between tradition and innovation, between form and impulse, between the society and the individual', and, in order to chart this aesthetic field, he [Abbs] proposes the four-phase model of making, presenting, responding and evaluating (Taylor & Andrews 1993, p. 14).

The notion of *making, presenting, responding, and evaluating*, or other similar ways or charting the aesthetic field, recur frequently in this book. As a set of signposts for understanding key aesthetic processes in arts-making, they are both simple and layered, and provide teachers with some useful guidance in their scaffolding of the arts education taking place in their classrooms. These organising principles appear in different forms in curriculum documents and arts syllabuses across Australia. It is worth noting, also, that different arts disciplines require different emphases. Consider, for example, the excellent Queensland Arts Syllabus (2002) and its approach to these organising principles for scaffolding learning in the arts that can be accessed on the web (http://www.qsa.qld.edu. au/downloads/syllabus/kla_arts_syll.pdf).

There are a number of things to be drawn from the naming of these key principles. Students come to arts understanding through engagements with the art form—they are the artists, and the process of exploring and creating (*making*) are as important as producing or displaying a product (*presenting*). John Dewey, educational philosopher and advocate for the arts, emphasised the importance of this balance, suggesting that the aesthetic experience associated with exploring and crafting expression through artform, finds its completion in the production (and sharing) of the art product (Dewey 1934).

Equally, in each art form, students engage aesthetically as audience, or *percipient* (*responding*). In fact, in a particular dramatic practice, *process drama*, students become audience and 'performer' through the same experience, as they are not only perceiving the events of the drama, but also generating and shaping them in the first place. According to John O'Toole, there is the potential for powerful learning through such a process.

> [When] the sensuous internalisation of meaning is … externalised and made cognitively explicit, knowledge is generated. The knowledge that emerges as dramatic meaning is

neither just propositional comprehension nor sensuous apprehension, it is a fusion of both (O'Toole 1992, p. 98).

The teacher's role

Within this dynamic aesthetic field the child, too, can move freely between being art-maker and art critic and receiver through responding to the art of others—but the teacher must facilitate the necessary access (Taylor & Andrews 1993, p. 15).

The kinds of scaffolding that teachers do as they assist students to negotiate the aesthetic experiences afforded by engagement through or with an art form depend on the learning context: the experiences that the children (and the teacher) bring to the work; the time and resources available in the school setting; and the specific learning and teaching objectives the teacher is responding to.

Some general principles that emerge repeatedly in the literature of this field, and in accounts of practice that teachers share (including the case studies to follow), are the importance of developing a repertoire of skills and techniques associated with the art form, including a discipline-specific vocabulary that enables them to negotiate through the art making, to communicate about it, and to collaborate on shared projects. This requires an understanding of the symbolic languages of the arts—each art form uses symbols to represent thoughts, ideas, emotions, and concepts; for example, the musical sound, the visual image, the 'stage picture', the sound scape, and the abstracted movement, and these are the raw materials from which arts-makers, regardless of age or experience, begin to build.

Some of the specific processes that help teachers to focus the work of 'making', 'presenting', and 'responding', drawn from the Queensland Arts Syllabus (QSA) document, are highlighted here (QSA 2002).

Making
- create, structure and organise
- engage in and reflect on aesthetic experiences
- explore ideas, feelings, and experiences
- control, manage, and synthesise the elements and conventions
- construct and produce
- using the languages and technologies
- develop the skills and processes
- recognise and interpret emotional and expressive content
- communicate ideas, feelings
- experience and observe of the world of the student
- document through sensory modes

Presenting

- develop
    - physical, expressive, and interpretive movements
    - positive self-esteem and build confidence in personal physicality
- engage in, and reflect on, performance
- informal and formal settings
- rehearse, refine, share, and perform scripted and student-devised works
- apply performance skills to convey meaning to audiences
- produce meaning for many audiences and contexts through a variety of forms and genres
- experience informal and formal display and exhibitions of images
- objects in personal, public, and community contexts

Responding (appreciating)

- analyse their own and others' dance across a range of contexts. Through dance appreciation, students developing an understanding
- analysis model that includes discerning the form, describing, interpreting, and evaluating
- elements and conventions used in their own work, and work produced by others
- develop an informed appreciation from a range of cultural, social, spiritual, historical, political, and economic contexts
- respond to meanings that they construct and represent
- use acquired skills and understandings to express and communicate ideas and feelings
- develop sensitivity, knowledge, and understanding of images and objects in relation to cultural, social, spiritual, historical, political, and economic contexts

The key to learning through the aesthetic lies in the ways in which the aesthetic can accommodate complex thoughts and feelings, as well as emotional, visceral, and physical responses to, and expressions of, experiences that a young person may not yet be able to find formal language for, or may not feel able or comfortable in expressing through words. Madeleine Grumet suggests that it is the 'non-logical, the non-verbal operations' (2007, p. 121) that precede logical, or cognitive thinking. Other theorists and practitioners also suggest that learning through the aesthetic remains in the memory far longer than learning that is encountered only in the cognitive frame (see Bruner 1990, Davis & Gardner 1992, Catterall 2002, and Deasy 2002).

Time and space

One of the recurrent themes to emerge in this book, particularly in the case studies to follow, is the importance of time and space. While each of these arts disciplines may be practised in the classroom, the development of an aesthetic space within that classroom requires an acknowledgement of the craft that informs the art—and for the teacher, this may come down to the question: what is the essential ingredient in achieving an aesthetic engagement in this artform? For the drama or dance practitioner, an uncluttered space may be sufficient. On the other hand, a sense of intimacy or 'safety' may need to accompany this—the school hall with the PE class at the other end of the room may be far less preferable to moving all the desks and chairs to the outer edges of the classroom, where students can at least establish a sense of ownership over the space.

Space is not only a literal term: the space between an idea and its execution, between a student and the artwork they have created, between an exhibition and a reflection, between two seemingly unrelated ideas, are all spaces that the teacher and students navigate. The ways in which the teacher might set up these spaces, and then guide the negotiation through them, may be one of the critical acts of teaching the aesthetic for that teacher.

Time is most frequently identified as a critical factor in the development of an arts-based program. Skills, techniques, and understandings develop over time, as does trust and confidence. While a short-term arts partnership with a visiting artist may have a profound impact in one term, if arts practice does not continue with students having the opportunity to refresh and extend existing skills and understandings, the momentum can be lost, and the gains across many areas of the curriculum and the social structure of the school can begin to recede. A recent study of teachers who use the arts in their primary classrooms in the US revealed that both time and space were critical factors in their ability to maintain arts activities in their classrooms.

> Limitations of time, space, and materials limited the scope and frequency of arts activities. Lack of time constantly challenged the teachers' use of the arts. Regardless of their personal values or interests the teachers knew that arts experiences need time and time is an increasingly limited commodity. Mark said, 'Time is precious to me. And although I love the arts myself and the kids seem to love it, I need class time to teach the basics …' Maria and Jane, who reported higher use of the arts, seemed somewhat able to disregard the time pressure because they … found efficient ways to make thematic connections throughout the curriculum.
>
> Teachers also mentioned lack of materials and appropriate spaces as severe limitations to the kinds of projects they once undertook. In Penny's and Jane's schools overcrowding had forced classes to use the gym and auditorium as instructional spaces during large portions of the day … Tape and CD players, art posters, musical instruments and drawing materials, where available, were purchased with teachers' personal funds (Oreck 2006, p. 16).

This study of primary teachers in the US also draws attention to another key factor in the construction of aesthetic experiences through the arts in schools: this is the role of the teacher as co-artist, as co-creator of art, and by implication, as co-learner.

> These teachers described their experiences as learners—taking risks, dealing with self-consciousness, gaining confidence and feeling successful—as the most lasting lessons taken from the arts workshops (Oreck 2006, p. 18).

This commitment to and engagement with the artistic practice underway in the classroom leads us to a closer examination of the teacher's practice. It prompts the question, beyond the making and co-facilitating of art in the classroom: is the actual practice of the teacher an act of artistry also? There is a growing body of writing, beginning with Eisner's development of the concept of *Connoisseurship* (Eisner 1991) that would argue teaching can indeed be artistic; that the artistry of the teacher is worthy of further consideration; and indeed, that the teacher of the arts needs to embrace the notion of artistic teaching.

The artistry of the teacher

After almost forty years of teaching, eminent Australian drama educator Jennifer Simons (2002) reflected deeply on her role as creator and facilitator of the aesthetic environment and, in attempting to better understand how this occurs, looked closely at the nature of her teaching practice. While her exploration focused on drama practice, her discoveries relate to all arts teachers and perhaps all teachers who choose to be present in the planned and unplanned moments of learning that occur in their classrooms.

When describing the knowledge base of the teacher, Simons opts for the term 'professional craft knowledge' to best describe her practice, because it evokes 'artistry, uncertainty and context specificity' (Simons 2002, p. 2). Professional craft knowledge emerges out of the day-to-day application of skills, of formal content knowledge, of an understanding of pedagogy, and of the teacher's own experience as an active participant in their own life and culture. Simons identifies a key principle for the artistry of the teacher when she describes the evolution of this skill set, from a body of explicit knowledges to 'embodied, tacit or unconscious knowledge'. It is in this evolution that artistry becomes possible because it is the teacher's capacity to respond 'in the moment' to the possibility of learning, or art making (or both), to shape, divert, nurture, or remain silent, in a seemingly intuitive understanding of what is necessary to harness the artistic opportunity.

The artistry of the teacher is not confined to the artistic 'teaching moment', however. It also relates to the teacher's capacity to manage the dynamic and multiple dialogues of the classroom. The building blocks of an arts class include the knowledge and experience of students (their 'cultural toolkit') and the teacher. While the teacher plans for how the class might begin, what resources should be available, what techniques need to be introduced or revised, what structural framework the class is to be contained within, he or she cannot predict how it might end and the direction future work could take. The dialogic encounters relate to exchanges between the teacher and the students, student to student, student and content, and an internal dialogue between student as learner and student as artist. The artistry of the teacher lies in recognising and supporting the 'dialogic improvisations' that take place in the classroom, and in drawing them into a constructive encounter with the arts practice at hand.

Chris Sinclair

Such encounters are not always comfortable for students or their teacher. Some of the ways in which the arts provide for students to take risks in a 'safe environment' are described in detail in the case studies, for instance in Chapter 12. In reading the body language of the students, interpreting sub-text and intuiting possible flashpoints, the teacher is the guardian of this 'safe space' and draws on tools of the different art forms to protect against the potential fragility of identity of the participant through framing, distancing, role protection, while at the same time leading the way for those students ready and able to leap into a metaphoric or literal unknown.

Jennifer Simons identifies a number of very specific examples of teacher artistry. The [arts] teacher:

- reads the body language of the students
- looks for potential metaphors in the topic
- guides learners to select a focus, research or reflect on a topic
- remains alert for the learning in the 'fun' activity
- and finally, according to Simons (and another arts educator, Brad Haseman), arts teachers also:

> Manage energy, lay trails, weave ideas together, sense what the learners want, withhold expertise in order to maintain tension and surprise, and 'smell' emerging scents … Teacher and task become inseparable: teaching becomes a form of artistry in which it is hard to tell the dancer from the dance (Simons 2002, p. 2).

The reference to Haseman provides us with a useful and somewhat challenging conclusion to this discussion on the aesthetic in arts teaching and the aesthetics of teaching. Haseman reflects on contemporary culture, particularly the highly digitised and mediated youth cultures that emerge, morph, and reconstruct almost before our eyes. He writes about the 'redactive creativity of artists and young people as they revise, adapt, remotivate, re-contextualise, sample, abridge, and counterpoint cultural materials' while successfully creating new symbolic forms 'rich with personal and shared meanings' (Haseman 2002, p. 128). Haseman identifies a dilemma in the ways that the new cultural forms are mediated, and poses the question to arts teachers about what our role might be as the future becomes our present:

> What is it to teach students whose sophisticated redacting skills outstrip our own and who in many cases are better at finding information, and certainly forbidden information, than we are? … As a teacher am I destined to become an expensive search engine, pointing students towards materials and discourses … out of which they can playfully edit their next collage performance? (Haseman 2002, p. 128)

While this provocation is certainly timely, perhaps it is also timely to recall John O'Toole's description in an earlier chapter, of the 'common aesthetic', to which Haseman's reference can be related, and to see this as the raw material of our arts programs. It is also the prompt for a clarification of the positioning of the arts teacher. It is the task of the primary teacher to help children make sense and meaning of their personal and social reality, and to negotiate and manage it. And, it is the arts and the 'common aesthetic' that are powerful conduits for this pursuit of new understanding, and the arts teacher who is fundamentally responsible for constructing the aesthetic environment to make it happen.

The overwhelming implications of this are that we must teach artistically. And we don't only mean while we are *teaching the arts*. For all teachers, one of our jobs in facilitating learning is to create an appropriate, congruent environment: a harmonious, inspiring, and motivating ambience where enthusiastic, embodied learning can flourish. Science, Maths, Social Studies, English, Languages, Health and Physical Education, and Technology also need the artistry to bring out the children's creativity, wonder, and imagination, the artfulness and the playfulness in those subjects. And we can do this in a conventional classroom—this book is not just about subjects labelled 'art', 'music', and so on. It is equally about how visually, aurally, sensorily, dramatically, and kinaesthetically we and the students can make our own aesthetic of learning. Our aesthetic classroom needs sophisticated understanding, not only of the pictures on the wall, but in how our bodies move and are grouped, and in how they interact in the space, and the semiotic of design and colour and pattern and their tensions. Our classroom needs to counteract the cacophony of sounds of hundreds of people thrown together, not with imposed wastelands of silence, but with harmony and rhythm, discriminating listening, and contrast of stillness and excitement—as the poet said, 'music has charms to soothe a savage breast'—at the very least, that's got to be worth a try! Then perhaps above all, there are the drama skills that are needed because the classroom is a performative space and must have a performative pedagogy—which does not mean a teacher up the front giving a monologue to a silent audience. Dramatic performance means dialogue, not monologue. The students are equally actors, and a performative classroom means maximising the opportunities for meaningful dialogue. The teacher is both playwright and key performer too, and must have some of the skills and range of both dramatist and actor.

Activities for students

Solo or whole group activity or assignment: teacher portraits
Either

Exhibition
1   Drawing from memories of great teaching and great learning experiences from childhood and adolescence, create a portrait of a 'great teacher'—using an artistic medium: pen portrait, 2D or 3D art work, multimedia, performance or movement piece, musical composition or song. This is for exhibition.

Chris Sinclair

Or

Reflection and discussion

2   Using the same starting point of memory, create individual brief pen portraits as a
     starting point for discussion: artistry and connoisseurship in teaching. Whole group/
     small group discussion.

Then

3   Take time out after having read this chapter, and before reading the next one:
     – create a piece of art
     – go to a gallery
     – see a play
     – bungi-jump
     – attend a festival
     (consider the notion of 'sensuous knowing').

Key references

Abbs, P. (1989) *The Symbolic Order*, Falmer Press, London.

Abbs, P. (1994) *The Educational Imperative: A Defence of Socratic and Aesthetic Learning*,
     Falmer Press, London.

Barrett, M. & Smigiel, H. (2003) 'Awakening the "Sleeping Giant"?: The Arts in the Lives of
     Australian Families', *International Journal of Education and the Arts*, 4(4).

Bredin, H. & Santoro-Brienza, L. (2000) *Philosophies of Art and Beauty*, Edinburgh
     University Press, Edinburgh.

Bruner, J. (1990) *Acts of Meaning*, Harvard University Press, Cambridge, MA.

Catterall, J.S. (2002) 'The Arts and the Transfer of Learning', in R. Deasy (ed.), *Critical Links:
     Learning in the Arts and Student Academic and Social Development*, Washington DC.

Davis, J. & Gardner, H. (1992) 'The Cognitive Revolution: Consequences for the Under-
     standing and Education of the Child as Artist', in B. Reimer & R.A. Smith (eds), *The
     Arts, Education and Aesthetic Knowing*, University of Chicago Press, Chicago.

Deasy, R. (2002) *Critical Links: Learning in the Arts and Student Academic and Social
     Development*, Arts Education Partnership, Washington.

Dewey, J. (1934) *Art as Experience*, Minton Balch, New York.

Eisner, E. (1991) *The Enlightened Eye: Qualitative Inquiry and the Enhancement of Educational
     Practice*, Macmillan, New York.

Grumet, M. (2007) 'Third Things: The Wondrous Progeny of Arts Integration', *Journal of
     Artistic and Creative Education*, 1(1), 115–39.

Haseman, B. (2002) 'The "Creative Industry" of Designing a Contemporary Drama
     Curriculum, *Melbourne Studies in Education*, 43(2), 119–29.

McLean, J. (1996) *An Aesthetic Framework in Drama: Issues and Implications*, NADIE Publications, Brisbane.

Nicholson, H. (1999) 'Aesthetic Values, Drama Education and the Politics of Difference', *NJ (Drama Australia Journal)*, 23(2), 81–91.

O'Toole, J. (1992) *The Process of Drama: Negotiating Art and Meaning*, Routledge, London.

Oreck, B. (2006) 'Artistic Choices: A Study of Teachers Who Use the Arts in the Classroom', *International Journal of Education & the Arts*, 7(8).

QSA (2002) *The Arts: Years 1 to 10 Syllabus*, retrieved 10 December 2007 from http://www.qsa.qld.edu.au/downloads/syllabus/kla_arts_syll.pdf

Reimer, B. (1992) 'What Knowledge is of Most Worth in the Arts?', in B. Reimer & R.A. Smith (eds), *The Arts, Education and Aesthetic Knowing*, University of Chicago Press, Chicago.

Simons, J. (2002) 'Drama and the Learner', in *Melbourne Studies in Education*, 43(2), 1–11.

Taylor, R. & Andrews, G. (1993) *The Arts in the Primary School*, Falmer Press, London.

6

Shower Singing and
Other Essentials

Julia Reid

In this chapter we provide a bridge between the theoretical discussions of key arts principles included in Part One of this book, and the practical applications of those principles explored through the case studies in the chapters to follow. In this chapter Julia Reid examines her own practice and elucidates not only what motivates her in her work, but the principles of her own arts teaching and her own artistry as a teacher.

> It's like driving a car at night. You never see further than your headlights, but you can make the whole trip that way.

> E.L. Doctorow

As a teacher of the arts, there is no sweeter moment for me than when the shy child steps to the front of the class and accepts the creative risk, or when the synergy of a group takes over and three plus three becomes sixty. There is potent electricity in a classroom that is fuelled by creative intention. The gauntlet laid down in the chapter before this one—that teaching is an art form and that every teacher needs to be an artist—is to me indisputable. But I also know without doubt that, as practitioners of this complex artistry, all teachers are equipped to reposition the arts to centre stage in their classrooms. A few additional skills in the tool kit are handy but not essential. I know, I know! '*I can't dance/hold a tune/act/…* (fill in your gaps)' is a statement I hear in many staffrooms. But please, just for a moment, find a quiet place and think about your own artistic qualities, creative preoccupations, performing moments. Write a list now.

There will be probably be one of those 'arts' areas with which you have at least a nodding acquaintance. Acting in your own school play, 'doing' piano for a year, shower singing, possibly just the crazy dancing you did to your favourite album in your bedroom might be the only tangible 'skills' you can easily bring to mind. But actually, even without these, *who you are* is good enough. Four principles inform my teaching practice—actually, they inform my life:

- encouraging and celebrating the self-directed learner
- modelling the creative process
- regular, allocated time for reflection

And the first, most vital principle:

- bringing the person to the classroom, not just the teacher

Bringing the person

What you have experienced unavoidably informs your teaching style, your particular passions that must flavour (and favour) the content. What stories do you bring with you to your teaching? How does the world you inhabit inform your pedagogy?

The more I experience as a teacher, the more I recognise that *who* I am, my storied self, does not limit, but rather *enriches* my ability to help students explore the arts. Bringing my whole person—narrative baggage and all—and not just the teacher into every class of students I interact with is the fundamental principle that informs my teaching practice ahead of all others … and it really works.

'OK,' you say. 'I willingly bring my whole self to the classroom. What happens now? Nothing has fundamentally changed in my skill base. I still can't dance/hold a tune/act. The students know more about this stuff than me!'

In many cases you will be right but really, this is of little issue.

Talent is only one part of a much bigger picture. *Creativity is for sharing* and skills waiting for perfection and locked away in cupboards touch no-one. As you now focus your attention on your classroom community of artists, look also for opportunities to share what *you* have, even if it is just your crazy lounge room dancing. We will discuss this in more depth later.

Encouraging and celebrating the self-directed learner

All aglow in the work (Virgil).

'What do we already know?' Discovering the artistic skills and interests within your classroom reflects the first vital step in any process of inquiry, and is the important first part of your arts curriculum. This may take some weeks, which is is good.

Within any contemporary classroom (and the likelihood is greater the further up the school you go) you may find the makings of a dance troupe, a band, even a small orchestra of sorts, an Actors Guild and—something lurking in every classroom I have ever entered—a stand-up comedian or two. Channelling this particular talent for good outcomes rather than 'evil' intent may be your finest hour!

Arrange your own version of *Australian Idol*; create a space for them to participate in *Dancing with the Classroom Stars*; and don't forget to provide room for genuine creative risk-taking—a good dose of *Red Faces*. All these will give your students authentic opportunities to share information that is not always revealed at school with celebration and such attention to detail, and critically they provide you with invaluable insights. You will also find out about the students who have next to no 'formal' skills in music, dance, or drama, but nevertheless follow a certain band, like one style of dance over another, or have a favourite comedian. This is all wonderful artistic fuel.

And now that you have discovered your existing talent pool and the interests that accompany them, you have created an artistic buzz in your classroom because hitherto private knowledge has been privileged, what next? My experience suggests that, with a little stage direction, some sensible organisation of roles and responsibilities based on skills, strengths, and interests, the most powerful educative way forward is to *let your students lead*. To negotiate how the learning happens in the arts, for the students to decide what and, to some extent, how they will perform, can sometimes be to watch a bunch of alchemists at work.

I have *felt*, and I'm sure you have also, the palpable change in intensity and urgency that surges through a room like a motivational tsunami when the direction of the learning shifts ownership, when the passion for the project becomes self-directed and when this is allowed to reach a satisfying conclusion. These are the moments when you decide to stay in teaching despite the lousy pay. This was confirmed again when I asked my three composite Year 5/6 classes to brainstorm what they valued (and did not) about my sessions. The one thing that came through more emphatically than anything else was the depth of ownership and responsibility given to them to prepare and present their work: from idea to final performance.

Yes, there is always room for skill acquisition and there will be time and opportunity for that—often in the arts it happens magically in the 'doing.'

How much of infinite value do we learn when we hit an educative roadblock and must find a way around, over, or through it? The early educator John Holt was emphatic: learning by doing. 'Try it and see what happens', is great teacherly advice. Enlisting 'expert' groups of students to teach their peers is a very powerful learning tool.

So if the students are doing all the work, what role do we have? I listen. I applaud. I encourage. Sometimes I suggest and scaffold.

> **Student:** *You help us turn our ideas into really good stuff.*
> **Translation**: *I help to give their ideas shape.*

And I also support them by articulating the creative process. You can too.

Modelling the creative process

> Creativity is allowing yourself to make mistakes. Art is knowing which ones to keep (Scott Adams—American cartoonist).

The question really is: What are *you prepared to risk creatively*? Which classroom talent event did you enter yourself? Did you share your shower singing?

Demonstrating your creative self at work (and at play) is the greatest of teaching gifts. If you do happen to be skilled at an art form, then share it freely, and often! Primary school children are the most rewarding of audiences to the adult's inner critic. When I whizzed off a very hackneyed version of *Fur Elise* on the piano the other day to counter the strange proposition from a Year 2 boy that all performances had to be comedic to be entertaining, the other children in the grade thought I was Rachmaninov. On another very different occasion, in a moment of some wistfulness for the holidays, I played my Italian cooking CD to the Year 5s and 6s and demonstrated how I dance rather lavishly around the kitchen. They of course joined in and now often request a reprise.

I talk a lot with students about aspects of this creative spirit. One of my favourite ways to start a unit of work is to have a really provocative quote waiting for them, lurking on the whiteboard. For example, 'Creativity is the ability to connect the seemingly unconnected' (William Plomer, South African writer) was the beginning of a hilarious journey of discovery where students matched unlikely performance genres to Olympic sports. They explored the heady possibilities of boxing as a Broadway musical, marathon running as a ballet, even swimming as a soap opera!

'Who sees the human face correctly: the photographer, the mirror or the painter?' (Pablo Picasso) was the prelude to a creative expedition into my favourite topic: story adaptation.

Julia Reid

'A work of art is never finished—it simply stops in interesting places' was the title of a reflection sheet about a three-day arts festival.

Sometimes the concepts are a little beyond their comprehension, but that's hardly the point. Creativity is more often about posing the excellent question: there is never a correct answer and it is of far less importance anyway than the robust discussions that occur.

Arts curriculum around the country asks us in various wordings to create and make; explore and respond.

Luckily, you've already started. By sharing yourself—stories and all—and by demonstrating that you are a creative risk-taker, your students will readily go on the journey with you. When heading into uncharted creative territory it is important to have a navigational compass and it is really useful to have a common language with which to discuss how you are going to arrive at your unknown destination. The creative map I follow is that of Wallas (1926):

Preparation

This includes brainstorming, researching, amassing anything you think might be relevant, and gathering resources together. Students are used to this concept from project work in other areas of the curriculum. It just needs a bit of tweaking to give it an artistic edge.

Incubation

This underpins the concept that things take their own time; letting the ideas 'marinate' and then 'cook away' consciously and unconsciously. My favourite representative quote here is: 'chance favours the prepared mind' (Louis Pasteur). Like 'preparation', incubation can last minutes or weeks (and for older creative minds, even years!). To do this properly, try to invest some time for students' ideas to soak up some interesting flavours, or to give the artistic 'bread' time to rise. This is when students can experience and discuss the importance of patience, perseverance, trust, concentration, and the art of sometimes just letting something 'be'.

Illumination

This is the 'Aha' moment—'I know what I'm going to do and it's going to be *sensational!*'

How do you know when you're on to something? Sometimes ideas arrive with an inbuilt knowingness. There's that little frisson of excitement that bubbles up in your solar plexus—maybe you want to squeal a bit with pleasure—and sometimes that idea is accompanied by a visualisation in your head like a 3D concept map, with tendrils rapidly unfurling and extending in all directions of artistic possibility. Talking to the children about this, asking them to describe what is going on in their heads when an idea 'hits' comes up with some startling imagery. One boy described the scene in *Charlie and the Chocolate Factory* when 'all the molecules fuse together to make the chocolate bar'.

But art is also about the 'not yet ready' aspects of creative thought and we need to model this for students too. It nurtures ideas that are not fully formed, not dressed properly for a public 'viewing'. Maybe the shape still only seems vaguely apparent in the mind's eye of the creator. One girl described this as 'a treasure in the centre of my brain surrounded by hazy stuff'. Or maybe the idea is like a nervous forest creature, needing encouragement to come out into the open clearing without the fluorescent torchlight of a '*correct answer*' highlighting or magnifying all its flaws. Maybe this little thought hiding in the shadows is the response to a *better question*.

Some of my favourite teaching moments are when I can *legitimately* model what's going on in my brain as it happens, as an idea begins to take shape. This captures students' attention, particularly if you are also waving your arms wildly. It's even better if you are able to articulate the excitement, the confusion, the struggle for words to name the concept, the uncertainty that the idea will work. Again, this is modelling gold, demonstrating the moment of creative risk, and tempting rejection or worse, ridicule. Scary, but real. As teachers, we do our students a great disservice if we don't prepare them for how to deal with creative doubt without succumbing to self-sabotage. It was the director John Newland who said dryly to a young artist, 'Doubt? It comes with the territory, kid!' (Cameron 2002).

Verification

This contains the hackwork. It involves working out the details: script writing, choreography, composition, and rehearsals; and presenting them in whatever format you have chosen and then getting feedback. This is the performance and the applause!

Reapplication

This reflects the cycle of creativity—nothing creative is ever linear, often we need to go back and reshape. Pieces of performance art are, by definition, transitory. A video-taped recording or photograph never quite captures the mood in the room that accompanies the work. I think it is to do with the nature of 'performance as gift'. Giving and receiving have unexpected complexities and undertones. As budding performers it is vital that students have regular opportunities to evaluate and receive feedback from others … and from themselves. To do this *they need to reflect*.

Regular, allocated time for reflection

> How can I know what I think until I see what I say? (Henry Forster)

'Reflective practice' can sound a bit like buzzwords. Observers might venture that 'creativity' is the 'New Black' of education and 'reflective practice' the chic accessory, but for me, as a reflective practitioner of many years, it feels more like an invaluable technique and life skill whose time has arrived. Children are all about 'the moment' and then 'what happens next?' Many of them deeply resent being asked to look backwards. But as we know, lived experience can only ever be described and explored *after* the event. By supporting students to develop the ability to investigate, to question and evaluate their actions and thoughts, we

Julia Reid

give them a key to *purposeful* learning though their own experiences and the skills to make more capable choices in their learning and responses.

Reflection can take myriad forms: *'I don't know how to'; 'I have a problem I can't fix'; 'I'm not sure about';' Working out how to … made me feel …'*. These can all generate a powerful awareness about how to live and learn in more resourceful ways. As adults we instinctively vary the depth of reflection, the frequency and the reasons for the introspection, but if reflection is to have true value for students learning the skill, it is of most benefit if practised regularly—and *it needs to be written down.* I think of reflective writing as creating the visible footprints of my learning and thinking. Here are some questions I ask myself:

> Where have I come from?
> What *did* I know/think/believe/assume?
> What has changed?
> What is my new knowledge?
> Why might this thought/belief/assumption have changed?
> *And then the million dollar questions …*
> How will I *use* this new knowledge to effect change?
> What is its worth to me?

While rehearsing for the performance of a short pop opera, students were required to record their progress towards this known goal, with indicators of what steps needed to be taken to achieve this. Early on in the process students responded to these sentence starters and then shared their responses with each other:

> Now that we have learnt a few songs,
> (CHOOSE ONE RESPONSE HERE)
>> I think …
>> I wonder …
>> I hope …
> (CHOOSE ONE SENTENCE STARTER HERE)
>> I'm not sure if …
>> Something I want to remember is …
> (ALL COMPLETE THIS)
>> Next week I would like to …

The nature of reflection changes throughout a learning process and sometimes the implications of the prompts need to be overtly articulated: 'Why am I asking you to respond to these prompts?' 'What information do you now have about yourself that you didn't know before this class?' In the final weeks the focus for reflection becomes more defined by time management concerns:

> Three specific things for me to do to prepare for the performance:
>> «
>> «
>> «

I will do them at these times:

(People help in big and small ways. ALL are significant.)

One way I know I can help Julia/my grade prepare for this performance is to:

_____

After the performance is over they responded to these:

When we started learning the songs, I thought …

When it was finally the day to perform, I felt …

The best part of the final performance was …

With the knowledge I have gained from this rehearsal process, I could teach someone else about…

After reading over my journal entries from the rehearsal weeks …

This work is complex. Young heads that are not usually asked *how* they approach their thinking need opportunities every day to step back and look at their learning from a new, altered perspective. Often they need to be visibly shown the square that they are being asked to think outside. Ongoing reflective practice is the teaching principle that provides me with the most challenges and the most rewards.

STUDENT: 'You work everyone's minds and push them to their limits; for example, you ask interesting questions that other teachers wouldn't worry about, and make us think.'

This final reflection sheet example was completed by a Year 5 boy who was a serial school avoider until the opportunity for a speaking role in the grade play appeared. I have kept his spelling but changed any names used.

Remember: A work of art is never finished—it simply stops in interesting places.

Table 6.1 'Now the carnival is over'—feelings and reflections about the Performing Arts Festival

The best part of the Festival was	• working with my peas and having a good time • because they all helped when I needed help
What stood out for me during the days of the Festival was	• the way people like Mick had to lean all thos lines and he dident have that much time
Something I have learned about myself as a performer is	• I am a good perefomer and I dident know that and I think the ordence agrees with me as well
I was most satisfied with	• the way that I dident start larfing when people made a silly mestake
Something I found hard was	• leaning my lines as good as other people
If I had the opportunity to go through the process all over again, this time I would	• make shor I lean all my lines erlia
In case you didn't notice, I want you to know that	• I am greatfull for what you did for us!! Thank you!!!!

Julia Reid

In the following year, this student had a leading role in his grade play and learnt all his lines really early! He *used new knowledge to effect change* that became the *new action* and the cycle of creativity started anew.

I love the work that I do, mostly. And I love it the most when these principles—that inform my life and work—affect students' work (and life) in stirring, sometimes provoking ways such that they are *inspired and motivated to transform.*

Activities for students

Individual reflection

Make the list that Julia recommends at the beginning of her chapter (see p. 55).

Practical task (learning to reflect)

Apply one of the sets of reflective questions Julia employs in her classroom to a current group creative project of your own; **or** to a creative project in a classroom setting at your next opportunity.

Key references

Cameron, J. (2002) *Walking in this World: Practical Strategies for Creativity*, Random House, London.

Holt, J. (1967) *How Children Learn*, Pitman, New York.

Wallas, G. (1926) *The Art of Thought*, Jonathan Cape, London.

PART TWO

Teaching the Art Forms

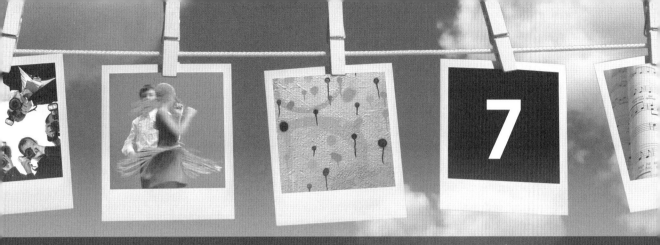

7

Drama: Social Dreaming in the Twenty-first Century

Chris Sinclair, Kate Donelan, Jane Bird, John O'Toole, and Kelly Freebody

This chapter illuminates the practice of a group of highly experienced drama teachers working with children and pre-service education students. The case studies chosen for inclusion here look at two very distinctive approaches to drama practice—a drama workshop, based on a rich and compelling 'pre-text', *Fox*, winner of the 2001 Children's Book Council Award; and the development of a multi-layered dramatic event redolent with learning possibilities across a number of disciplines. The case studies are framed with a brief overview of some key principles of drama education: the place of dramatic play; dramatic elements; and embodied learning; and a series of questions, activities, and provocations designed to broaden and extend the way the newcomer to drama teaching might think about possible applications of drama in the classroom.

Introduction

Chris Sinclair and Kate Donelan

Drama provides a space in the curriculum for young people to imagine and actively engage with human experiences from the past, present, and future. It is a place for exploring and re-making old stories, and for embodying new stories, for creating and projecting into fictional worlds where the rules can be changed and new possibilities appear. When you seek out the syllabus or curriculum documents of various Australian states, drama is defined in terms of:

- expressing and communicating understandings about human issues and experience;
- interacting in a range of roles, relationships, situations;
- investigating feelings, actions and consequences contexts;
- developing confidence and self-awareness.

These are all addressed through such activities as:

- the enactment of real and imagined events;
- collaboration in the preparation and presentation of drama performance;
- and the manipulation of and understanding of forms, styles and purposes of drama (QSA 2002).

The key words to emerge in the curriculum documents, and in the various statements of purpose and significance that begin this chapter are: imagination, engagement, embodiment, fictional worlds, expression, communication, enactment, exploring and inventing, and change and possibility. It seems that as we launch into this discussion about drama in the primary classroom, we are destined to encounter a dynamic, interactive, compelling learning landscape in our quest to better understand the nature of drama and its various practices in classroom contexts.

Dramatic play

In Chapter 1, John O'Toole persuasively proposed a paradigm in which art and play sit alongside one another as fitting companions in artistic production and the development of a common aesthetic. In order to understand drama in the school setting, one must first look at *dramatic play* and its pivotal role in the cognitive and social development of children.

> Children use play to re-create [the] world and model the social behaviour they see in it. In this way they can experience the world without risking the consequences (Toye & Prendiville 2000, p. 11).

In their dramatic play, which is called *social role-play* by Toye and Prendiville, young children create fictional contexts, use symbols to represent places and objects, take on roles and generate narratives, and the outcome of this activity is the intellectual and social development of the child. One of the most notable characteristics of dramatic play is that it is not a taught activity, but arises independently, like language acquisition, as part of the 'learning blueprint' (Toye & Prendiville 2000). Much has been written about young children and their propensity towards dramatic play, with a particular focus on links to learning and language development. Peter Slade's seminal work, *Child Drama* (1954), provided a landmark in the evolution of drama education, drawing attention as it did to the particularities of children engaging in dramatic play. He proposed the distinction between two forms of dramatic play: projected and personal.

In the projected play of the very young, according to Slade, a 'dream or fantasy of the mind' is projected into or on to objects outside the child him or herself. Toys, dolls, or puppets take on this imagined life, as the child, 'god-like' gives them voice and action. In personal play, 'the child is able to become a constructive hero in fantasy and overcome situations in physically active creation'. In other words, the child becomes the imagined hero and is able to take action in the fiction for him or herself (Slade 1977, p. 122).

The significance for the drama specialist or the classroom teacher is the rich heritage of dramatic play that the children themselves bring to the classroom. They are already familiar with the ways in which the fictional setting can allow the individual to explore what it might be like to have superpowers, or, to be the 'mother', the 'father', or the 'teacher'—all holders of power over the child. They also have an understanding of how dramatic play allows space for exploration of what it might be like to be the villain, or the 'naughty child', without the consequences that these actions would bring outside a fictional domain. They also understand how tan-bark and leaves can become a three-course meal; or valued currency; a stick, sword, or magic wand; or how a sheet draped over a table can become the cave of the mysterious dragon. The use of space and symbol, key tools in the lexicon of drama, are already stored in their own lexicon of 'make believe'. 'Let's pretend this is a cave and you're the princess and I'm the baddie' has signalled the formation of many a contract between players in the complex preparations leading to dramatic play. Children engaged in such play have made another important discovery—that it can be both serious and fun.

The study of dramatic play informs many drama programs and is given additional focus in early childhood, where the boundaries between dramatic play and a more formal approach to 'drama' are tantalisingly blurred. While the organic nature of dramatic play is foregrounded, serious and considered attention is also given to teacher 'interventions' and their consequences for learning. These can range from teacher intervention causing the cessation of the play, to the judicious intervention assisting the children to encounter what Vygotsky described as the 'zone of proximal development'(Vygotsky, cited in Toye & Prendiville 2000, p. 11). When the teacher identifies an opportunity to heighten the drama, re-focus or re-direct it, without disempowering the 'players', it is possible for the children

Chris Sinclair, Kate Donelan, Jane Bird, John O'Toole, and Kelly Freebody

participating to move beyond their known experiences and to encounter new territories of learning, skill, or understanding, in their 'zone of proximal development' (Toye & Prendiville 2000, p. 11).

Negotiating meaning through drama

Over the past twenty years drama has found its way into formal school curricula across Australia, often under the umbrella of the 'key learning area' of the arts. While there has been some variation of emphasis from state to state, and over time, at the heart of the teaching of drama is an embodied art form, with the child standing in the shoes of someone else, entering into fictive situations, negotiating meanings for the real world through the lens of the imagined world. The child manipulates dramatic elements to explore and express those meanings, and finds a dramatic form to house and communicate these understandings. In negotiating these meanings, the teacher draws on the repertoire of dramatic conventions to shape the experience of the learning.

Defining drama

> Drama is the enactment of real and imagined events through roles and situations. Drama enables students both as individuals and in groups to explore, shape and represent ideas and feelings and their consequences. Students make, create and re-create drama through improvisation, role-play, characterisation and interpretation of texts. They plan, rehearse, present and reflect on their own drama and the dramatic work of others, past and present.
>
> In drama students take on roles and learn actively through the process of stepping into someone else's shoes or looking at the world through somebody else's eyes. By imagining themselves to be other people, or in other situations students can explore their world, speculate on possible futures, and deepen their understanding of themselves and others. Drama is a natural extension of the play of small children (Victorian Curriculum and Standards Framework II, 2007).

Drama is potentially powerful within the school curriculum because it can be an art form, a medium for learning (a pedagogy), and a socio-cultural experience (dramatic play)— sometimes the teacher chooses to focus on one of these approaches, sometimes all three are incorporated in the same lesson or unit of work. The case studies that follow in this chapter provide a glimpse of how this might be possible in the primary classroom. There are, of course, many other ways of approaching the use of drama, including the ubiquitous end-of-year school performance, the reading and writing of scripts in the classroom, the historical re-enactment of the Eureka Stockade, and the embodied reconstruction of the process of photosynthesis. Regardless of the purpose, the teacher and the students are engaged in negotiating meaning through drama. In order to do so, it is necessary for them to begin to engage with the dramatic 'toolkit' that underpins the art and craft of drama. Central to this 'toolkit' is a selection of dramatic elements.

In this introduction we will touch briefly on each of them, but will also include references to some of the many texts that have devoted themselves exclusively to describing drama as a learning medium, an art form, and a socio-cultural activity across time and culture.

Dramatic elements

The dramatic elements are the fundamental building blocks of drama—they are present to a greater or lesser degree in all dramatic activity, and it is their presence that signifies that an activity is dramatic, carrying with it the potential for aesthetic engagement associated with art form, and cognitive engagement associated with a learning medium. These are the dramatic elements: *role, focus, tension, climax, transformation of space and objects, and the symbolic use of space and objects.*

In the literature and practice of drama in classrooms, much attention is paid to the first of these elements, *role*, as it is the taking on of roles that enables students (and their teachers) to step into another's shoes, to consider the world and an issue from another perspective, to try out an otherwise risky attitude without real consequence, to explore the feeling domain that underscores a story, image, picture book, current, or historical issue in a 'protected' way, distanced from themselves, and with the knowledge that it is temporary and in the careful hands of the teacher they trust. From the seminal works of Dorothy Heathcote and Gavin Bolton (for example, 1995) to leading contemporary writers like O'Neill (1995), Morgan and Saxton (1989), Saxton and Miller (2004), Ackroyd and Boulton (for example, 2001), Nicholson (2000), and Neelands and Dickenson (for example, 2006), and O'Toole (for example 1992), 'role' as a construct and a vehicle for learning through drama is considered, analysed, and unpacked. There are levels of role, strategies for building belief in role, managing and modelling roles (Bolton 1998) and de-roling. It is not possible to do more than signal this rich discussion with a brief description from John O'Toole and Julie Dunn and to recommend further reading.

Process drama

In the classroom there is no outside audience. Most of the time we are improvising with the children, exploring fictional situations through various kinds of role-play, mixed with theatrical conventions, games and exercises. We call this working in 'process drama', which is like children's play, with all the players actively involved. Acting or demonstrating drama work in front of other people and being an audience are sometimes involved, but the audience is often informal and the performance unscripted. Working in this way, with all

Chris Sinclair, Kate Donelan, Jane Bird, John O'Toole, and Kelly Freebody

the children taking part in the dramatic situation, allows you to maximize the learning opportunities in the classroom. (O'Toole & Dunn 2002, p. 2)

It should be noted that many classroom teachers work with their students on developing scripted and improvised plays for performance to their peers and sometimes to the wider community. Sometimes this performance work emerges from the process drama work described by O'Toole and Dunn, and sometimes from published texts, scripts written by students or teachers, or work created in collaboration with visiting artists. In the primary school, there is a continuum of drama practices, from dramatic play in 'home corner' to process drama where there is no outside audience, to a rehearsed performance staged in a public venue for a community-wide audience. Regardless of where it is placed on the continuum, the dramatic elements identified here are the first building blocks to practice.

The manipulation of the other dramatic elements: *focus, tension, climax, contrast, conflict, transformation of space and objects, and the symbolic use of space and objects* all relate to the teacher's understanding of the art and craft of classroom drama and to their own artistry (see Chapter 5). They are elements that do not require specialist facilities or resources, and can be manipulated within a five-minute drama exercise employed to frame the reading of a new story or to reflect on an issue from the study of the environment or history, or, across an entire term's work. Just as teachers develop greater confidence and expertise at the manipulation of dramatic elements to explore and communicate meaning, so too can children. Through the development of a 'dramatic vocabulary', students can take greater control of their own expressive skills, can negotiate more complex territory and can become architects of their own learning, through drama and beyond.

Two non-drama elements that have been discussed elsewhere in this book also have a place here: *time* and *space*. While the classroom teacher may not need specialist facilities to create alternative worlds in their classroom, time is a critical factor. This is time spent in establishing a safe space for drama to take place—where there is trust and mutual regard among students; time within the drama activity to fully explore the possibilities that unfold (not always easy within the 'crowded curriculum'), and time to reflect when the drama activity is completed. The reflective component is essential in order to contextualise and consolidate the learning that has taken place within the drama activity. Also, if students have been deeply involved in a role-play activity, it is essential to take time to de-role, to place the experiences of the fictional world at a safe distance, to understand the challenges of the imagined world without them impinging in harmful ways on the student's personal world.

Space is a factor because of what it can signify literally, imaginatively, and aesthetically. Drama is an embodied artform, and space is one of the elements that can be manipulated to generate meaning. Transforming the classroom into Botany Bay can be the precursor to a sustained engagement for students in a historically informed re-imagining of the past, in and out of role. Equally, when the teacher and the students push back the desks and chairs of their classroom, they are symbolically signalling the transformation of the classroom space into an agreed *aesthetic space*, with the possibility of travelling to other times and places at will.

The case studies included in this chapter signal a number of ways in which classroom teachers and their students can explore this agreed aesthetic space. The artistry of students and teachers emerges as a powerful theme in both of the case studies, as does the willingness to explore inner and outer worlds through the medium of drama. The case studies also hint at the challenges and complexities involved in bringing a drama workshop or unit of work to life, with differing cultural perspectives, backgrounds, purposes, and agendas all impacting on the fabric of human interaction and understanding that underlies meaningful education.

Looking forward: drama in the twenty-first century

So where is drama situated within the twenty-first century Australian curriculum? McLaren and Giarelli (1995) write about the role of contemporary schools in helping young people to expand their sense of self. They argue that an individual's identity is not static or predetermined by race, class, or gender; and they call on teachers to build 'new social spaces' within their classrooms so that students can participate in 'an 'arch of social dreaming' (McLaren & Giarelli 1995, p. 8). Drama is well situated to address this challenge. Learning in drama is active, social, and experiential; it involves critical inquiry and creative problem-solving. Also, drama engages the whole person—the intellect, the emotions, the imagination, and the body—and it develops socially useful skills and knowledge. Drama thus provides a space for 'social dreaming', where young people can participate in an open-ended and dialogic search for meaning.

CASE STUDY 7.1

The *Fox* workshop—reflective practice in drama teaching

Jane Bird and Kate Donelan

Introduction—about the research

This case study examines the teaching of a university-based drama workshop and the responses of participants who were tertiary primary education students. The two-hour drama workshop, taught by Kate in collaboration with Jane, who was the co-researcher, explores the text of an Australian picture storybook, *Fox* (Wild & Brooks 2000). For us the practical drama workshop is a learning site; it is an opportunity for student teachers, through their active participation and reflection, to discover drama as a powerful pedagogy—a way of building cognitive, affective, aesthetic, and kinaesthetic engagement with written and visual texts.

This workshop uses *Fox* as a 'pre-text'; through a sequence of drama activities, students explore its characters and story from a range of perspectives, as well as dramatising parallel social situations. *Fox* tells the story of three animals living in the Australian bush: Dog is blind in one eye, Magpie has a charred wing, and Fox is a lonely and destructive outsider. Dog rescues Magpie from a bushfire and stays with her even after she rejects his help. They form a close friendship with Magpie riding on Dog's back as he runs through the bush. Filled with 'rage and envy and loneliness' Fox tries to persuade Magpie to leave Dog and 'fly' with him. Magpie twice refuses but finally succumbs. Fox carries Magpie to the middle of the hot red desert and abandons her there so that she 'will know what it is like to be truly alone'. The final page of the book shows Magpie, thinking of Dog's grief when he finds her gone, setting out on her long journey home.

Data for this case study was drawn from Kate's teaching of two drama workshops. It includes Jane's descriptive field notes, Kate's planning notes and post-workshop reflections, written products generated during the workshop, discussions and informal interviews with students, and their written evaluations of the workshop experience. We analysed significant moments, problems that participants encountered during the workshops, and themes and questions that emerged from the data.

An account of the workshop sequence follows, constructed from Jane's observational field notes. Inserted through this text are extracts of data from the students and Kate's comments as a reflective practitioner. Following this, Kate discusses some pedagogical issues emerging from her experiences of teaching the *Fox* unit in different contexts. A detailed outline of the full drama workshop structure is provided at the end.

Background to the *Fox* drama

Inspired by their reading of *Fox*, the 2001 Australian Picture Book of the Year, Kate and her colleague Noel Jordan devised this drama unit for the upper primary and middle years. The unit was also informed by the work of PETA (Philippine Educational Theatre Association) whose creative arts workshops are designed to empower children who have experienced physical and emotional abuse and social deprivation.

The *Fox* workshop

Introducing the drama through warm-up activities

A circle is formed to mark the beginning of a drama class. These tertiary students don't have a strong experience of drama and for many it is quite a new way of learning so there is a mixture of excitement and nervousness. The teacher checks that everyone knows the rules, asking various students to explain their understanding of the game.

> I was aware of the international students in the class and wanted to encourage cross-cultural sharing of versions of this childhood game. I was surprised that everyone seemed to have the same understanding of 'paper/rock /scissors', but it had been worth checking this to avoid confusion before starting to play ... (Kate)

The students' interest level increases when the teacher introduces the roles of animals for the 'evolution game'. Now the students are asked to transform into a cockroach, bird, monkey, and then a human once they win their game of 'rock, paper, scissors'. Applying this familiar childhood game to this new context provides a clear structure and generates high energy, competition, and physical action.

> The games played at the beginning of the workshop were good to 'break the ice' and make
> people feel more comfortable taking risks. I felt more at ease after the games (Student).

Again, the teacher shifts the game, using the same evolution structure, but changing the characters. This time the hierarchy is more complicated, but the class is eager to participate and bombard the teacher with questions, 'Is there anything lower than a one-eyed dog?' and 'If I become a fox do I still keep playing?' They are highly engaged, and committed to the physical detail of the injured animals. The room is filled with crawling, hopping, limping shapes trying to improve their status within the world of the game. Once there are a few foxes, the teacher pauses the game, asking the animals to form groups of their own kind. They create a still image to represent 'the essence' of their animal character. The teacher then places the groups of injured and uninjured dogs and magpies in the centre of the room. She instructs the foxes to circle the others in silence; some students giggle and the teacher insists on silence as the foxes stare at those in the centre of the circle.

Introducing the 'pre-text'

The teacher opens up a discussion: 'What does a fox mean to you?'

Feral

Cheeky, cunning

Night dwellers

The lights are dimmed and images from the cover and first pages of *Fox* fill the wall at the end of the drama room. Like a primary teacher introducing a new book, this teacher asks: 'What do you think this book will be about?' Students respond:

The dingo eating other animals

The bird has something to say

Friendship

The Australian bush

The teacher reads the first page of the book, and highlights Magpie's rejection of Dog's help. The students move into pairs to select and try out a human situation where help is rejected—a clearly defined task with open-ended content. A few students look at others

Chris Sinclair, Kate Donelan, Jane Bird, John O'Toole, and Kelly Freebody

to check what to do. The teacher side-coaches, encouraging students to focus on the moment of rejection; she asks them to reduce their dialogue to two lines, to find and communicate the essence of this situation. This intervention adds more structure to the activity and the students work hard trying to shape their short scenes.

> Encouraged by the focus and energy of students working in pairs throughout the drama room I decided to ask everyone to perform in this collaborative context. I put the emphasis on the content—asking the audience to note the range of social contexts selected and to identify the reasons for the rejection of the offers of help … (Kate)

The pairs form a large circle to present their ideas; this keeps things moving, and provides a safe, non-confronting performance environment. The scenes range from helping elderly or disabled people on public transport to a young adult wanting to drive home a friend who has drunk too much. The group selects one scene: a woman's brother has died and a friend wants to take her out to get her mind off things. When this scene was originally shown, students laughed uncomfortably; interestingly this is the one they now want to explore. The pair replay their original scene and the audience considers how the offer might be delivered in a different way so it is accepted. The mood in the room shifts as the students take this task very seriously. The first attempt is tentative; the student who volunteers looks awkward moving from the audience to enact the role of the friend in the scene. A second student jumps up quickly and tries out his idea more confidently. The students are engrossed in content that relates to their world and they seem more comfortable taking risks in performing.

> I found that the activity where we offered and rejected help was a very good way to make people transfer issues from a book about animals to our own lives.
>
> When we spent a long time doing activities on the first few pages I almost forgot about the text, where we had to deny help from someone. It was a good activity though.
>
> The planned sequence asks participants to move back and forth between social situations that parallel those in the story and drama activities that draw directly on the written text. I know that I have to work hard to retain students' interest in the narrative so that they can reconnect with it after each point of departure. Although this presents a teaching challenge, I find that the structure works well—enabling participants to develop an emotional engagement with the world of the story while also applying the themes to their own knowledge of the social world … (Kate)

The class's attention is drawn back to the text of *Fox* through projected images and the teacher's reading of the next four pages. She allows plenty of time for the class to absorb and interpret the visual information in the illustrations. The class is organised into groups and the teacher asks them to create sculptures (or tableaux) with their bodies to represent Dog and Magpie 'flying'. One group create a pyramid with a small woman standing on the knees of other group members, her arms spread wide, reaching for the ceiling. Her legs are held as the group experiments with creating a sense of movement inspired by the music now playing in the background. Again, the teacher places the groups in a large circle for performance; this time they all perform at the same time while the music plays and some look across at the other 'flying creatures'. *Requiem for a Dream* creates an atmosphere of soaring and the performers respond with bodies stretched, gracious arm movements, and focused facial expressions.

One group is selected and placed in the centre of the room as the teacher dims the lights, shaping the space and heightening the mood, projecting an image of Fox's eyes. The students as the collective Foxes form a circle around this 'flying creature'. The teacher asks the Foxes to begin whispering their inner thoughts as they circle:

Mmm Magpie

I'm waiting, just waiting

I'm going to kill you

One student later commented on the dramatic intensity of this moment:

We surrounded the flying animal and circled it, glaring like a fox, very dramatic. The whispering at Dog and Magpie while circling them was very effective, quite sinister and powerful.

The students constructed scenarios involving three characters similar to Fox, Magpie, and Dog. They improvised scenes about sexual temptation, financial gain for evil deeds, and the lure of alcohol and socialising in inappropriate situations. Again, they seem very committed to subject matter that relates the theme from the text to situations from their contemporary world. The teacher intervenes to remind them to attend to the aesthetic form of their drama. She offers a guiding structure:

Limit the use of language in your scene and instead focus on using the space. Experiment with physical movement in the space …

They consider how to manipulate the dramatic element of space more effectively. One group moves two rostra boxes, exploring the possibilities of using height and space symbolically. Another group starts playing with the dialogue, using short phrases repetitively. Three girls deliver their lines via phone calls, limiting their verbal interaction to: 'You haven't told anyone' and 'I really shouldn't'. They develop their storyline through varying their intonation and tone as they repeat these two phrases. Before sharing the different interpretations of 'temptation' the teacher asks the audience to focus on how space is used and how this impacts on the story being told. They discuss the use of different levels and the specific movements of the performers. The teacher looks at her watch; she tries to push the lesson to its dramatic conclusion, not wanting the students to miss out on the final phase of exploring the story.

Chris Sinclair, Kate Donelan, Jane Bird, John O'Toole, and Kelly Freebody

I was aware of the limited time that was left, and was determined to complete the writing of messages of support for Magpie following Fox's treachery and the ritualised walk on the desert stones. The full workshop is impossible to complete within a two-hour session, and I always need to omit and truncate some planned activities ... (Kate)

She skips a section of the plan. Two volunteers take up positions as Fox and Magpie, while the class forms a circle around them. Another two students 'sculpt' Fox and Magpie at the end of their journey into the hot desert; they move each character into a precise physical position in the space. The teacher passes a cue card to the student representing Fox; she narrates the next section of the story and asks him to speak when the time is right:

'Now you and Dog will know what it is like to be truly alone.'

Fox leaves the circle and students voice the inner thoughts of Magpie as she reacts to Fox's words and his departure. The students speak softly of abandonment and longing for Dog.

Figure 7.1   The pathway is formed by the students' messages to guide and encourage Magpie home

The final three pages of the book are read, and the teacher moves quickly, handing out earth-coloured pieces of paper cut into the shape of a rock. The students write messages for Magpie to read as she begins her long journey home. The students concentrate, heads down in private contemplation. As each message is completed, they are placed across the length of the room to create a long winding pathway. Some students place their 'rocks' randomly, but the teacher quietly moves these in a deliberate shaping of the space. She adjusts the lighting slightly and turns on the music. Each student is asked to walk the pathway, reading the messages on each of the rocks in silence. The teacher places two rostra blocks at the end of the pathway and stands at this 'doorway' to greet each of the students as they arrive. Some students giggle as they wait and the teacher encourages them to join her homecoming greeting. Finally, the last student arrives and there is a hug. They briefly discuss the messages they liked:

> You are his eyes and he is your wings.

Some students comment on the emotional nature of this last activity:

> I was affected by the strength of feeling that came across in people's messages.

> Magpie's walk home gave a satisfying conclusion that the story itself lacked.

> I felt a little awkward writing a message to a fictional character, good that we didn't have to put our names on them though.

Figure 7.2   The students pause to read each of the messages on the rock-shaped paper, considering how Magpie would feel as she travelled along the pathway

Chris Sinclair, Kate Donelan, Jane Bird, John O'Toole, and Kelly Freebody

The students consider whether they would teach a version of this unit themselves:

> I would conduct a version of this workshop with a group of children because the story is wonderful and it works as a great way to enter into issues about human nature, no matter what dramatic ability.
>
> Probably not, I feel I would struggle teaching in that style.
>
> Definitely, it's engaging, exciting, and would lead to some great discussions on human nature, which could be related to real life or other literary characters.
>
> I would teach it because I think it creates a safe and friendly way of exploring philosophical questions/ideas about human nature.
>
> Yes, but not until I had become a far more experienced teacher as it requires a lot of class management.

The *Fox* workshop is over and participants help clear the space after sharing an intense two-hour drama experience. Later they reflect on what they have learnt from the content, the pedagogy, and the aesthetic form of the experience.

> It opened up a lot of opportunities for deeper learning.
>
> The workshop made me think greatly about human actions and motivations: how easily emotions can be stirred up in groups, how people can transform in a dramatic role with ease.
>
> Drama is not just about acting and poses, it can be developed to analyse what a character is thinking.
>
> Drama can be used to explore any issue in society, whether it be big, small, or controversial.

Reflective teaching and learning

Fox is an evolving drama structure, with cycles of reflective practice. A drama workshop, like a performance, is an ephemeral aesthetic event with roles and dramatic meaning constructed by each participant within the negotiated social space of the class. As a teacher you hope your students will experience the drama event meaningfully, that they will engage with the fictional situation, create new narratives, and use dramatic form to express and embody their ideas.

Each time Kate leads a *Fox* workshop, participants respond differently, drawing on the particular understandings they bring into the drama room. In one workshop Kate led, Year 6 students imagined and represented the symbiotic relationship between Dog and Magpie, and then explored the plight of Magpie left alone by Fox in the relentless desert heat. Their messages to Magpie as she travelled on her long journey towards home ranged from the practical: 'Stop after about every 20 minutes or so to rest your wing because it may not of healed properly', to the responsible: 'Magpie you must go to Dog, he's hurting. You must help him like he helped you *fly*', to the inspirational: 'Don't ever *give up*. You will find Dog! One day you will arrive at his cave.' They transcribed the messages on to paper, cut them into the shapes of 'gibbers', and placed them in a spiral on the classroom floor. In turn they undertook Magpie's journey, following the pattern of desert stones. Many of these Year 6 students or their parents had travelled as migrants or refugees to Australia, and their classroom teacher felt that the metaphor of a long and dangerous journey, explored within the aesthetic space of the drama workshop, resonated strongly for them. Their messages indicated their empathy for Magpie, but they wondered about Fox and the reasons for his actions. They considered the scream that Magpie hears after Fox has shaken her off his back and left him in the burning desert heat. They created physical images to depict the scream and to express its qualities of triumph or despair. While reflecting on these shared images one student said: 'I think Fox is the worst off because he's got no friends, nothing but a heart of bitterness.' They imagined alternative endings to the open-ended text. Their versions had Magpie eventually completing her journey and being reunited with Dog, and Fox finding a form of redemption.

EXEMPLAR: *FOX*

Resources

Wild, M. & Brooks, R. (2000) *Fox,* Allen & Unwin, NSW.
Lee, R. & Doyle, M. (1997) *Wild Honey Dreaming,* New World Productions, Qld, Track 2.
Kronos Quartet, *Requiem for a Dream,* Track 3.

Workshop outline

Evolution game

- Explanation of traditional hand-game of *paper/stone/scissors.*
- Whole group physicalises four evolutionary life forms in the following sequence: cockroach, bird, monkey, and human.
- Students play *paper/stone/scissors.* The aim is to move up the evolutionary life forms by winning. If you lose you revert to a lower life form. All start as cockroaches. Teacher stops the game when some participants have reached human form.
- Groups join with their own kind. Each group makes a physical image of the essence of their life form. Share these images.

Dog, Bird, and, Fox game (adaptation of the Evolution game)

- The teacher shows images from *Fox* of Dog, Magpie, and Fox. Discuss the qualities of each animal from different cultural perspectives.

Chris Sinclair, Kate Donelan, Jane Bird, John O'Toole, and Kelly Freebody

- Introduce the concept of damaged animals: one-eyed dog and one-winged magpie.
- Display the sequence of animals that will apply to this version of the Evolution game:
  - Dog.
  - If lose: One-eyed Dog.
  - If win: Magpie.
  - If lose: One-winged Magpie.
  - If win: Fox.
- Stop the game when there are a few foxes.
- Group with your own kind and physicalise your creature.
- The Magpies and Dogs groups in the centre of the space. Foxes circle the room in silence staring at the Magpie and Dog groups.

Law of Nature game

- The aim is to avoid being eliminated from the game.
- Respond to the following commands:
  - *Fire*: whole group physically link, spread out to fill the space, and move as if a bushfire.
  - *Heatwave*: find shelter in some protected place.
  - *Drought*: slow motion crawl across the room.
  - *Dust storm*: make a physical shape in threes that protects everyone in the group.
  - *Predator:* try to put your hand on top of someone else's head and to protect your own. Eliminated if the top of your head is touched.
- Class practise responses to each term.
- Teacher invents a story about the Australian bush incorporating these terms.
- Tell the story and students respond when commands are mentioned.

Offering and rejecting help

- Show images on the first few pages of *Fox*.
- What are our expectations of the dog and the bird from these images?
- Read the first page of the text: from *Through the charred forest* ... to *melting into blackness*.
- Form pairs and decide A and B.
- Select a human situation similar to the one in the book; that is, an offer of friendship or help that is rejected.
- A—offers and B—rejects. Pairs simultaneously enact their situations.
- Reduce the exchange to a couple of lines—communicating the essence of the offer and rejection.

- Set up pairs in a large whole group circle. View brief scenes in sequence around the circle.

Forum theatre

- Select one or two scenes to work with.
- Each pair repeats its scene in the centre of the circle. The audience assists by finding ways for A to make the offer in a way that B will accept.
- Try a couple of versions with different people being A.
- Discuss the social implications and link with the situation in the book.

A sense of flight

- Read the next four pages of text: from *Days, perhaps a week later*, to *through Summer, and Winter*.
- In groups of four form a physical conglomerate structure and create a strange flying creature. The aim is to represent a sense of flight.
- Music: *Requiem for a Dream*, Track 3.
- Perform the Flying Creatures simultaneously to the music.
- View and discuss each one and choose one for the next task.

Fox—the outsider

- Read the next four pages of text: from *After the rains*, to *rage, envy, and loneliness*.
- Show the image of Fox's eyes.
- Put one of the Flying Creatures in the centre; the rest of the class represents Fox. Two members of the Flying Creatures represent Magpie, who is unnerved by Fox, and two represent Dog, who feels comfortable about his presence. (The small group decides this, but doesn't yet reveal it to the class.)
- The group, as Fox, circles the Flying Creature twice, trying to intimidate through eye contact: the first time in silence, the second time they verbalise the inner thoughts and sounds of Fox.
- Discuss the experience from the perspective of each character: Magpie, Dog, and Fox.

The temptation

- Read the next three pages of text: from *Magpie tries to warn Dog* to *I am ready*.
- Form groups of three.

Chris Sinclair, Kate Donelan, Jane Bird, John O'Toole, and Kelly Freebody

- Identify a human situation involving a temptation; the scenario involves a trusting and naive character (Dog), a tempter (Fox), and a vulnerable character (Magpie).
- Develop a scene that conveys the phases of temptation through the use of space and symbolic objects. Use minimal language. Tempter makes three offers until the Magpie character succumbs.
- Perform and discuss the social context and how space was used to heighten dramatic tension.

Conscience alley

- Form an alley—two lines facing each other. One student represents Magpie at one end. One side represents the views of Dog and the other of Fox. Magpie walks slowly along the alley looking from side to side at each person; each speaks a phrase or sentence as Dog or Fox try to persuade Magpie to stay or leave.
- At the end of the alley Magpie decides which direction on the basis of what she's heard.

Abandonment

- Read the next four pages of text: from *While Dog sleeps* to *He turns and looks at Magpie, and he says …*
- One volunteer plays Fox and another Magpie. Two students sculpt Fox and Magpie into a physical position for this moment in the desert; the class forms a circle around them.
- Fox is given a card with text from the book: *Now you and Dog will know what it is like to be truly alone.*
- The teacher re-reads this section of the text.
- Fox speaks these words to Magpie and then leaves the space.
- The circle of participants voice the inner thoughts of Magpie after the Fox has left, trying to make sense of what has occurred. Continue until there is silence.
- The teacher narrates from the text: *In the stillness, Magpie hears a faraway scream. She cannot tell if it is a scream of triumph or despair.*

The scream

- Discuss interpretations of the scream that Magpie hears.
- Groups of four create a physical (moving) image of the scream. Add a soundscape if required.
- Arrange groups in a large circle with one volunteer as Magpie in the centre.

- Each group in turn recreates their image of the scream.
- Silence is held for ten seconds.

Ritual journey on desert stones

- Read final three pages of text: from *Magpie huddles, a scruff of feathers adrift in heat* to *Long journey home.*
- Each participant takes a piece of paper and cuts it into the shape of a large desert stone.
- Each writes a message to Magpie to encourage him on his journey home.
- Lay out the desert stones in a large spiral with a marked end point.
- Each participant makes the journey on the desert stones in silence, reading each message.
- Each is met by the workshop leader at the end of the journey.

Conclusion: picture postcard and thought tracking

- Set up a physical space as *Dog's place one year later.*
- In turn students take up a still position as an animate or inanimate object, naming what they represent.
- The group decides where Fox is in the space and decide how to represent him in some way.
- As they are tapped by the teacher, Dog, Magpie, Fox, and the other animals and objects speak their thoughts.

Each participant reflects on the workshop and chooses a phrase or word about the story, characters, or the drama experience.

Activities beyond the case study

Begin a collection of examples of useful drama practices (draw on texts, personal experiences, observation, and classes). Some starter terms:

- teacher-in-role
- theatre in education
- building belief
- process drama.

Chris Sinclair, Kate Donelan, Jane Bird, John O'Toole, and Kelly Freebody

Finding the way—a theatrical adventure of found lands, lost cultures, and a sky full of constellations

John O'Toole and Kelly Freebody

The Vikings swept with fearsome power and discipline down the hill—their bemusement at the failure of their legendary navigation that had brought them unaccountably to an unknown island quickly overtaken by their curiosity to explore this strange environment. Then the realisation halted them that they had lost their standard and standard-bearer, apparently kidnapped by one of the weird white-coated figures they had briefly encountered. They cautiously approached the white-coats' building ... Little did they know that close by a canoe of Polynesian explorers was having an identical experience. The two warlike groups were about to meet, and would have to deal with each other—first, of course performing their Viking war-chant and Haka to raise the support of their gods—before they were both confronted with the white-coats and their mystery. Even when those had been triumphantly overcome, for Vikings and Polynesians alike there was still much debate to be shared, many stirring speeches to be made, and a great decision to take.

Figure 7.3   Fearlessly confronting the dilemma

In this case study we wanted to explore how drama combines art and learning, and the potential tensions between them. We chose to work within a complex context: pedagogically, with two different learner groups, where we could explore the possibilities of older students peer-teaching younger ones with both engaged in the dramatic fiction; and artistically, in a naturally theatrical setting outside the classroom. Our 'A' group of primary learners comprised two classes of Year 4 students from an inner-city school, studying 'explorers and navigation' and 'Vikings'. Their 'B' group 'teachers' were a class of primary teacher education students, learning how to use drama in their teaching. As researchers, we would be participant researchers, planning the overall learning experience for both groups, and preparing the B group to lead the A group and take over the responsibility for the drama experience.

Our plan was to engage all the participants in an exciting and problematic fictional situation, where as the characters in the situation, they would carry out tasks towards their purposeful goals, providing dilemmas, conflict, surprise, mystery, and the urgency of the task as dramatic tension. The participants would be responding naturally, identifying with

Figure 7.4   The Polynesians realise their star charts have led them astray

Chris Sinclair, Kate Donelan, Jane Bird, John O'Toole, and Kelly Freebody

their characters, not as actors, for there was no external audience to perform to. Our data would comprise:

- the documents that the project would generate: course and teaching plans, planning notes, and production schedule
- the B group's reflective assignments
- online follow-up interviews with the B group
- our reflective journals and observation notes, cross-referenced with ongoing discussion
- feedback interviews with A group students and teachers
- photographs taken by ArtPlay staff.

The context

This context was literally beyond the classroom, a site redolent with rich artistic opportunities and learning opportunities. ArtPlay is a heritage railway shed by the river in central Melbourne, redesigned exclusively for children to play and work with professional artists. A very child-friendly building, it has the added advantage of being set in the middle of a newly landscaped river park, beside a large adventure playground.

For the tertiary students, we wanted to stretch their range of classroom drama skills and to raise their awareness of the aesthetic and theatrical possibilities of participatory drama. They and we wanted to have an experience of drama with children, outside their practice classrooms—somewhere they could take risks.

We presented the B group with this brief: to create and lead the A group in an interactive adventure theatre, where the children would become historical travellers who lose their land, find a new one, are confronted by strange people, and face problems and dilemmas that must be dealt with. Navigation and the stars was a potent theme. This adventure would involve the children moving round ArtPlay, and if the weather was fine, the park outside. The B group fleshed the following out: that the travellers would be two clans, previously unknown to each other, of Viking and Polynesian explorers, whose sophisticated navigation would forsake them and they would find themselves on an unknown island. Unbeknown to both, they had been led there by some modern scientists, sinister or inept (to be decided in rehearsal—in the end it turned into a combination of both!) whose experiments had rearranged the stars, and who then kidnapped the two clans' standard-bearers, to find out more about these historical specimens. Tasks, problems, and dilemmas aplenty faced both clans: First, they had to confront each other and find that in fact they shared a common cause.

Then they had to confront the scientists and deal with the problems and threats they posed, and the blandishments they offered. Finally, they had to decide whether to stay on the island and colonise it according to their cultures, or return to their families and homes

Figure 7.5   Your war-chant doesn't scare us—wait till you see our haka

far across the seas. None of these decisions would be made in advance; the children in their roles would have to surmount their challenges and make the decisions.

For such a complex and short-lived experience, considerable preparation was needed in building background knowledge, trust in the drama, and a strongly shared belief. The adventure began earlier in the school classrooms, with the first meetings comprising a one-and-a-half hour session with the Year 4 classrooms the week before the ArtPlay expedition.

Prior to this, we led the B group in a range of drama activities, both role-play and performance, to help them prepare for their roles, and to lead the A group in the ArtPlay experience. Then the B group divided itself into three teams. One of these researched Vikings, and backgrounded a Viking history and characters for themselves; they studied Viking navigation and religion, and wrote and rehearsed a Viking war-chant to teach their A group class. The second team researched historical Polynesian travels, and backgrounded a Polynesian history and characters for themselves; they studied Polynesian navigation and religion, and wrote and rehearsed a Haka for the other A group class. The third B group team fleshed out the backgrounds and motivation of the imaginary scientists, planned

Chris Sinclair, Kate Donelan, Jane Bird, John O'Toole, and Kelly Freebody

Figure 7.6   A time for making speeches and decisions

the challenges they would set for the visitors, and took charge of planning the timing of the encounters, and ensuring that ArtPlay was ready and represented the island and their laboratory. In addition, splitting this group into three teams, which worked separately, largely solved a problem of group dynamics within the B group that had previously affected this group's participation in drama, and could have disrupted the theatre work. The group split naturally and with some mutual hostility into a sub-group of keen students (the Vikings, who also took on production management and liaison), a smaller sub-group including two who brought into the class some resistance to drama (The Polynesians), and a third sub-group, mainly visiting Asian students, who were new to drama and Australian classroom dynamics, and unassertive, though led by one very confident Australian student (the scientist). This was summed up in retrospect by one of the students:

> There was disunity in the group ... It appeared that perhaps their (the two resistants') motivation was only to pass the subject ... Other students appeared to only accept ideas by others ... Input by everybody is a very important attribute when planning these productions. If we feel a sense of ownership in the piece, then we will be more motivated.

We had already put this perceptive advice into practice. The responsibility of preparing and delivering an exciting and effective learning experience to a real class of children actually gave the 'resistants' that ownership, and they threw themselves into researching, backgrounding, and preparing the Polynesian segment, and in the performance they manifested unexpected skills. One of them noted afterwards:

> By the end of the performance we were interacting much better as a group, and a variety of people were putting forward ideas. I believe this was a result of the smaller groups that we formed.

The Vikings gave themselves the added challenge of delivering the preparatory lesson through drama. The scientists also rose to the demands of driving the narrative in the actual performance without that added stress of the preparatory lesson. Since trust within the group is one of the essential prerequisites for students to commit themselves to drama—particularly to take the risks involved in jointly suspending disbelief—where that trust is missing, the teacher sometimes has to create a diverse range of tasks to fit the dynamics, as we found in this case study.

On the week before the ArtPlay visit, the B group Vikings arrived with a sequence of dramatic role-play activities designed to teach the Year 4 children about Vikings and to provide them with background roles. These activities were closely based on those that we had used in their own prior training. To their initial discomfiture, they found the children already knew more about Vikings than their would-be teachers; the children, used to artwork, quickly picked up the tasks, and responded with energetic engagement. The teacher, obviously unused to drama, and the levels of noise and movement necessary, was uncomfortable and intervened to 'discipline' the children far more than was warranted—a factor that disturbed the B group 'teachers' much more than his own children, who showed their engagement by largely ignoring the interruptions.

The war-chant that the B team had laboured over received a tepid reception, as the children in turn taught their teachers an authentic Viking chant they already knew, which they clearly thought was better. The lesson finished on a note of high ritual: a banner was decorated with blood-red handprints from each Viking as they stepped forth in turn with their oath of commitment and a one-sentence statement to leave with their families.

In the other Year 4 class, an enthusiastic relief teacher and his children were ready for drama, but this B team was not confident enough to use drama yet. Instead, they took the children through a careful talk lesson about Polynesian culture, before taking them into the yard for an energetic session teaching and rehearsing the Haka. An attenuated form of the commitment ritual and oath then completed this very different enrolment process. Though less dramatic than the Viking team's lesson, its leaders felt it had created enthusiasm and belief:

Chris Sinclair, Kate Donelan, Jane Bird, John O'Toole, and Kelly Freebody

The *enrolment* process was a fantastic idea … the children got really excited and they were already getting in-role when they were practising the Haka. In addition, it was good to get an understanding of the class, the teacher, and a bit about the school. (Donna)

Figure 7.7   Moments of shared concentration

The proof was provided when both groups of children arrived at ArtPlay and met their B team leaders. For Year 4 children, the excitement of a joint class bus trip, a half-hour picnic, and free riverside playtime could be very unconducive to focusing on learning, so the B group teams had prepared careful re-enrolment exercises. These were barely necessary, for as soon as the classes met their leaders, they were ready to step into the shoes of the Vikings and Polynesian adventurers, and sail off (metaphorically—the voyage was actually a landbound symbolic walk, with the mariners enthusiastically miming the rowing and sailing, oblivious to the startled glances of passers-by). The in-role engagement was sustained throughout, with complete concentration by the B group, and almost no off-task activity from either A group class.

Their involvement and learning were confirmed by one of the A group teachers:

> I thought it was terrific, the opportunity to integrate all the various stuff in the drama, I thought that was really wonderful. Because as a teacher you're always looking for ways to make learning interesting and engaging for the kids, so it covered stacks of content and in a way that was obviously engaging for them; there was music and dance with the Haka and there were connections with our space-integrated unit with the star charts; and there was the use of imagination, cooperative skills, and problem-solving (Year 4 teacher).

The A group students themselves remarked on the involvement and learning taking place. We interviewed one Year 4 student because his teacher noticed a marked difference in his behaviour during the performance:

> he is very softly spoken in class and doesn't put himself forward to speak up, you couldn't shut him up (Year 4 teacher).

He explained simply:

> I loved arguing with the scientists, I had a great time doing that.

From another:

> I learned the Haka and I also learned how to improve my acting and get into my character a bit more quicker (Year 4).

From a potentially resistant Year 4 A group member:

> I thought it was going to be really stupid and boring, but it was fun …

It seems that for many students their previous experience of drama had not been based on role-play and improvisation, but on more stressful teacher-directed script-work:

> I like the ArtPlay drama better than normal drama where you go 'oh no you don't do that, remember you have to do that and that', you don't need to worry (Year 4).

Chris Sinclair, Kate Donelan, Jane Bird, John O'Toole, and Kelly Freebody

Figure 7.8   Intent participants in a moment of crisis (spot the researcher, quite ignored)

Another key point of drama pedagogy was underlined by the A group classes' speedy re-engagement with the adventure after their lengthy enrolment the previous week. To spend enough time in drama on enrolment—what is often called 'building belief'—is crucial. This was re-emphasised the following week, when the B group held a second performance at ArtPlay for a scratch group of 7–11 year olds who just turned up for the morning. The children were keen on drama, but had no commitment to the subject matter, no special interest in Vikings or navigation. The B group spent nearly an hour on engagement and enrolment activities, but throughout the actual adventure theatre these children were noticeably less involved and more quickly distracted.

The last word on the production should be given to one of the initial B group resistants, for what she observed in her peer-learners, but primarily for what she found for herself: that not only is drama a valuable pedagogy, but actually inspiring for the primary teacher … and fun, too.

> The performance was absolutely brilliant. I enjoyed it thoroughly and was so proud of what not only I but all group members achieved. It isn't until the actual performance that you can see exactly how everything works together, and I was thrilled to see the enjoyment on each

and every child's face. From the minute we enrolled the students they worked fantastically as a group and remained so focused. Although being a *teacher-in-role* was a daunting task, and I feared how students would actually respond to this, it worked so well. I felt totally in control without the students even knowing that there was someone of 'authority' with them at all times. We worked in unison rather than being that 'boring teacher'. It was a collaborative learning experience, which allowed me to interact with students and guide the learning of the students without simply telling them what I wanted them to do (Amy).

EXEMPLAR

The reconfigured exemplar below has tried to take all these findings into account, in devising a much simplified version of this drama, with a further option of peer-teaching. You don't have to start with three classes at two different age groups in a far-off location. Nor is it confined to Year 4—it is quite practicable for years 3–7, with different levels of challenge in step 1 below. Give yourself at least an hour a day for a week—there is much cross-curricular learning in this. There is one unusual teaching technique you will use: teacher-in-role—joining in the drama with the children, possibly in two different roles. Don't be afraid of this; it will work as long as you take it seriously yourself, and give it the respect that you expect the children to give you; you can use a single simple prop or dress signal if it helps you—a lab-coat for the scientist, a shoulder-wrap for a Viking Elder. And remember, step 1, the enrolment, will take most of the time you have available—steps 2–4 will take perhaps an hour, or at most two, but will only work properly if you have built deep belief.

The bones of this drama, taught by a single teacher in your own classroom, are:

Before the drama

1   Decide according to your own class and curriculum whether to investigate Vikings or Polynesians (we'll use Vikings to explain—it works just as well for Polynesians). First, if you are not already, inspire yourself with interest in the subject—it will certainly help the children (for Vikings, try reading Kipling's *The Harp Song of the Dane Women* to yourself).

2   Decide for your drama why the modern scientist would have monkeyed around with the stars, and drawn the Vikings to his/her island. Is it accidental ineptness, or are there ulterior motives? You might try getting ideas from the children. The main dilemma for the travellers will be whether or not to stay on the island and leave their families, but you might be able to give them other, harder dilemmas or tests of their loyalty to each other.

Chris Sinclair, Kate Donelan, Jane Bird, John O'Toole, and Kelly Freebody

Step 1: Backgrounding and building belief (Enrolment phase)

- Create a Viking village: read and research the customs, stories, and legends; draw a map of the village with all the important features, and make artwork with typical Viking patterns.
- Use drama to people it with Viking families over three generations:
  1 The group freeze-frames to depict its activities.
  2 Pairs role-play within the families to explore the daily problems they might face (all pairs working simultaneously—these don't need an audience).
  3 Short scenes are acted to the other groups to show a precious moment or a typical crisis in the family history. Try framing these in the play-within-a-play role-play of 'a long winter night's entertainment for a special visitor'—perhaps with a group member as a Viking elder or distant traveller, to give him or her practice as teacher-in-role, which will be needed for later, though all he or she has to do is listen appreciatively. This is also useful practice for the ritual and discipline necessary later. Activities such as boat building, weaving, and laying feasts can just be pretend, but should be practised to look real. (Chopping and sawing trees is hard work!)
  4 Craft work and backgrounding: make a decorated bracelet for each person with an individual motif. This is a talisman in fact and fiction—putting it on signals we are in-role; perhaps make a Viking shield each; compose and rehearse a war-chant invoking the gods; compose an oath of solidarity and valour for all Vikings to use in the rituals. Try some in-role writing: diaries of their journeys, letters back from newly conquered lands, or poems about the gods, victories, or fallen heroes.
- This could take two sessions or up to a week, depending on how much time you have.

Step 2: The voyage and exploring the island (play and discovery phase)

- With the students, map out the area that you are going to use as the island—the cleared classroom is probably as good as anywhere unless you have a dedicated drama space. Outdoors is actually difficult—drama is easier in a circumscribed and private space even if restricted, and the outside is distracting. Together, try to envisage where the important places will be, and somehow signify physically your precious boat, and the scientist's building. Some children may need to change roles, so that all can become 'the members of the family who are going on this dangerous journey'. Perhaps select the exact role, task, and social position of each mariner on this journey—from the Captain down.

- In-role (with you as that Viking elder, who is *not* travelling), hold the farewell ritual, with each of the Vikings imprinting his hand in blood-red paint on the banner that they will take, and speak a solemn message for their families.

- Step into the boat, stow the banner, and when seated ready to row, ask the children to close their eyes, and rhythmically pull together as they listen. When the rhythm is established, briefly but vividly narrate them through the journey of many months, where somehow their navigation goes wrong, and after storms and adventures, they arrive safely … where? Stop rowing, tell the children to open their eyes and let them explore the island in groups, remembering that they need to find food, fresh water, and shelter. Let this be playful or serious as the mood takes them.

This will take a session, and you can cut the drama and invite them to report back what they have found.

Step 3: Confronting the scientist (experiential learning phase)

- Before re-starting the drama, explain that you are going to join it in role as the scientist, and that the Vikings will confront a new kind of foe, who, they will discover, has stolen their banner, and has powers to withstand their war-chant and their spears, and who will force them to make a difficult decision. Make it clear beforehand how they will know you are in-role—perhaps donning the lab-coat.

- Re-start the drama: 'Gathering together at the end of the day, we repeat our oath and our war-chant, before telling each other what we have discovered.' Let this run, and at a dramatically appropriate moment, step forward as the scientist, showing that you have taken their banner. (Perhaps they will have discovered already!) Watch unmoved while they make their war-chant and challenges, then explain who you are and what the situation is (whatever you have decided).

- From here, you will find that the action will probably run itself, turning into a long council-of-war debate as the Vikings wrestle with the problems and dilemmas you have set them—you may need to make occasional in-role interventions to turn the screws, re-focus them, or set the tasks, but this should be minimal. The final decision (if more than one) should be whether or not the Vikings will stay and colonise this island, or sail back—with their navigational stars restored—to their families. When this is made, cut the drama.

- There is a good, solid session here, or if you have set up a series of really tough dilemmas and the students are deeply involved there may be two or three.

Chris Sinclair, Kate Donelan, Jane Bird, John O'Toole, and Kelly Freebody

Step 4: Reflection-in-action (transforming and understanding the experience)

- While the Vikings are still more or less in-role, gather them in a circle, and ask each in turn solemnly to describe in a sentence what they see themselves doing one year or two years hence. This might be preceded or followed by the Viking oath and war-.chant, to create a ritual climax and finale.
- Out-of-role, look at how this voyage will be re-told as legend in fifty or one hundred years on.
    - Discuss what would be remembered, and what would be changed, as memory dims and the story is retold by those who were not there. Together, or in groups, create a dramatic storytelling of the tale—narration with vivid illustrations in freeze-frame and theatrical enactment. Take the role again as the grandchild of the Viking elder, now yourself an elder, and be the audience, as the 'long winter night's entertainment' unfolds once more. (This second part will take another full session.)

And then, for the brave, a big leap:

Step 5: Theatre-in-education

- Persuade a colleague to join you in peer teaching, for the older students to lead younger classes. Then adapt it as theatre-in-education by just following the version that you have read in the case study, adding step 1 above, and whatever bits of steps 2–4 seem appropriate. You may need to study both Vikings and Polynesians, if you use the three-group format of the case study!

Activities beyond the case study

Planning tasks

1   Develop a lesson plan/workshop outline for a 'process drama' inspired by a picture book.
2   Build a collection of pre-texts suitable for use in drama classes—across a range of ages and year levels. Include:
    – a list of 'arts-rich' picture books
    – a catologue of evocative music tracks/sound recordings
    – poetry
    – newspaper items
    – images.

Conclusion

Kate and Jane reflect on *Fox*

As a classroom teacher using drama to explore texts, you need to plan a sequence of tasks, be familiar with your material, organise the space and your resource material. As the drama workshop leader you need to be open to the responses of your students, the quality of their attention and energy, their levels of engagement, the things that distract or confuse them, and the moments when they are focused, identifying with the characters and situation, and transported to a fictional world. You may need to adapt your teaching style and presence, to modify your planned activities, to intervene with a different strategy, to ask different questions, to shift the mood or the rhythm of the workshop. Your students' responses will inevitably be unpredictable; at times they will disappoint you, as will your teaching performance. Sometimes you will be exhilarated by the quality of students' insights, their fresh and original interpretations, the integrity of their drama work and you will be proud of crafting a richly satisfying creative event. You will know there is artistry in teaching a fine drama lesson.

Every drama class is different, and every time we teach we learn something about our students and ourselves. We encourage you to begin your risky, bumpy, and exhilarating journey as a reflective drama teacher!

John and Kelly reflect on the ArtPlay project

When one of the Year 4 students commented that he preferred the ArtPlay drama to 'normal drama' because you didn't have to worry about remembering what to do, it provided a reminder of the considerable evidence that structured improvised role-play is not only more effective than scripted drama or acting to an audience as a learning tool, but the children value it more. In this form of drama the teacher (or in this case 'teachers') helps the children to construct an original dramatic fictional situation, then make up the action, and live it experientially, not as actors—just as children do naturally in their own dramatic play. A Viking team member clearly concurs:

> I was really overjoyed at the result. The students taking on the roles in such a manner that they really acted as Vikings was fantastic … The children gained a deeper understanding of the characters of Vikings, voice projection, communication skills and problem-solving (Brooke).

And another added:

> It compounded my belief that drama education can foster teamwork and interpersonal skills in children (Phuong).

Another significant element of the pedagogy in this case study related to peer group teaching. Large-group peer teaching is still a relatively rarely used teaching technique—

Chris Sinclair, Kate Donelan, Jane Bird, John O'Toole, and Kelly Freebody

often for structural reasons within schools relating to timetables and space. This case study reinforced what is almost invariably the case in peer-group teaching: the primary learning content may be intended for the younger students, but the greatest learning benefits accrue to the peer-teachers themselves.

> I gained a lot of new understandings, skills, and experiences, from something as simple as making props to something as major as choosing the educational purposes for the students (Thao Thanh).

It is useful to consider the ways in which the teacher researchers who conducted these two case studies reflect on their practice. In the *Fox* case study, Jane played the role of observer and was able to reflect-in-action, as did Kelly on occasion in the ArtPlay study. This enabled them to capture moments of insight from the position of privileged observer—watching with an understanding of the teacher or workshop leader's process, but with the opportunity to retain some distance. In the writing of both of these case studies, the thoughts of the teacher's reflecting on action are also captured: in the *Fox* case study we have the critical moments of decision revealed in Kate's boxed meta-commentary. In the ArtPlay case study, we have the considered reflections of John, Kelly, and their student teachers as co-researchers, recorded as they look over their data and other triggers for memory of their practice. This provides the readers with a privileged 'insider-view' of the experienced drama practitioner revealing the mechanics of pedagogy and artistry 'on the floor'.

There are other facets to the issue of reflection that are worthy of attention here. The first is that the teacher as 'reflective practitioner' learns and grows through a reflexive process of action–review–analysis–action. Through 'reflective practice' the teacher develops strategies for reviewing his or her own practice in a constructive and productive pursuit of better practice: better teaching and better learning outcomes, in an aesthetic framework. This process is potentially regenerative for the teacher. In some ways their students become co-researchers and co-artists with the teacher, in response to the questions: what happened here, why did it happen, what it does it mean, what do I do now?

The process of reflection is critical to student learning in drama. Through transforming drama experiences into another form—either another creative form, a discussion, or even a new application of a skill or technique—the potential for drama as a learning and an expressive medium is played out.

> For teacher and children, the drama is virtually never complete in itself as a learning experience. It must be reflected on and transformed into explicit knowledge, through reflection and transformation—sometimes through performance or sharing of the drama. These are often interdependent … (O'Toole & Dunn 2002, p. 23).

The case studies examined here are contemporary examples of 'social dreaming': drama practice occurring in schools and universities at the present time. As children and young people find new ways to navigate the south seas or guide Magpie home, they interrogate the challenges of their own lives—what it means to be a loyal and true friend, to belong, to go into the unknown, what it means to be a leader, or a good teacher. They are invited to reflect and share in the 'social dreaming' of their present moment, to make new stories out of old ones as they actively engage with human experiences in a shared aesthetic space of their own making.

Questions for students to consider

1 What strategies would you would use in teaching a drama workshop like *Fox* to primary children?
2 How does reflective practice enhance drama teaching?
3 What are the benefits for students of exploring the characters and situations in a story through drama?

Key references

Ackroyd, J. & Boulton, J. (2001) *Drama Lessons for Five to Eleven-year-olds*, David Fulton, London.

Bolton, G. (1998) *Acting in Classroom Drama: A Critical Analysis*, Trentham Books, Stoke on Trent, UK.

Heathcote, D. & Bolton, G. (1995) *Drama for Learning: Dorothy Heathcote's Mantle of the Expert Approach to Education,* Heinemann, Portsmouth, NH.

McLaren, P.L. & Giarelli, J.M. (eds) (1995) *Critical Theory and Educational Research*, State University of New York Press, Albany.

Miller, C. & Saxton, J. (2004) *Into the Story: Language in Action through Drama*, Heinemann, Portsmouth, NH.

Morgan, N. & Saxton, J. (1989) *Teaching Drama: A Mind of Many Wonders*, Stanley Thorne, London.

Neelands, J. & Dickenson, R. (2006) *Improve your Primary School through Drama*, David Fulton, London.

Nicholson, H. (ed.) (2000) *Teaching Drama*, Continuum, London and New York.

O'Neill, C. (1995) *Dramaworlds: A Framework for Process Drama*, Heinemann, Portsmouth, NH.

O'Toole, J. (1992) *The Process of Drama: Negotiating Art and Meaning*, Routledge, London.

O'Toole, J. & Dunn, J. (2002) *Pretending to Learn*, Pearson Education Australia, Frenchs Forest.

QSA (2002) *The Arts: Years 1 to 10 Syllabus*, retrieved 10 December 2007 from http://www.qsa.qld.edu.au/downloads/syllabus/kla_arts_syll.pdf

Slade, P. (1954) *Child Drama*, Cassell, London.

Slade, P. (1977) *Natural Dance*, Hodder and Stoughton, UK.

Chris Sinclair, Kate Donelan, Jane Bird, John O'Toole, and Kelly Freebody

Toye, N. & Prendiville, F. (2000) *Drama and Traditional Story for the Early Years*, Routledge Falmer, London.

Victorian Curriculum and Assessment Authority (2007), Curriculum and Standards Framework II, State Government of Victoria, Melbourne, retrieved 24 April 2008 from http://www.vcaa.vic.edu.au/prep10/csf/index.html

Wild, M. & Brooks, R. (2000) *Fox*, Allen & Unwin, NSW.

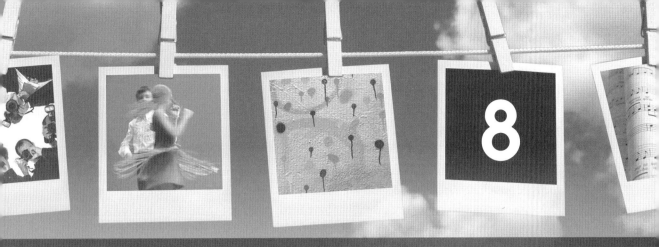

Making Music and Cultural Connections

Neryl Jeanneret and Andrew Swainston

This chapter draws attention to a number of key themes present in this book, and puts them in the context of contemporary music education in the primary and middle school. The case studies consider the impact of the artist bringing both music and cultural experience into the classroom. In Andrew Swainston's case study, an Indigenous artist in residence works with several classes of 'challenging' Year 8s in a middle-school setting, with exciting results and powerful changes in understanding. In the second case study, Neryl Jeanneret looks at the impact of the Musica Viva schools program (in this instance the visit of a local gamelan to a small multicultural primary school) and places it in the context of a beginning teacher's first experiences as the music specialist in a primary school. The case studies are framed by a discussion of the recent *National Review of Music Education*, and the various approaches to music education in schools in Australia.

> Music is fun. Everyone had musical ability. Even if you can't sing, you can be musical. Everyone has the ability to compose.

> I think the most important thing I learned is to just try different musical activities. It was hard before to even think of doing any of it and now I'm comfortable trying anything once.

> (Pre-service generalist primary students)

Introduction

Neryl Jeanneret

The issue of the quality and quantity of music education in primary schools has been the focus of much research and debate for many years. There have also been a number of government research reports released that have focused on both arts and music education (see the *National Review of School Music Education* [NRSME] Report for elaboration). The stark reality of the music programs in schools is that you will encounter the full spectrum of provision. Some schools offer comprehensive classroom programs with a range of extra-curricular activities, while others will have virtually nothing, regardless of what curriculum authorities might specify. It is possible that Australian students can complete thirteen years of education without participating in any form of music education, particularly in Victoria, Western Australia, or the Australian Capital Territory, where there are no mandatory requirements for music education (Stevens 2003). At the same time, the *Australian Attitudes to Music* survey (Australian Music Association 2001) found almost all the parents in their survey (95 per cent) felt that the study of music should be part of a well-rounded education.

The problem is not isolated to any particular state or territory, or country for that matter, and this seems a rather gloomy start to a chapter about music education. The fact is that the quality and quantity of music in primary schools in Australia is one of the foremost issues identified in the *National Review of School Music Education* (DEST 2005). On a more positive note, in schools where music is valued, where there is enthusiasm among the staff, and where sufficient resources are allocated, music flourishes.

In this chapter we will examine some of these identified issues and discuss ways you might overcome them, with a special focus in the case studies on the resources you might call on. In this way we are mindful of a study for the Australia Council for the Arts where Hunter (2005) identified the attributes of effective arts that include student-centred learning, administrative support, integrated professional development, diversity, continuity and sustainability, and artists as effective partners.

Teaching music

There are all sorts of challenges you will face, particularly as a beginning teacher and certainly your first year, when you finally have the excitement of your own class, will be an adjustment. Teachers at the beginning of their careers sometimes have a different outlook on music curriculum (and perhaps curriculum in general) than their school principals and more experienced colleagues, and they often feel that their teacher education has not prepared them fully for the realities of full-time employment in a school. The number of hours of music education you will or have received in your tertiary course is probably very small. The Stevens Report (2003) found pre-service teachers receive on average only 23 hours of music over their teacher education courses, and tertiary music educators understand only too well how little time they have when their students frequently have little prior music experience. This does not mean your teacher education can't have an impact as the quotes above from students with 12 hours of music education demonstrate. You need to remember that the nature and the diversity of schools are extremely complex, and it is difficult to talk in much more than general terms about music education when the time is so limited.

When new to a school, it is important that you work at establishing and maintaining a professional dialogue with your colleagues and establish communication with your principal. Chapter 2 presented the benefits of learning in the arts and you need to be able to articulate what the benefits are of a music program to some principals. We have strongly advocated the need for a 'creative' teaching approach to the arts where children are actively involved in experimenting with and creating music. Not all teachers have this view of music education, nor have they had the benefit of a pre-service education that embodies this principle. You may encounter colleagues with a more conservative, traditional approach, but do not be disheartened—persevere. Teaching is full of challenges and rewards, and your first couple of years will be particularly challenging.

Generalist versus the specialist

Although some school systems maintain music specialists in primary schools, the reality of the situation is that a large number of generalist primary teachers in Australia, Great Britain, and North America have the responsibility for teaching music in their classrooms. Childhood music experiences have a powerful influence on the development of future adult attitudes about music and can be predictive of musical involvement in later life. The primary teacher is an important source for these early music experiences and she or he has the powerful potential to affect students' opinions about music. I acknowledge that at the same time, primary school teachers' own musical experiences frequently shape their attitude towards, and confidence in, teaching music. There has been a lot written about the debate about generalist versus specialist music teachers in primary schools, so let us just consider some of the advantages you have as the classroom teacher. The generalist teacher has the capacity to include many more music lessons within a week, and there is evidence to suggest that this is significant in improving the level of student achievement (Runfola & Rutkowski 1992). The generalist teacher also has an advantage over the specialist in that he or she knows the children in the class better than any specialist does. The generalist is also able to integrate music into the general school curriculum, making it more relevant to real-life experiences. Of course, the ideal situation is where a specialist works with the classroom teachers, providing support, ideas, and the opportunity to team-teach.

Neryl Jeanneret and Andrew Swainston

The confidence (or lack of) in the generalist to teach music is a common problem and probably one that many of you might be feeling. The important thing is to remember what has been said above. Embrace your music subject at university and experiment with music ideas in your classroom. You also need to remember a number of music education writers assume that musical expertise will automatically ensure success in teaching music, but they fail to acknowledge that non-musical teacher traits and competencies also play an important part in the teaching of music. For example, Greenberg (1972) found that despite a limited musical background, some teachers taught music to very young children as competently as those with a considerable music background. Similarly, Young (1974) identified teacher traits such as willingness to take the initiative, determination, and industry as having more effect on children's improvement than the teacher's musical background.

Approaches to music education in the primary classroom

There are a number of methodologies in music education you might encounter. Two such approaches are those developed by the German composer, Carl Orff, and the Hungarian composer and ethnomusicologist, Zoltán Kodály. More commonly referred to as the 'Orff–Schulwerk' and 'Kodály method', they have had a strong international influence on music education programs in primary school settings. Space is too limited to expand on these approaches here, but I suggest you make yourself familiar with their principles and practices as a number of primary teachers use these methods in their classroom programs. There are national and state organisations for both the Orff–Schulwerk and the Kodály methods, and they offer many valuable workshops for generalist primary teachers throughout the year.

Another approach is what originated as comprehensive musicianship in the US in the 1960s, which has had a significant influence on the development of music curricula and resources in the UK, US and Australia. This method focuses on students becoming actively involved in the study of music through participating in performance; perceptive listening and analysis; and compositional and improvisational processes and techniques—and these activities are integrated rather than taught separately. The musical elements are examined in a broad range of repertoire that includes music from different eras, styles, and cultures, and children are encouraged to be active learners, making discoveries and applying this knowledge to their own music-making.

In more recent years, ideas from general education have become more prominent in music education; in particular, the developing of critical thinking, problem-solving, and the inclusion of Vygotskian constructivist learning. Jackie Wiggins, a leading figure in music education, especially the area of children's composition, suggests teachers and students should work as collaborative partners in solving problems that can be performance-based, listening-based or creating-based (Wiggins 2001).

Most recently, the NRSME Report summarises approaches to music education by stating

> In broad terms, student learning in music is categorised under two general headings:
>
>   *Music practice* (making music, exploring and developing music ideas, skills, processes, conventions, composing and performing music)
>
>   *Aesthetic understanding* (listening and responding to music, and understanding music's social, cultural and economic significance) (DEST 2005, p. 91).

Figure 8.1   Integration of music practice and aesthetic understanding

Composing in the primary classroom

In making a special mention of composing in the primary classroom, I tend to focus on creative activities as a tool for understanding music throughout my pre-service classes because of what I see as neglect of this area in schools. The more I became involved with primary music, the more I noticed the tendency for activities to be whole-group, teacher-centred, involving, for example, singing songs or listening to recorded music. My research and experience in early childhood music brought home some serious questions. With the focus on play and exploration that is frequently characteristic of early childhood programs, why was it that the same notions weren't extended to music? Why did so many teachers revert to the whole-group, teacher-centred focus when it came to music activities? Why weren't there music centres in the classroom where children could explore sound and sound-makers in the same way there were other learning area centres in the classroom?

The research data of Louie Suthers at the Institute of Early Childhood Education provides wonderful video footage of young children experimenting and exploring sound in a variety of music centres. They are curious and completely absorbed, and it showed me that very young children could spend extended periods of time in the music centre, either alone or with others, if the opportunity were provided.

There seems to be a perception both in the community and the teaching profession that music education is about learning an instrument and performing only. It is essential that children are given the opportunity to explore and experiment with sound and making

Neryl Jeanneret and Andrew Swainston

their own music. Perhaps it would help if composing in this music education context is not the 'pure' act of composing from an external or internal inspiration, but a structured activity aimed at internalising and understanding the concepts of music by manipulating sound. Christensen's (1992) conclusion from her study of Year 4 students cannot be put any better—'the music composition process … is a powerful means for developing elementary music students' ability to perceive what is musical about music, their ability to engage in collaborative musical production, and their metacognitive awareness of the composition process'. If children are expected to create art works and write stories, they should also be given the chance to create music. The creative aspect is as important to the understanding of music as listening to and performing the music of others.

Guidelines for music in the classroom

As a final point to this section, I have included the guidelines for teachers taken from the NRSME Report. Table 8.1 provides a useful guide for both the generalist primary teacher and the music specialist with a series of questions for reflection.

Table 8.1   Guidelines for teachers in specific phases of schooling (NRSME Report, DEST 2005, p. 106)

Phase	Role of all teachers	Role of specialist music teachers	Key questions for all phases
Early childhood	Provide opportunities for a number of different modes of expression in the arts in general and music in particular. Each child has the opportunity to sing, play, move, create and think as a musician Build on the musical experiences that students bring with them to school while extending and developing the repertoire of music that students experience and come to know and understand Value music as a form of expression and communication Work collaboratively with other teachers, community members and other providers of music learning for students	Introduce students to basic musical concepts Ensure that this music learning is engaging and meaningful for students Work collaboratively with other teachers and providers of music learning for students	Is my teaching of music age/development specific? Does my teaching include a range of approaches? Is my teaching of music inclusive? Do I include a range of music styles, forms, genres, periods and sources including those of students' home cultures Does my music teaching challenge students?

Table 8.1 (continued)

Phase	Role of all teachers	Role of specialist music teachers	Key questions for all phases
Middle childhood	Provide a range of music opportunities that build on their learning in early childhood including: • Singing; • Playing music using instruments; and • Creating/composing music Provide music opportunities that continue to challenge each student to explore and experiment with music ideas, extend their musical skills and understanding of musical processes Provide music opportunities that encourage students to make connections, to become aware of music and the other arts in the world around them Work collaboratively with teachers with specialist knowledge and experience in music, parents and community partners who can provide relevant music experiences Build in each child an understanding of music as an arts language Work collaboratively with other teachers and providers of music learning for students	Provide relevant musical experiences to enable students to engage with key musical concepts Provide performance opportunities for students as performers and audience to engage practically with musical concepts Ensure that this music learning is engaging and meaningful for students Work collaboratively with other teachers and providers of music learning for students	Do I show and share my values about music with students? Do I respect the learning needs of each student? Do I work collaboratively, effectively and efficiently to teach music? Does my work with students recognise the value of music education in assisting and supporting learning in all other areas of the curriculum? Do I recognise the role music can play in the whole learning program of all students, especially those who may not be specifically studying music at school?

Neryl Jeanneret and Andrew Swainston

Gongs, angklungs, and Indonesia: integrating music as a whole school project

Neryl Jeanneret

About the research

This is a case study of a music project implemented in a small metropolitan primary school in Victoria with the assistance of the Musica Viva in Schools (MVIS) Program. The purpose of the study was to examine how a cross-years, cross-curricular study about Indonesia could include a significant music component that involved professional development for generalist teachers, activities for children, and a performance by a local gamelan (Indonesian musical ensemble). The study took place over terms 3 and 4 in a school of two hundred students and nine teachers. The study also observed the first three terms of a beginning teacher in her first appointment.

The case study

Cathy is a newly graduated music specialist with an appointment two-days per week in a small inner metropolitan school. Cathy has done most of her teaching rounds in secondary schools, and in preparation for taking on a primary appointment she attends a couple of primary music professional development workshops. One was a two-hour workshop I offered at the end of the university year for secondary graduates who were taking up primary positions. The second Cathy attended was the Victorian Orff Schulwerk Association's January conference in Melbourne, which provided her with lots of ideas and resources.

The school's demographics comprise children who come from very diverse backgrounds and an interesting mix of teachers, some new, some very experienced, and all with a variety of attitudes to music in the classroom. Although Cathy sees the entire school for a single music lesson in her two days there, a number of the teachers also engage children in music activities in their general program.

While at university, Cathy was exposed to the MVIS Program in her methods class with a performance/workshop given by Byar, a local gamelan group of four musicians. She and her peers were given the opportunity to engage with a number of activities with the group as well as observe the demonstration of instruments and performance of a variety of Indonesian music.

The nature of the MVIS Program is to conduct a two-hour professional development workshop with teachers that takes them through a number of music activities outlined in a teaching kit that comes with a CD containing pieces performed by the group. The teachers take these activities back to their classroom and work through them with their students, familiarising the children with the style and sound of the music. The teaching kit is designed in such a way that it presents an integrated approach to music education with listening, performing, and composing activities. Some weeks later, the group returns to perform for the whole school and takes the children through a number of activities. Musica Viva has a range of groups representing different styles and genres available for these workshops.

Setting the scene

As fate would have it, this school had a specialist LOTE teacher, Jane, who taught Indonesian, and a cross-curricular program where some time was spent on the study of Indonesia. Cathy suddenly thought of Musica Viva and Byar, and we began our case study.

Musica Viva kindly provided the professional development and the performance by the group. Now we had to convince the principal and the staff that this was a good idea. New to the school and fresh out of university, Cathy bravely approached the principal early in the year. The principal responded enthusiastically, pledging her support. Buoyed by the reaction, Cathy set off to approach the staff, who initially were not quite so enthusiastic. Typical questions included:

- When would this happen?
- How would it happen?
- How did it all fit with what we were already doing?
- What about the Term 3 concert? How would it fit in? Where were they going to find the time?

Cathy was a little deflated. The whole plan of bringing Musica Viva into the school *and* a real, live gamelan to support what was already happening was a *great* plan. It was a gift—why weren't these teachers just as delighted as she was? She pressed on with hours of hunting for resources, planning lessons, and coping with a heavy teaching load for the two days she was in the school.

> There were just no breaks in the school day for me to catch up on things. Recess and lunchtimes were spent getting ready for the next group of children. Even though it was a relatively small school, I saw every student over the two days I was there, from Preps to Year 6.
>
> It was a bit of baptism by fire, constantly adjusting to the different year levels and the management issues.

In spite of this, Cathy persevered with trying to enthuse and organise the staff for the Musica Viva professional development workshop. A saving grace was that Cathy kept in touch with Andrew and me at the university, and we offered extra advice about resources, management, and generally lent a sympathetic ear. Cathy had found herself teaching in a portable building in the schoolyard with little musical equipment. The room was too small to comfortably do group work, and she often found herself moving between indoors and the

Neryl Jeanneret and Andrew Swainston

playground among groups of children, some of whom seemed to think that being outdoors was a license to do anything except be on task. She started the year by fixing some of the broken instruments, extending her CD collection to include music she thought would be appealing to the different levels, and making lots of colourful and appealing teaching aids for her lessons.

> Management with these kids is a pain in the neck. I just get everyone settled and listening to instructions, and someone disrupts things again and we start all over again about 'When I'm giving you instructions, you need to listen otherwise you won't know what to do. How hard is that?' The real shock was realising this was all *my* problem now. Not like on rounds when you had a supervising teacher looking out for you. Only being there two days a week makes it hard to catch up with students and follow up with other staff on how to deal with some of the chronically naughty ones—and what is it about some Year 6 girls?
>
> I don't think some people were prepared for the level of noise you get in some music classes. I was in the middle of a lesson and all the kids were working away on things and the noise level was pretty high. A couple of prospective parents were touring around the school, looked in for a few minutes and then left. The next minute the Assistant Principal came bursting in. The parents had told him I was in trouble. I just said to him, 'This is what a music classroom looks like—if you hand 25 children a percussion instrument, what would you expect to happen?'

But there were rewards as well:

> Some of the kids starting coming up to me in the playground and chatting about all sorts of things. It was a bit hard to work out why they could be naughty in class one minute and the next minute chatting away happily about this and that … like I was a real person (laughs).
>
> The Preps absolutely loved the song. The minute I started playing it, they started to sway with the music. They couldn't get enough of it.

Professional development workshop

Meanwhile, there were a few dramatic changes in the school and a new principal arrived. He was also supportive of Cathy's ideas but in a quiet way. The afternoon of the professional development session with Musica Viva arrived and all the teachers attended with an extra two from another school nearby making eleven in all. There were some grumblings about waiting at school until five o'clock, but the teachers noted later that it was obvious that the musicians were enjoying themselves, which was infectious and inspired their own enjoyment. One teacher said she was prepared to stay half an hour and then go home, but she was enjoying herself so much she stayed for the full time: 'It was much easier than

I thought it was going to be and there were activities I thought I could use'. Afterwards the teachers all agreed that the session had been worthwhile and enjoyable. They said it had made them far more likely to try the activities with their own classes and they were surprised how readily they had learned from the activities. For example, they were happy to try the Kecak and the soundscape with their class and the session had given them the confidence to attempt these in the classroom. The teachers all commented it was clear from the presentation that there was no need for highly developed music skills to implement the activities.

What happened next?

Over the next few weeks the school was in a frenzy, preparing for the annual school concert towards the end of Term 3. This was a whole school event and every class and year was busy with its contribution. At the same time some of the classroom teachers attempted various activities from the Byar professional development session with their classes. Andrew was invited to attend one young teacher's (Alice) years 2 and 3 classes with whom she had been developing the soundscape idea used in the workshop, but using a dinosaur theme. It was clear from the outset that the bulk of the development and composing work had already been done and the classes were putting the final touches to their performances. Both classes were highly organised, they were focused and very motivated. Alice had drawn a grid involving seven groups (rows down) representing the roars of different dinosaurs or sounds such as a storm, wind, or river. There were about ten steps or events (columns across) where the different dinosaurs or sounds occurred. The children used a range of instruments, mainly classroom percussion and vocalisations and body percussion.

Figure 8.2 Dinosaur soundscape

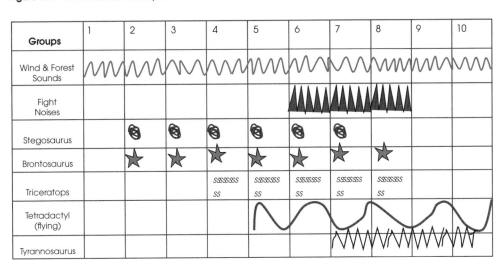

Neryl Jeanneret and Andrew Swainston

At first each group performed their sound. The performance was then run through a number of times. Each time it was discussed and evaluated with students making suggestions like: 'Maybe we could get louder at this part and softer at that'; 'Maybe it could get faster'; 'I think the Tyrannosaurus Rex should be stamping its feet like this …'. Alice's achievement here underlines just what a primary generalist teacher with little or no musical background is capable of with a little support and appropriate teaching materials and resources. Alice herself was very positive about the experience, somewhat surprised by the results, and said that she felt she this had opened up a new aspect and dimension to her teaching.

The school concert

Andrew and I arrived at the community hall amid a throng of parents, grandparents, aunts, uncles, younger and older siblings, and carers. The hall was packed and the atmosphere wild with excitement as the lights dimmed and the curtains parted. There were many items that night, but one of the highlights was the Indonesian segment. The children performed Kecak, there was the piece using anklungs and some of the girls danced using Indonesian movements and gestures.

Byar performs for the school

Figure 8.3   Byar performing

It is a mild November day in Term 4. A group of Year 1 children sit on the concrete in a covered outdoor area. The children gather closely in front of the musicians setting up; they are curious about the instruments and ask questions such as, 'How many songs are you going to play?' The temptation to touch the instruments is almost irresistible. The children are asked to move in anticipation of the rest of the school arriving and they express disappointment about losing their prime seats in favour of the Preps. The Preps arrive and are seated in front of the musicians. There is a lot of talk and general noise; it is the organised chaos of a whole school event. The noise becomes deafening—how will the musicians gain everyone's attention and hold it? The musicians wait patiently—they are used to this. Those children seated and ready are fascinated by the drummer who begins to play quietly. The Assistant Principal settles everyone and introduces the group. The musicians begin to play.

The children watch intently; a few move; some crane their necks for a better view while others comment to each other and point at aspects of the performance. The repetitive music is quite mesmerising (a deep gong and repeated patterns). There is movement, slight chatter and exclamations every so often. Cathy notices

> the Year 2–4 boys (the 'naughty' ones Kate used to call 'the puppies', because they liked roughing and tumbling on the carpet so much) are patsching on their legs and air drumming'. Two of the boys from Year 4 have worked out the timing and pattern of the drumming, and are using both hands to reproduce it. (Yay!) …
>
> I'm incredibly proud!! They should know where Bali is, thanks to Jane, but I actually wasn't really expecting them (foolishly perhaps) to know or remember what percussion is, and how it's played. But they do! Did I actually manage to teach them something?!

Gideon demonstrates a number of the instruments—the double-sided drum, cymbals, and bronze gongs—noting the different pitches of the instruments and what they are made of. Jeremy takes over. He is very animated and engaging, and the children respond. He tells them, 'We're going to play a short piece of music for you now, and I want you to tell me something about it at the end'. Cathy watches the children as the musicians play and wend their way though the seated children. Chatter starts up, and children turn around to follow the procession with their eyes.

> Oliver K is mimicking the drums, frantically smacking the air in front of him. He is another 'naughty' one. There's a funny kind of trend I'm seeing here: like the ones who were most likely to be disruptive and unfocused are the ones who are obviously physically responding to the music, more so perhaps than some of the other children who were deeply interested, or demonstrated innate musicality.

Jeremy engages in a question and answer session and the chatter builds. It's interesting that the minute the musicians engage in a more conventional teacher mode of interaction with the children, some of them seem to switch off and become restless, but then there is

Neryl Jeanneret and Andrew Swainston

a change. There is more widespread chatter as the children spot Jo with the anklung, an instrument they recognise. Some start to shout out the name, and put their hands up. The musicians begin to sing along with the anklungs. Some of the children join in and some imitate the actions of playing the melody. Some girls standing at the back imitate Balinese hand/dance gestures—they must be the dancers from the school concert.

Jo starts telling the Kecak story. The 2/3/4 children have done a dramatic version of this with Jane and Fran. Jo gets a giggle when she explains that the warrior is a monkey. Jeremy separates the group into three sections and each group will be following a different musician. The musicians work through the story with different groups using different sounds to represent the characters. This activity grabs the children's attention and the excitement builds as the full performance comes together. One Prep/1 teacher tells the Year 6 girls next to her on the steps that they (the Prep/1s) did this for the concert. The children and teachers clap wildly at the end of the piece and the concert comes to an end. The Assistant Principal thanks the musicians and the children again burst into applause and cheers. The children are encouraged to disperse for recess but a number of them mill around, talking to the musicians as they pack up the gear.

I talk to some of the teachers who are excited about the concert. One teacher says, 'That was awesome!' Another teacher tells me how great it was that the children were able to share what they knew, 'The performance brought together what they'd done in class and what they'd done at the school concert. It worked really well!' And Cathy reflected,

> Using Byar at this school was particularly appropriate, due to the LOTE factor. The older children should have been particularly aware of various things such as the geography, culture, performing arts, history, and so on of Indonesia, all of which linked in with this specifically musical performance. In another situation, with a different LOTE, the response to 'Where is Bali?' may not have been so quickly and correctly answered, for example. I suspect that a lot of the understanding going on in this performance came from the LOTE program, rather from just the preparation in the PD booklet.

Concluding thoughts

While you mightn't feel very confident about bringing music into your classroom, there are many resources available to help you. Musica Viva in Schools is but one program available to primary teachers, and the attachment of professional development for generalist teachers is an important feature. A number of orchestras and ensembles have education programs, and it is worthwhile checking with your local education authority, council, or community arts organisation about programs of artists in schools. In the case of world music groups, it is a powerful way of bringing other cultural dimensions into the school. And, of course, ask the children and parents—you'd be surprised how many musicians, professional and amateur, are more than willing to share their knowledge with their local primary school.

If you want to build your musical skills and knowledge, there are many professional associations that offer workshops for the generalist primary teacher with a limited musical background, as I mentioned in the Introduction. There is wonderful warmth and support among music educators and they are more than willing to share their ideas.

Activities beyond the case study

Resource building

1   Create a resource directory for music:
    - artists who visit schools
    - sites for students to visit.

Resource-sharing session

1   Bring resources to a class, talk to the group about your ten most useful/interesting resources.
2   Compile a resource directory drawn from the whole group and distributed to the whole group.

CASE STUDY 8.2

Contemporary Aboriginal music

Andrew Swainston

Music is more than just sounds. It is invariably an expression of the culture of different societies and peoples within societies. It is bound up with social and personal identity. This is especially true for indigenous music, which expresses the history, ideas, hopes, and aspirations of peoples. While it is an expression of cultural distinctiveness it is can also be seen as a particular expression of our common humanity. I think this in part is what informs the view that one important way of seeing music education is to define it as cultural studies (Dunbar-Hall 2005).

About the research

A key issue in Australian education is the incorporation of Aboriginal studies in the curriculum. Some states mandate the study (New South Wales) and other states and territories make recommendations about the inclusion, but the implementation of such studies appears to be ad hoc at the best. This case study examines the design and implementation of

Neryl Jeanneret and Andrew Swainston

an Aboriginal arts/music module at a mixed inner city school, which would engage and enthuse students in years 7 and 8. The central research question was: 'What are the main characteristics of an engaging and significant unit on Aboriginal contemporary arts/music aimed at the middle years?' The project was informed and enriched through substantial consultation with local Aboriginal educators and community groups, and through the direct participation of leading Aboriginal musician, Kutcha Edwards. The aim was to provide students with an encounter and experience of Aboriginal music and culture that would be stimulating, memorable, and enjoyable. Emphasis was on investigating, understanding and modelling Aboriginal ways of approaching music-making through listening, playing, and composing. Recognition of the social, historical, and cultural contexts would be a central consideration. Data were collected in the form of photos, videos, audio recordings, student work samples, questionnaires, and interviews.

Introduction

Anecdotal evidence suggests that teachers are often reluctant to implement Aboriginal Studies in their classrooms. One of the problems is that they are conscious of issues of appropriation. There is material still in existence from early anthropological studies that is considered inappropriate for public viewing by the Aboriginal community. Another concern expressed is that with Aboriginal culture being so diverse, depending on the region, there is a risk of presenting information that is relatively superficial, as well as not in keeping with local Aboriginal customs. This study endeavoured to address this concern by consulting with Aboriginal educators and the local Aboriginal community in the design of a program for Year 8 music classes.

This study took place at an inner-city metropolitan school. The school has a mixed demographic, as well as a range of ethnic groups represented. It has a strong classroom music program that has developed over the last five years to include a number of elective classes, in addition to the mandatory program, and a growing number of ensembles covering traditional groups as well as popular and world music. The *Aboriginal Music Module* which formed the basis of this study has been a part of the Music Curriculum Years 7 and 8 for a number of years, but we made a decision to develop and extend the module. I felt a more authentic, in-depth approach was needed; one that delved deeper into the social, cultural, and historical contexts of Aboriginal music, and that would be linked to Aboriginal communities and musicians. The intention was to build students' awareness of Aboriginal approaches to music making and the distinctive qualities of Aboriginal arts culture.

Consultation, planning, and preparation

From 1985 to 1989 I taught at Preston East Technical school, which has a high proportion of Aboriginal students (25 per cent of the school population). I worked closely with two full-time Aboriginal educators, Dedrie Buk and Lynne Thorpe in the Aboriginal and Torres

Strait Islands Pedagogy Project, and an after-school program for Aboriginal students and their friends, which had involved music lessons and band rehearsals. Preston East Technical school, now called Northland College, was recognised by 'The Royal Commission into Black Deaths in Custody' (1992) as an example of what can be achieved at a mainstream school when the needs of Koori students are accommodated.

Consultation with Dedrie and Lynne, who are both still at Northland College, resulted in the recommendation that the Aboriginal musician and community leader, Kutcha Edwards, be approached for an 'artist-in-residence' program with the project. Another recommendation was that an important objective of the module should be the building of awareness and understanding of Aboriginal arts and culture, and of a recognition of the centrality of social, cultural, and historical contexts. We discussed at length how this might be achieved.

I also contacted the Aboriginal radio station 3KND, Kool 'N' Deadly. Program Manager, Cheryl Harrison, provided me with a CD of recent Aboriginal music, which had an emphasis on youth. Tracks included *Down River* (The Wilcannia Mob), *No Dedication* (J Mac), *Stolen* (Local Knowledge), *Invasion Day* (Little G), and *Black So What* (Mary G). I also searched Aboriginal arts websites, and compiled a list. 'Dusty Echoes' on the ABC website combined brilliant animations and music around Aboriginal Dreamtime stories, along with classroom activities and lesson plans. 'Morganics.com' is the web page of a 'rap artist and community worker' who travelled remote Aboriginal communities recording Aboriginal youth including the 'Wilcannia Mob'.

The principal's support from the outset was strong and enthusiastic. As the arts coordinator, I had been keen to pursue and develop an integrated arts project across the various arts disciplines: drama, visual arts, and music. The intended Aboriginal arts project was full of potential and it acknowledged that in Aboriginal communities, music, dance, drama, and visual art often exist side by side and are often seen as an integrated whole. The teachers agreed that all of the arts learning areas would develop activities and programs around Aboriginal arts, and that they would seek to integrate their efforts as much as practically possible.

The next step was the selection and consideration of some key questions. For example, what are the defining features of Aboriginal art? How has the history of the Aboriginal people shaped their arts/music culture? Is there a distinctive Aboriginal approach to music making? How are the traditions of Aboriginal music passed down and learned? Why is country music and reggae popular with many Aboriginal people? What particular themes and issues can we identify in Aboriginal contemporary music? What is the role of music in expressing the culture, history, and stories of Aboriginal people in contemporary society? Answers include the land and the environment; identity, friendship, and community; hardship and injustice; and stories of struggle. Which songs particularly stand out as being important in this respect? How has Aboriginal music influenced the mainstream Australian music culture?

A critical element of preparation lay in the setting out of principles of learning and teaching Aboriginal music. We decided that the emphasis would be on team teaching and collaborative learning, as well as group music making. The teachers' roles would be, in part, as facilitators, collaborators, advisors, and co-learners. The emphasis would be on oral (discursive) and aural learning; for example, aural transcription and learning through imitation. Emphasis would be placed on practical activities, composing, playing, performance, listening and discussing, and on formative assessment such as verbal, informal, and ongoing assessment procedures. The learning outcomes for the module are listed in Table 8.2, and with these in mind a range of curriculum documents, maps, and charts were created.

In the first instance three classes would take part in the program: a Year 7 'girls' group', a Year 7 'accelerated learning group', and a Year 8 group, who enjoyed the description of being one of the most 'challenging' in the school. The timeframe of the unit would be approximately three weeks, around eight to ten 50-minute periods per group.

Table 8.2   Outcomes for the Aboriginal studies module

At the end of the module students will:	• have completed a negotiated research project into an aspect of Aboriginal music, as well as a practical project and recording
	• have taken part in class discussions, performances, individual and/or group composition
	• have had the opportunity to use ICT and multimedia facilities (for example, I-Life)
	• demonstrate increased awareness and understanding of Aboriginal art/music as narrative (storytelling), of the significance of the social cultural context, of the 'healing' function of the arts within Aboriginal society, and its importance in reinforcing personal and social identity.

Implementing the program

The teachers began by explaining their ideas behind the unit, a summary of all the above, to each of the classes taking part. It was pointed out that parallel work would take place in Drama classes and Visual Arts classes. The whole project would culminate in a school assembly, performance, and arts exhibition. We listened to and discussed a selection of traditional and contemporary Aboriginal music. This included video footage of live performances, often including scenes that placed the music and lyrics into relevant and particular contexts. For example, in the Yothu Yindi *Treaty* video (original version) there is footage of a smiling Australian prime minister visiting remote Aboriginal communities, as well as demonstrations, traditional dance, and 'live' music performance by Yothu Yindi. In the Warumpi Band/Midnight Oil *Blackfella, White Fella* YouTube clip, band members are standing in a small boat singing and playing a guitar somewhere in the swamp lands of the 'top end' while crocodiles circle the boat. The metaphor for the dangers of racism and disunity are clear.

Lyrics and chord charts were given out. The discussions, which ranged from musical characteristics (such as the chord structures, rhythmic characteristics, diversity of musical styles, combination of traditional and contemporary music) to lyrical content and social cultural meanings, were animated and enthusiastic. Students were engaging and enjoying the experience while forming an acquaintance with some of the classics of Aboriginal music, and with Aboriginal stories and history.

After about an hour the students formed groups and began work on composing their own songs with simple chord structures, which would tell their own stories or stories from the local community. We suggested that they might wish to base their song on one of a number of recurring themes often found in Aboriginal songs, such as the land and environment, identity, friendship, and community. Students were quick to take on the 'spirit' of group music-making and composing activities with enthusiasm and with a noticeable lack of reticence. At the end of the double lesson some groups were able to perform rough drafts of their own original songs to the class. We promised to return to these activities at a later stage.

Figure 8.4 Creating a song

In the following double period, students were asked to choose an Aboriginal song to perform as a whole class. The Year 7 'accelerated learning group' chose *Treaty*, which was later mixed with another Yothu Yindi song, *Wirrkul Girl*. After listening carefully and jotting down the chords and bass lines, they began to play along with the recording on guitars,

Neryl Jeanneret and Andrew Swainston

keyboards, and percussion. Some sang while others worked out dance moves. In the end they were performing without the recording. In the following lesson students were asked to work again in small groups, on their own compositions or to choose an Aboriginal song from 'the list' to learn, rehearse, and perform. Some worked on computers to create their own songs or rap. A pair of boys, using Garageband, composed and recorded a rap *How the tortoise lost its tail*. Others created their own backing tracks for songs such as *Treaty* and *From Little Things Big Things Grow*.

A group from the girls' class wrote and recorded a song entitled *When the Big Ships Came*; another group wrote a song about the appreciation of *Nature*. A group of about six boys from 8C took a number of chants (in an Aboriginal language) from the song *Wirrkul Girl* and used them in a call and response pattern, as part of a their own percussion composition. Another group of boys decided to learn the original lyrics of the song *From Little Things Big Things Grow* which tells the story of Aboriginal stockmen who went on strike at the Northern Territory Wave Hill station. The dispute over wages and conditions turned into a demand for land rights. The boys recorded themselves singing all eleven verses and choruses over a Garageband arrangement produced with the assistance of the teacher. A mixed group of about eight girls and boys sang, performed (on guitars, keyboards and various percussion) and recorded the No Fixed Address song *From my Eyes*.

Kutcha Edwards

Kutcha Edwards made his first visit involving 8C for a double period on a Friday afternoon. From the moment he entered the class this affable, intelligent, and knowledgeable man commanded respect and attention. For over an hour students listened enthralled as Kutcha spoke about the traditions of Aboriginal music, its role in Aboriginal society, and how Aboriginal music is taught from generation to generation. Kutcha spoke about his own life, his experience as part of the Stolen Generation, his family, his life as a musician, and his approach and philosophy to songwriting. He sang a song about his father.

Kutcha related stories of collaborations with musicians such as Paul Kelly, Renee Geyer, and the Warumpi band. He told stories of adventures on overseas tours, of observations of different countries and cultures. Kutcha talked of big gigs such as 'Dreamtime at the G' (Melbourne Cricket Ground), where Australian Rules football pays tribute to indigenous players. He related his feelings walking on to the ground, flanked by Aboriginal kids. When asked why is it that musicians are so respected within the Aboriginal community, he said, 'We are the healers'.

After nearly an hour had passed, Kutcha requested 'Let's all write a song!' Taking the whiteboard marker in hand, he began to canvass for topics and titles. Minutes later, after numerous suggestions and following a democratic vote in two stages, the joint themes of *home* and *friendship* were selected. Through brainstorming techniques, two verses and a chorus were constructed. Somehow an agreed tune for the song emerged. Different chords

Figure 8.5   Writing a song with Kutcha Edwards

were tried on guitars and keyboards. Before too long the song was being sung by the whole group. 8C (who at first looked on in disbelief) were hooked. After the third singing of the song, *Home is Where the Heart Is*, Steve (another teacher) talked excitably about performing it at the whole school assembly, in front of over 1000 people in the Town Hall. The bell had gone five minutes earlier; no one seemed to notice. What a way to end Friday afternoon. The 8C home teacher made the following comment:

> The theme of home and friends really got them. I think what happened was the simplicity of the lyric and the repeated themes of home and friendship, 'Home is where the heart Is'. That was what really sunk (in) in the end, when a real empathy began to develop, come together (8C Home group teacher).

Kutcha repeated this with the two other groups. He came back again for a day to mingle, to encourage, enthuse, advise, and collaborate with students as they sang, played, composed, arranged, and recorded.

Whole school assembly

> I will let you know that this particular home group is one of the few, if not the only one, in which not one of the students take part in any after-school extra-curricular activities. They do not do sport, they do not go to the swimming carnival, they do not do music. They do not do any activities outside of the classroom, because for them that is uncool (8C Home group teacher).

Neryl Jeanneret and Andrew Swainston

A few weeks later the whole school assembly took place in the Town Hall. A highlight was a short talk and performance by Kutcha, whose original song highlighted the situations facing many Aboriginal people, particularly many in remote outback communities. Waiting behind the stage, eagerly and nervously, was 8C. After Kutcha's performance they came on and sang with him the song they had created together that previous Friday afternoon.

> Every staff member has written me an email. They were astounded. For them to get up at assembly in front of the whole school and participate in a performance was the most mind-blowing thing any of the staff had ever thought of (8C Home group teacher).

Responses and analysis

The student responses to the unit, both formal and informal, were very positive. Many students indicated they had learned that Aboriginal songs told their stories and that music was an important part of their society, that through this work they had developed some knowledge and understanding of Aboriginal people and culture. A great many positive references were made to composition activities and the performance aspect of the work. Students indicated a high sense of achievement through their musical endeavours, playing,

Figure 8.6   Ready for the concert

composing, and performing, and many indicated a strong and increased desire to pursue music in the elective options the following year. A high percentage of students indicated that they would have liked the unit to have been longer.

The following comments highlight some of the student responses in the interviews.

How did you feel about getting up on stage?

> G3: Scary (laughs).
>
> B1: Yeah.
>
> G2: Embarrassing.
>
> B1: I was nervous.
>
> B2: I was embarrassed too; the pressure was on.

What did people say to you after that?

> G3: That they really liked it.
>
> B3: Yeah, thought it was cool.

They thought it was cool? Even the kids?

> All: Yeah, A-huh.

And what about the teachers, what did they say?

> B1: They were amazed.
>
> G2: They said it was really good.
>
> B2: They were complimenting us for the whole week.
>
> B1: Yeah.
>
> G3: It's like it's over, but it's not.

In response to a survey question asking 'Was the project worthwhile?', 100 per cent of the students answered in the affirmative. This was surprising. When we mentioned this to the school principal, he said, looking a little surprised himself: 'Well, they've already got their reports so they have no reason to lie to you'. The Middle Years Campus Principal was very positive about the project, especially in respect to Kutcha Edwards.

> I really think it's important for Middle Year students to be exposed to people who are experts in their field. And Kutcha is one of the leading proponents, as a musician in Australia. So for kids to work directly with such an inspiring figure, it is a great opportunity and it's going to open up their eyes and their experiences, and enrich their education.

He was determined to see the program go ahead again the following year,

> With any new initiative you want to try and embed it in the school culture. It's a bit like now, every year we have Medieval incursions for a week, that's just booked. It doesn't matter who the new coordinator is, it is just something we do as a school. So if we can get someone like Kutcha, who becomes a regular, embedded part of the curriculum, then you've made a permanent change.

Neryl Jeanneret and Andrew Swainston

One of the interesting aspects of these comments lies in the recognition that the project has made an important contribution to the cultural life of the school. For one of the teachers, Steve, the emphasis on composition:

> enabled the students to see how simply a composition can be constructed, including from a lyrical point of view, and how they could go about doing it. To see kids writing stuff in groups and writing from the perspective, a lot of the time, they were trying to put themselves in the place of being an Aboriginal person, at different times throughout history.

Steve spoke with enthusiasm about a group of boys in the 'accelerated learning class' who were singing a particularly poignant Aboriginal song *From Little Things Big Things Grow*.

> That particular group in the accelerated class, to me, they were quite amazing. They are looking at this song that is telling this incredible story and they took that story very, very seriously, and the lyrics that they were singing took on a very, very important meaning to them. So when they sang that song they sang it with a great deal of heart and compassion, and I found that quite amazing—some of those kids are not really renowned for that. It was a real eye-opener for them.

Concluding thoughts

Peter Dunbar-Hall (2002, p. 173) refers to the problems that face many classroom music teachers in introducing popular music to their students. He makes a number of crucial points:

> Popular music, despite its existence in syllabuses in various forms, is still a problem area for many music teachers. This is due to a number of factors: both the study of popular music styles and methods for teaching them are missing from many tertiary courses; the mainly art music backgrounds of many music teachers act against an understanding of popular music; there is a shortage of critical material in this area to which teachers can refer; and an accepted model for teaching popular music has not yet been developed.

In many ways these same 'problems' apply today to the teaching of Aboriginal music, in addition to the further issues relating to cultural and political aspects and sensitivities. As Mackinlay and Dunbar-Hall (2003, p. 39) point out:

> To teach Indigenous musics is also to teach the historical, social and political contexts in which they exist, to raise debates over the efficacy of the pedagogic act, and to uncover the dialectic and musical tensions.

All this should not be reason to avoid or skim over what is potentially a rich but often underutilised area of the curriculum. In my view it is all the more reason to take it on. On a different but related point there is a tendency within mainstream society to talk of Aboriginal culture as if it were something very different, very remote, far away and removed from the rest of 'us'. Aboriginal stories are distinctive and particular to Aboriginal people, but they are also part of the collective consciousness, part of the well of Australian experience, of all experience. The development of cultural and social 'empathy' is an important aspect of connecting with and understanding any culture. It would appear that this unit of study had a profound impact on all those who were connected. The principal realised the positive impact the module had on the students, particularly the at-risk group and wishes the program to continue with even greater support. The teachers were drawn into the project in the same way the students were, albeit on the sidelines, and were astonished at the level of engagement on the part of the students. Most important was the level of engagement of the students and, from their comments, what they took away from the experience.

EXEMPLAR

Aboriginal art, drama and music, and the Dreamtime stories

This project centres on a study of the culture of Aboriginal peoples' traditional and contemporary art, music and stories (including the legends of the Dreamtime). Students demonstrate personal responses and understanding in class and small group discussion, and by creating original art works, music, and drama. They document the process, which may be presented as a collage, in an integrated digital movie format as a live performance, or through an integrated live and multimedia presentation. As a crucial and central part of the project an Aboriginal artist or artists should be invited to give a presentation and run workshops for the students involved.

This is an overview of *possible* activities, which can be developed in detail by individual teachers in respective subject areas involved in the project.

Step 1

Students view a multimedia (photos, video, audio, stories, music) demonstration of Aboriginal arts, history, and culture. (For example, the Yothu Yindi *Treaty* video, Warumpi Band documentary, and Albert Namatjira documentary.) They write a short personal response and discuss as a group.

- What are the defining features of Aboriginal arts?
- How has the history of Aboriginal people shaped their arts and culture?
- Internet research tasks.

Neryl Jeanneret and Andrew Swainston

Step 2

In their respective arts subjects, students set about creating a work based on, or inspired by, particular examples of Aboriginal arts.

Step 3

Individually and in small groups, using any range of available resources and materials, students create their own original work in response to their experiences of Aboriginal arts and culture.

Step 4

All works are presented to their respective classes and discussed. All are recorded in a suitable digital format.

Step 5

Representatives from all classes involved in the project work together to assemble, edit, and arrange final presentation.

Step 6

A final product incorporating the digital multimedia presentation, art exhibition, and 'live' performance is to be prepared for a special school/public performance.

Step 7

Create art in an Aboriginal style. Create a landscape for the school grounds or mural. Try out face painting and dance, storytelling, or performing an Aboriginal song. Compose music in an Aboriginal style. Listen to 3CR 'Songlines' program, Thursday (12–2 p.m.)

Digital ICT component

Use multimedia software such as:

- Windows platform: Moviemaker, Sonar Home Studio, Vegas Movie Studio or Flash
- Apple platform: Garageband, iPhoto, iMovie, Final Cut or Flash.

This gives students the chance to combine traditional art and music skills in a digital format.

Researching an aspect of Aboriginal music using the internet (extension work)

Your task (should you accept this mission) is to find, compile, organise, and present information (fact and opinion) on an aspect of Aboriginal music. To start you off is a list of Aboriginal websites for you to explore. And here's a list of possible topics to get you thinking. Your presentation should be in a digital multimedia format.

• Create a profile of an Aboriginal band or musician such as Yothu Yindi, Jimmy Little, Christine Anu, Sally Dastey, or Archie Roach.

• Research traditional Aboriginal music and instruments.

• Describe and review one or more Aboriginal websites.

• Compile a history of contemporary Aboriginal music.

• Compose a report, 'Stories of the Aboriginal Dreamtime'.

• Report on the work of musician 'Morganics' as he visits outback communities and records Aboriginal musicians and rappers such as The Wilcannia Mob.

Internet sites

Dusty Echoes: Ancient stories, new voices: http://www.abc.net.au/dustechoes/

Morganics Website: http://www.morganics.info/live/

Checklist for teaching Aboriginal Studies across the Curriculum: http://www.teachers.ash.
        org.au/wattle/abstuds1/chcklist.html

VISIBLE with Kutcha Edwards and Jali Buba Kuyateh and Diyaa Looloo: http://www.
        multiculturalarts.com.au/events2007/visible.html

Teaching Aboriginal art: http://www.araratcc.vic.edu.au/shodo/page7.htm

Australian Indigenous Spirituality, Dreaming and Dreamtime: http://www.trinity.wa.edu.au/
        plduffyrc/indig/dream.htm

Dreamtime legends: http://www.muenster.org/abendgymnasium/faecherprojekte/
        projekte/aborigines/dreamtim.htm

Aboriginal Art, Culture & Spirituality: http://www.ciolek.com/WWWVLPages/AborigPages/
        Art.html

Art of Australia: http://www.princetonol.com/groups/iad/lessons/middle/austral.htm

Aboriginal Australia Art & Culture Centre:
        http://aboriginalart.com.au/didgeridoo/songs.html
        http://www.aboriginalaustralia.com/aboriginal.htm

Stories of the Dreaming: http://www.dreamtime.net.au/dreaming/index.htm

Neryl Jeanneret and Andrew Swainston

Aboriginal Art and Culture: www.moederdegans.be/Aboriginal.htm

Links Pages:

> http://www.mythinglinks.org/ip~australia.html
> http://www.didjeridu.com/wickedsticks/links.htm
> http://www.trinity.wa.edu.au/plduffyrc/indig/culture.htm

Table 8.3 Mapping for a contemporary Aboriginal music unit

Listening analysis	Learning, rehearsing Aboriginal music	Composing
Discussion: Key questions (See outline) **Video/Repertoire:** Warumpi Band documentary, Buried Country, 'Australian Story', Yothu Yindi clips, YouTube. Kutcha Edwards *Friend of Mine, Treaty, From My Eyes* (see outline) Radio 3CR Songlines, 3KND (Kool 'N 'Deadly)	Whole group, small groups **Repertoire:** See outline (*Wirrkul Girl, Blackfella Whitefella, Treaty, From Little Things Come*) **Resources:** Music, multimedia software, instruments, breakout spaces Aboriginal artist in school	Individual and small group work Theme/story-based songwriting Workshop/jamming/informal Simple chord progressions **Resources:** Acoustic, electronic instruments Music ICT software Digital recording Aboriginal artist in school
Research project	**Performing and recording**	**Reflection**
Researching an aspect of Aboriginal music. Open task Online web-based List of web links Artist in school Multimedia presentation	Class-based performance and school assemblies Public/community events Computer sequencing (for example, GarageBand, Sonar Home Studio Acid) Digital video/multimedia presentation Aboriginal artist in school	Discussion Key questions Interviews, surveys Students work/recordings Photos, videos to record document process

Activities beyond the case study

Build electronic/virtual resource kits as an assignment

Discuss the following questions:

1 What professional development opportunities are available to you in music and arts education generally?
2 How might programs such as Musica Viva in Schools work in your school?
3 What is the local music scene like? What sorts of opportunities are there for making connections with local musicians?
4 What possibilities are available for bringing these musicians into the school?
5 What are the main characteristics of an engaging and significant unit on Aboriginal contemporary arts/music?

Ideas to consider

- Authenticity and depth: through consultation the program is linked to the Aboriginal community, and it includes involvement by Aboriginal musician(s). It covers a rich and wide repertoire.
- Hands-on, practical emphasis: playing, composing, listening responding, and performing.
- Informal learning: small group work, peer-to-peer tuition, open-ended tasks, teacher as collaborator and facilitator.
- Recognition of the centrality of personal, social, cultural and historical contexts.
- Sharing of personal stories, encouraging open expression.
- The creation of a 'classroom community' mutually constructed (Marshall 2004).

Conclusion

In this chapter we have explored how teachers might make connections with the wider community and bring musicians into the school not only to support a music program, but also to explore wider cultural issues. As Neryl noted in Chapter 2, music and the arts are a way of exposing children to a variety of cultures, and the experience can have a powerful impact on they way in which they think about those cultures, equipping them with inter- and intra-cultural understanding.

Neryl Jeanneret and Andrew Swainston

It is also important to remember that although you might not possess specialist music knowledge and skills, you can still implement worthwhile music programs by taking advantage of the many community resources and professional development opportunities.

Key references

Christensen, C.B. (1992) 'Music Composition, Invented Notation and Reflection: Tools for Music Learning and Assessment (Composition Notation)', *Dissertations Abstracts International, DAI–A*, 53(06).

Department of Education (2005) *National Review of School Music Education: Augmenting the Diminished*, DEST & Centre for Learning, Change and Development, Murdoch University, Perth.

Dunbar-Hall, P. (1996) 'Designing a Teaching Model for Popular Music', in Gary Spruce (ed.) *Aspects of Teaching Secondary Music: Perspectives on Practice*, Routledge in association with the Open University, London, pp. 173–81.

Dunbar-Hall, P. (2005) 'Colliding Perspectives? Music Curriculum as Cultural Studies', *Music Educators Journal*, 91(4).

Greenberg, M. (1972) 'A Preliminary Report of the Effectiveness of a Pre-school Music Curriculum with Pre-school Head Start Children', *Council for Research in Music Education Bulletin*, 29, 13–16.

Hunter, M.A. (2005) *Education and the Arts Research Overview*, Australia Council for the Arts, Sydney.

Mackinlay, E. & Dunbar-Hall, P. (2003) 'Historical and Dialectical Perspectives on the Teaching of Aboriginal and Torres Strait Islander Musics in the Australian Education System, *Australian Journal Indigenous Education*, 32, pp. 29–40.

Marshall, A. (2004) 'Singing Your Own Songlines: Approaches to Indigenous Drama', in M. Mooney & J. Nichols (eds), *Drama Journeys: Inside Drama Learning* (pp. 55–76), Sydney Currency Press, Sydney.

Runfola, M. & Rutkowski, J. (1992) 'General Music Curriculum', in R. Colwell (ed.), *Handbook of Research on Music Teaching and Learning* (pp. 697–709), Schirmer, New York.

Stevens, R.S. (2003) *Trends in School Music Education Provision in Australia*, The Music Council of Australia in collaboration with the Australian Society for Music Education and the Australian Music Association, Sydney.

Wiggins, J. (2001) *Teaching for Musical Understanding*, McGraw-Hill Higher Education, New York.

Young, W. (1974) 'Efficacy of a Self-help Program in Music for Disadvantaged Pre-schools', *Journal of Research in Music Education* (22), 158–69.

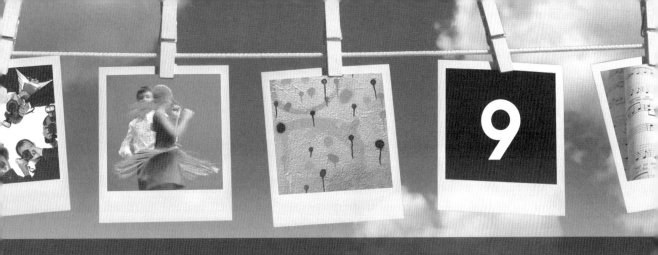

Valuing the Visual Arts

Robert Brown, Wes Imms, Marnee Watkins, and John O'Toole

In this chapter readers are introduced to two very contrasting ways of looking at visual arts practice in schools: the first, a close-up view of an inspired and inspiring primary school art teacher; the second, an immersion program, with pre-service primary education students specialising in visual arts, bringing a whole day of art practice into a whole school curriculum. This latter experience provides powerful learning for all involved: primary-aged children, classroom teachers, and the pre-service education students. The case studies provide some glimpses of the ways in which art in the primary school can infuse all areas of the curriculum, be informed by them, and promote learning in and through the practice of art. The chapter is framed by a discussion of key principles in visual art teaching and learning.

Introduction

Robert Brown

Across cultures, and in past and present contexts, we have imagined, understood, and communicated through the creation of expressive images, models, and architectural forms. The visual arts have enabled us to contemplate, explore, and communicate human responses to life, ranging from the timeless sculptures by the Italian Renaissance artist Michelangelo to the transitory coloured sand mandalas created by Tibetan monks.

Views on art are continuously changing and contested, and this is no different for art education, which has been informed by varying theories on why art is important to young children and how it should be taught. Franz Cizek, considered the father of child art, was a Viennese art student when he came to appreciate the unique aesthetic qualities of child art. His appreciation of the natural artistic abilities of children led to the development of a pedagogy later known as free expression or self-expression, which was 'based on the premise that children are artists and that their art, like all art, is inherently valuable. And yet it was a vulnerable art, one easily corrupted by adult influences' (Efland 1990, p. 195). John Dewey aspired to make education relevant to children and consequently inquired into how intrinsically motivating 'occupations', such as handwork and the arts, could help children acquire skills in an integrated curriculum. Following the horrors of World War II, Victor Lowenfeld (1947) began his longstanding promotion of the visual arts as a form of therapy that supports individual expression and play, psychological and social harmony, and cultural tolerance. Later, the Cold War and the launching of Sputnik led to an increased scientific study of human learning (Weiss 1992), which continued to prize individual innovation, but also emphasised society's needs to develop technical skills. It was at this time that creativity became a central tenet for art education that added to the earlier established values and goals, free-expression, and 'learning through doing'. Contemporary theory and research such as Howard Gardner's theory of multiple intelligence (1983) continue to frame and re-frame how the visual arts are conceptualised in relation to human development.

This brief survey only captures a 'Western' view on art education that is now challenged to take into account diverse social and cultural practices and perspectives (Golomb 1992; Bresler & Marm 2003). In essence, how children learn and what they learn through art is largely influenced by the values of the surrounding culture: families, teachers, and the local community. These values impact on the emphasis given to the visual arts in relation to manipulative skills and creative thinking, copying and originality, vertical thinking and lateral thinking, control and freedom, product and process, and collaborative art making and individual art making.

Teaching and learning through the visual arts

In the quest to 'make sense' and to understand, children observe, question, explore, and record using visual arts media and techniques including drawing, painting, clay-work, collage, construction, textiles, printmaking, photography, and, more recently, a range of digital technologies. These art forms promote individual invention, aesthetic exploration, problem-solving and skill development, and offer children many opportunities for direct and open-ended manipulation. Importantly, they provide an array of 'cognitively rich' media (Wright 2003) that enable controlled symbol making and the development of a 'visual language'. Other art areas, including textiles and woodwork, are also significant in relation to manipulative skills and sustained concentration while computer-generated art has the potential to engage children in sophisticated and complex visual design processes.

What is and isn't a quality art experience is a contentious issue. Activities that direct children through predetermined processes to a teacher-prescribed and uniform outcome may develop manipulative skills, but do not promote independent and creative learning. Conversely, laissez-faire art rooms may encourage imagination and experimentation, but arguably children miss out on skills-based instruction. We believe that art experiences that combine and contextualise teacher-led skill-based instruction with student-centred and open-ended learning provide the optimum balance. What is commonly accepted is that such experiences should be introduced in a variety of ways, essentially moving children from simple to more complex forms of manipulation and symbol development. Materials and processes are selected by the teacher to match the interests and readiness of children. In summary, a visual arts program needs to address several *key principles* if it is to be effective:

- the content should include both student and teacher interests
- skills-based learning should be linked to creative expression
- inquiry-based teaching and learning and immersion are supported by in-depth projects
- both the learning environment and the materials are aesthetically stimulating
- responding to art should regularly be linked to making art
- visual arts experiences need to be linked to other learning areas
- collaborative learning promotes creativity and problem-solving
- critical reflection is stimulated by supportive peer-group feedback
- the program should demonstrate a commitment to reflexive teaching.

The two case studies presented here explore these important principles. The first tells a story through the words of an experienced art teacher and artist. It focuses on an in-depth unit of work, Under the Sea. The second study intentionally diverges from looking at how children learn through art, to exploring how pre-service teachers learn about quality teaching practice through an art program: ArtBlast. While these case studies differ

Robert Brown, Wes Imms, Marnee Watkins, and John O'Toole

significantly, they both elucidate issues and challenges related to effective art teaching and point to a multi-layered and reciprocal relationship between teaching and learning.

Journey under the sea

Robert Brown

This case study we focus on an experienced visual arts teacher in primary education. We present a multi-layered story of Jeanette, who trained first as an artist and later as a teacher, and survey the personal and professional elements that have stimulated and evolved her art practice. Presented largely in the voice of the teacher/artist, the study was developed from a series of meetings, interviews, and informal observations. It draws from extensive documentation collected by Jeanette that illustrates the theories, processes, and outcomes of her longstanding work with young people and other members of the community.

A multi-layered visual arts program

At the age of sixteen, Jeanette took on an apprenticeship in graphic design and photography, working in advertising. She later qualified with a fine arts degree, majoring in ceramics, graphic design, advertising, and photography, and followed this with a graduate diploma in teaching. Jeanette has now taught for seventeen years, first working as an artist-in-residence in a number of schools while her children were young, and then as the sole visual arts teacher in her current school, which forms part of a large metropolitan multi-campus non-government school. Jeanette considers her varied background as helpful, in that she has 'been able to stand back from teaching and look at it from another perspective'. She notes how her experience as artist, educator, and parent inform her philosophy for teaching art:

> One of my experiences came from my own young children. I allowed a space for them to work that was full of creative materials. It was a bare floor off my kitchen, full of cupboards, recycled materials, everything that I could get my fingers on, and from the time they could walk literally there was an easel up. They spent all their time playing in our home environment, and I didn't have any reservation about the mess involved. What interested me was that both of my children did not follow my art profile. I gave them lots of materials, books, space to play with and to solve problems, but I didn't encourage them to become young artists. It interested me that they both became academics and excelled in the maths and science areas. I asked 'Why is that so?' because I don't see myself as an academic. So, it interested me.

Jeanette's experience and subsequent belief in the value of arts, in the connection between art and later development in other 'academic' areas, stimulated her to become a community artist who has now worked with diverse age groups, including people with disabilities. This experience confirmed for her the importance of the visual arts, particularly for young children, which led her to teaching. Jeanette notes:

> I went into schools and worked as artist-in-residence on very large community projects, and I could see that schools were very isolated. They weren't reaching out to the community to find what was out there, what the possibilities were. I felt that schools could promote themselves and their children's learning far more broadly if they connected with the outside world.

Framed by a clear philosophy, Jeanette set out to develop a multi-layered school-based visual arts program.

> Initially I wanted to develop an art learning program that linked with other areas of learning and the classrooms. That was my first stage. The second stage involved helping people understand that children have the potential to change the environment around them. So I started off by looking at integrated units of study, and working with the teachers to develop their units in a visual way using all the modalities: maths, science, literacy, and other areas. I then thought, let's now have a look outside the art room, at our local environment and the school grounds. I set about trying to change our environment here. The students were developing works of art that not only beautified the area, but also required them to use their maths, science, and literacy skills in the process.

Jeanette's program continues to evolve. It comprises three 'different streams of teaching', including general classroom practice, large group artworks developed for the school outdoor environment, and other collaborative art projects involving students and community groups who together create sculptural installations for public spaces. For Jeanette these collaborative community projects support life-long learning, in that they bring diverse multi-skilled groups of children and adults together by 'living through something'. For Jeanette such projects 'bring in visitors and parents and other people into our program, and show them what we can do through art', and also provide a significant opportunity for her students to make a permanent creative contribution to a public space.

> Such an experience is there for them to remember for the rest of their lives. They go back to those places they have helped create. Hopefully, in the long term, we're creating environments that they have learnt from. It's a powerful message really to be able to go to a space and see a large mosaic developed from children's drawings.

This overview of the background, philosophy, and key elements of a visual arts program helps to contextualise Jeanette's classroom teaching.

Under the Sea: A whole school art unit

As the sole visual arts specialist teacher in the school, Jeanette has developed a close relationship with children whom she has taught for several years. Jeanette teaches in a

Robert Brown, Wes Imms, Marnee Watkins, and John O'Toole

dedicated art room for up to twenty hours per week with children from preschool to Year 6. The younger children have a one-hour workshop each week, and the Year 4 to Year 6 students undertake art workshops for two hours once a fortnight, which Jeanette notes 'gives us a lot of time for conversation, for delving into the learning behind what we're doing, and also for reflection'. Jeanette has also taught one-hour workshops, which are common in other schools, but notes that 'It's very hard in an art room to be productive in an hour, as this gives you and the children only half an hour of time with materials'.

Jeanette bases her visual arts program largely on one theme-based integrated unit that is explored throughout the year, particularly in terms 1 and 2, and culminating in the transformation of the art studio into an art installation by the end of second term. Past unit topics have included Maps and Memory Grids and the Australian Outback. One earlier topic, Black and White, led Jeanette to gradually 'drain' colour from the art room so as to concentrate the students' attention on line, shape, and pattern. This topic emerged from an investigation of black and white photography that revealed to the students that some things can be seen more clearly in black and white than colour. The outcomes of each project are exhibited, both at the school and in many cases in community galleries.

Figure 9.1   Mermaids at play

Unit topics are generated in response to student interests and these are conceived normally late in the year prior to beginning the unit. The Under the Sea project was stimulated by a nine-year-old child named Rebecca who at home had written and illustrated a story about the friendship of two mermaids, dedicated to her grandmother and friend. Jeanette notes that

> Rebecca made two copies of the book, all beautifully bound and well presented, and when I read the story I thought we should celebrate this child's story, so that's when we went on the journey. I'm always looking to take what I do from a child, wherever that might come from. I thought that her book was well written and that it's the sort of thing that a lot of children can relate to. They go on holidays with families to the seaside. They explore the seaside.

In response to Rebecca's artwork, Jeanette put together a newsletter inviting children and families over the summer holidays to collect materials relevant to a future study about the sea.

> I thought what a good opportunity to send them off on their holidays to explore the sea and to come back with fresh ways of seeing the topic. So the parents, children, brothers and sisters worked together finding creatures, finding out about creatures, listening to the waves, feeling the sand, and looking for things that are in the environment around the sea. They brought in bags of kelp and shells, everything they could find and it was a wonderful experience for everyone in the community.

During the holiday period, Jeanette, with assistance from the school librarian, also researched the topic extensively, including making direct contact with a lobster fisherman during her holiday trip to a coastal fishing town. This search for materials and ideas formed part of a larger plan that had the goal of developing a series of individual and collective artworks that would ultimately transform the art studio into an Under the Sea environment.

Led by the question 'What does the sea represent to us?' Jeanette developed a structure for the unit based on the idea of 'levels of the sea' that travelled from the shoreline to the depths of the dark sea. The unit began with Jeanette reading Rebecca's story to all of her classes to acknowledge a creative work and stimulate the children's imaginations. Then they started planning together.

> There was an element of how do we create the fish swimming under water? So we might have a discussion about that and what is the sea like, what are the colours of the sea, and what materials might we use? So then we looked at a series of images. We had an enormous range of resources from the library about the sorts of fish that you might find and places where you might find them. The same with the turtles. A group of children were asked to explore the Internet for information. So I sent the children out as scouts to find resources, and what happened was that different children became fascinated by a variety of creatures.

Robert Brown, Wes Imms, Marnee Watkins, and John O'Toole

Jeanette encourages students to act as researchers, and in doing so to find and follow their own interests. Student choice is framed, and in some ways limited, by Jeanette's planning, which she calls a 'safe boundary' and 'success-orientated structure' that is based on 'set achievable tasks that match the individual abilities' and still allow for 'freedom of expression'. As an example of this 'balance', Jeanette refers to a three-dimensional paper sculpture activity where children with reference to the template shape of a fish modified and extended it to create a wide range of undersea fish forms that, as Jeanette states, are 'totally different' from each other in terms of shape, colour, and pattern.

Over two terms the children throughout the entire school produced a wide array of individual and collaborative artworks including:

- sea horse paper sculptures (Prep and Year 1)
- three-dimensional paper 'colourful fish' and 'water mobiles' (Year 2)
- digitally manipulated coral reef fish (Year 3)
- starfish sculptures (Year 5)
- wire and plaster crayfish, lobsters and crab sculptures (Year 6).

Figure 9.2   Neptune's table

Jeanette and the children, at times with help from parents, produced a number of cross-group artworks, including a giant jellyfish made from a cane structure covered in silk. A full-scale King Neptune dining setting was installed in the art room with the help of children who created everything from clay goblets and candle holders to printed fabric seat covers. The end outcome of prolific art-making was the transformation of the art studio into a playful and theatrical set-like environment.

Figure 9.3   Fish painting

Throughout her program, Jeanette, both directly and indirectly, introduces students to visual arts elements and principles. She does not teach specific art knowledge in dedicated lessons; instead, she prefers to explore this knowledge subliminally, 'so that it's just part of everyday life that we're learning about all these things, we're learning about them in a way that makes sense and hopefully they remember'. Through regular discussions with children regarding the feeling and mood created in other artworks (both children's and adult's), Jeanette encourages children to question and articulate their aesthetic choices. For example, when looking at fish the children were asked questions such as 'Why are things certain colours in real life?' and 'Why do artists choose to interpret things in different colours?'

Robert Brown, Wes Imms, Marnee Watkins, and John O'Toole

In response to these questions the children were engaged in a discussion about 'strong and bold colours', 'camouflage', the 'effects of light and shade and reflections on the water', and the changing 'graduations of tone and colour' the deeper you travel into the sea. As Jeanette notes, this discussion could come from 'a sharp response to a painting'.

Illustrated picture books provide a significant resource for Jeanette, who refers to these to critically examine the aesthetic choices of the artist both in relation to imagery and story.

> Why has the illustrator used that illustration for those words? Why has she placed the central figure of the story in that position? How has she used the background to support the character's story? All those sorts of issues come up when you're looking at books. I'm able to challenge the students—'Why do you like it? What is it about?'—encouraging them to make critical artistic visual decisions and relate to the story. And this gives them the space to use their imagination and use the same criteria for their own artworks.

In Jeanette's program the children not only respond to the works of artists, but also regularly view and discuss each other's artworks.

Figure 9.4 Mermaid

Often what we do with pieces of artwork is lay them down somewhere when we are finished. I try to speak to each child about their own piece of work, and ask them to choose another piece of work that they really like and tell me why they like it. What is there about it that you like? All the children are privy to that conversation and it makes them think about what other children have done, and they say, 'Oh, yes, I can see what you're talking about. I can see why you would choose that, but I probably wouldn't have chosen that.' It's quite interesting how many choose quite different works, and for different reasons.

This ongoing investigation of the choices artists make, both adults and children, informs the practical art making. They are encouraged by Jeanette to engage in a design process, similar to that of an artist, one that requires planning and problem-solving, and in the case of group work, negotiation and agreement. Practising artists provide a direct model of how the design process works, and guided by this belief Jeanette invites artists (most of whom are also parents) to create artworks at her school. In the case of the Under the Sea project one artist constructed a large mermaid in situ in the art studio.

Jeanette notes that first-hand experience with an artist 'is always a good thing for children because students respond to them differently', and artists bring a different 'wisdom' to the program. This comment reflects Jeanette's background as an artist and designer, which frames her teaching.

Something that I really love is doing design. I'm always on to the students to develop as many of their ideas as possible, and then to choose from those. When I studied I often did twenty designs or more and selected from these.

To support this process Jeanette always gives her children 'thinking paper' so as to encourage them to 'play' with ideas and 'think through' and decide which designs work best. A key part of this process is 'problem-solving', which Jeanette considers before she sets challenges for the children.

I mean, I myself started to work out how they could make a lobster, and I stood there after all my years of experience, and I thought, how much I need to know to make this lobster! How many legs does it have? How large is the head? How many sections are there to this lobster? What are the pincers like? Are its legs long or short? Where are the eyes situated? How do I use these materials? How do I hold it all together? How do I make the shape long enough or strong enough? And I was trying to solve all that, and that's what I expected from the children!

Working from a design brief, Jeanette's students have to solve problems and make decisions, both in relation to construction techniques and their visual representations, and in doing so use a wide range of manipulative and thinking skills that support interdisciplinary learning. For example, in the process of constructing a wire and paper fish sculpture the students have to create individual designs and transfer these on to two sides of the one

Robert Brown, Wes Imms, Marnee Watkins, and John O'Toole

three-dimensional form, taking into account size relationships, mirror-image, and positive and negative shapes.

Jeanette believes there is increasing awareness of the importance of thinking skills across the curriculum and this has created an opportunity for others to see the value of using the visual arts to promote observation and problem-solving skills. Throughout Jeanette's art program, emphasis is given to reasoned thinking that supports mathematical processes. For example, as part of the Under the Sea project one group of level 5 students were involved in designing a large turtle sculpture, which included exploring how to divide the shape into thirty-five parts. This, as Jeanette notes, was a 'simple example of putting maths to work' that required the students to think both about pattern, placement, size relationships, and spatial relationships. Through projects that Jeanette describes as 'learning journeys', she teaches other areas of the curriculum including literacy, numeracy, and science. This integrated approach to learning, which is in contrast to her own school education, is supported by projects that make the exploration of knowledge relevant and interesting.

> The learning that they do is relevant to them. I know that I would have done much better with numeracy had I had the experiences that I give the children now through visual arts experiences. I could see no relevance in what I was learning, but if I could have gone to find what I needed to learn for a particular reason its relevance would have had a powerful effect.

The opportunity to focus on a topic in depth in an art studio dedicated to one project is liberating for Jeanette.

> I have the freedom of a room that I can change completely and leave it to remain like that for the period required. In a (general) classroom you're trying to turn the space over all the time into other spaces, because the curriculum dictates that you have to do different topics each term. I think that's difficult for the teachers who do not have the freedom to extend what they're doing with the children.

Throughout the unit the art studio transformed into a mesmerising set-like sea environment, providing an ongoing stimulus for the children's play and imagination. Filled with child-created sculptures and images, it provided a space both for creation and reflection on the children's achievements, which Jeanette describes as individual and shared 'histories'. She notes, by fourth term 'we've created the space, and we virtually live in this space and enjoy it for the rest of the year. I think that's really what it's about.'

An important element of the whole project is the public exhibition of the work, which occurs one evening with parents and friends invited, and an accompanying program of music and artistic presentations. By this time, the undersea locations stretch from the hall itself, to the art studio, to the library. The work is treated seriously as one of the public centrepieces of the school year.

The process of dismantling the art studio installation occurs gradually in the final term, and this creates mixed responses from the children, with some eagerly wanting to know what will happen next year, while others express an interest to explore the topic further. As one child said to Jeanette, 'The sea is coming down and we're only halfway through it!'

Figure 9.5   Jellyfish

EXEMPLAR

The following exemplar, which focuses on 'sea creatures', presents a collection of visual arts ideas drawn from the Under the Sea case study.

1   Provide

a well-organised and stimulating aesthetic environment, including good quality two- and three-dimensional art media. During art-making provide a collection of relevant photographs and artwork copies for student reference.

Robert Brown, Wes Imms, Marnee Watkins, and John O'Toole

2   Plan and collaborate...

with other teachers to share knowledge, time, and resources. Consider topics that stem from children's interests and your own, and develop these further through group discussion. Create a 'concept map' or 'curriculum web' that outlines the key subject matter you want to explore. This will help you and the students understand how their work 'fits into the whole' and provide a sense of direction for the program.

3   Research...

thoroughly into the topic. For example, what varieties of sea creatures exist? How do they differ in colour, texture, and shape, and how do their designs help to achieve the effect of camouflage? What do sea creatures eat and how do they breed? What is their habitat?

4   Explore...

materials and techniques directly yourself before presenting to children. This is particularly important for a step-by-step building process such as building a wire frame and papier maché sea creature sculpture. Consider how children with different levels of experience will manipulate and control materials. Allow time for students to explore and play with ideas, materials, and techniques.

5   Provide clear starting points...

that stem from observation, memory, and imagination For example, provide a sea creature for students to draw from different perspectives and encourage individual responses. Have other tasks available for those students who complete their artworks before others. This may include contributing to an art room display and ongoing group projects.

6   Stimulate engagement...

through the use of a variety of stimuli. For example, if the emphasis is to depict form and movement a video of sea creatures swimming and moving could be used to encourage students to express, swimming, diving, and floating, first through physical actions and then through 'action' drawings of moving sea creatures. Another idea is to create a 'water' picture that focuses on repeated and rhythmic line, first drawn with a light-coloured wax-resist crayon, and later washed over with thin transparent paint. The famous artwork *The Great Wave* by the Japanese artist Hokusai would provide a stimulating reference.

7   Respond to specific adult artworks and illustrations...

for example, artworks created by the Australian Indigenous artist Bronwyn Bancroft in the picture books *The Whalers* and *How the First Children Learnt to Surf*. These books engage children in stories and also provide rich illustrations to discuss design and art techniques. The visual simplicity of Bancroft's imagery provides an accessible style for children to interpret simply in their art making.

8   Encourage children...

to view themselves as 'designers'. For example, present students with a 'design brief' that involves creating a sea creature that has many different colours and patterns and exists in a coral reef. Discuss with the children the problems they are likely to encounter such as achieving balance and symmetry in their drawing.

9   Demonstrate techniques...

for example, how to develop a sea creature image using simple oval shapes and, if need be, introduce light horizontal and vertical grid lines to show the children how to achieve symmetry and balance in their drawings.

10   Guide...

the children's art-making through open-ended and probing questions that stimulate extended thought. Encourage students to use 'thinking paper' (white cartridge) to explore various ways of communicating ideas and feelings.

11   Integrate...

discussion of the art elements—line, shape, colour, texture, pattern, tone, and form—into art-making.

12   Share and appreciate...

all of the children's responses including playful, imaginary, and realistic representations. Regularly invite students to select and comment on their artworks and those of others, and to share their reasons with the rest of the group.

Robert Brown, Wes Imms, Marnee Watkins, and John O'Toole

13   Create collaborative artworks...

both in and beyond the school. Seek out grants from local government and other organisations that support community-based projects.

ArtBlast: A day in a school

Wes Imms, Marnee Watkins and John O'Toole

About the research

The second case study describes a project we call ArtBlast, where pre-service teachers design a learning unit in collaboration with teachers, descend in force on a school and implement that program in a single day (a 'blast of art'), and then jointly reflect on the learning that occurs for all participants. The case study exemplifies, we believe, where practicum experience should be heading. Because of the educational issues it raises, it is as relevant for schoolteachers and pre-service teachers as it is for university lecturers trying to make practicum 'more relevant'.

ArtBlast is a project that has run annually for a number of years. We have treated the most recent episode as a case study, drawing from the pre-service teachers' journals and research diaries a vivid description of the benefits of its 'inverted practicum' approach. By inverted practicum we mean that in ArtBlast the classroom teachers learn from the pre-service teacher as well as vice versa, and in the process assessment is a rich and authentic educational experience that helps to develop skills in being a reflective practitioner. ArtBlast showcases the visual arts as a medium for exemplary teaching in the primary school.

About ArtBlast

The ArtBlast project has four equal partners as its participants. The first but by no means most important are the visual art lecturers in the university's primary program who are keen to maximise the limited time available to train pre-service teachers clearly eager to specialise in primary art education. The lecturers want to take full advantage of any opportunities available to them in terms of having their pre-service teachers plan and implement art programs, and develop the skills of critiquing the effectiveness of the curriculum that they develop. ArtBlast is conceived as a means to address these issues.

The second partner is actually a large group of people—the twenty or so pre-service students in the last year of their generalist primary education degree. While some specialist practicum experience in visual art education is available to them, a variety of systemic factors frequently combine to make these opportunities unavailable, to the extent that most of the students who are enrolled in the specialist visual art options in third and fourth year of their Bachelor of Education program do not have an opportunity to teach specialist art lessons during their teacher education.

The third partner in ArtBlast is the school that hosts the program. When first approached, this school had only small visual art programs in operation due to a variety of factors related to staffing and resources. The school recognises the value of art to the overall development of their students, but feels they lack the opportunity to improve on their situation. ArtBlast would provide rich student experience in visual art and valuable teacher in-service training in this subject.

Finally, the fourth partner is the university. Faculties of education in many universities are now actively seeking to improve the quality of their relationships with schools based on a mutual sharing of skills and expertise. Sometimes referred to as 'knowledge transfer', ArtBlast is an exemplar of this concept. This case study reflects the role visual art can play in linking these four partners in a particularly practical and mutually beneficial sense, while at the same time opening all partners' eyes to a more rewarding and beneficial model of practicum.

What does ArtBlast look like? The pre-service teachers pair up early in the first semester and are allocated a class at the school and a host teacher with whom to liaise. Each team plans a unit of work in consultation with their lecturers and the host teacher, with the aim of developing a sound art education activity that successfully supports the theme or area of study in which students will be engaged at the time of ArtBlast. This planning usually involves some early meetings with the host teacher, a viewing of the classroom and an assessment of available resources, the writing of a draft unit, and the submission of this draft for review (and eventual assessment) by the lecturers. This is a timely experience—the unit is conceived and developed through discussion over many weeks. Given the luxury of a full day to run the unit, the pre-service teachers plan a combination of activities that sequentially develop knowledge across time. The revised unit is discussed with the host teacher, and resources such as teaching aids, art materials, and the like are organised for the day. Normally, pre-service teachers will visit the school the day before ArtBlast to put up displays and organise other requirements.

On the given day the pre-service teachers, with considerable enthusiasm, take over the majority of the classes in this 400-pupil school. It is a blast of art for the students and teachers. Students, being well aware of the planning that has taken place, come to the day with a keen sense of anticipation. Teaching begins under the direct supervision of the host teacher with the university lecturers moving from class to class to observe. Teaching and observation duties are swapped between the two pre-service teachers in each class, as the day progresses. Most often there are parent volunteers to act as teaching assistants, and the classroom teacher observes and often takes part in the art activity. Recess and lunch times are used to re-organise materials, and to meet to discuss progress in the staffroom. Informal teaching occurs as the lecturers and teachers discuss with the

Robert Brown, Wes Imms, Marnee Watkins, and John O'Toole

pre-service teachers issues that emerged during the previous session. The day concludes with a mandatory exhibition and review of work by the whole school, often lasting well past the normal close of school. The artworks are left as a display, and the pre-service students meet for a de-briefing.

The session is critiqued some weeks later. This is a critical component of ArtBlast; students are never externally assessed on their teaching performance, but are expected to critically analyse their planning and teaching. This allows students, once in the classroom, the freedom to refine and experiment with pedagogy. The eventual critique (held up to eight weeks later) is an evidence-based activity that uses data from the observations to identify strengths and weaknesses. A set of guidelines provided at the start of the year to help the observers frame their observations now acts as the assessment criteria. The critique is a formal presentation with an accompanying short written report. The presentation, given in front of their peers, with lecturers and teachers from the school in attendance, is given some weeks after the ArtBlast day. It takes the form of a 10-minute PowerPoint presentation to the class and invited teachers from the school.

The strategy of co-teaching the classes supports this approach very well. It allows for the pair to actively assess teaching as it progresses. One pre-service teacher is required to be an observer, but can swap the observer/teaching roles as often as they wish. Guidelines for the observer's role based on standard ethnographic practices for observational research are provided prior to the ArtBlast day, together with some simple techniques such as the use of an observer's diary, and gathering digital photography and video evidence. The assessment of the pre-service teachers in ArtBlast is based solely on this presentation and the quality of the unit plan (assessed prior to ArtBlast, as part of the reviewing process); no grade is given for actual teaching during ArtBlast. This allows students the freedom to focus on teaching practices in a manner not enjoyed during any of their normal practicum rounds.

A degree of procedural support is provided to the pre-service teachers. Due to the time needed to liaise with the school staff, to write the units and prepare for its implementation, and to actually teach for the day, in lieu time is provided from normal lecture time. Resources from the art department are made available to the project, with the school providing a negotiated cash amount to help cover costs. Some voluntary workshops on video editing are provided, and a full two-hour lecture is allocated to host the PowerPoint critiques.

In summary, pairs of students planned units of work, taught the units of work to a whole class of primary students over the period of a whole day, analysed their performance, and presented the results of this professional reflection to their peers and the school's teaching staff.

Some comments on research

This case study advocates the importance of keeping a rich mix of theory and practice, and has been written deliberately using two different, yet interdependent voices: the academic, scholarly voice, underpinned by theoretical perspectives, functioning as a critically reflective narrator voice; and the personal, in the spirit of bearing the signature and voice of personal interpretation (Connelly & Clandinin 1996).

In our study we adopt Emery's tenet that as researchers we need 'to probe deeper and to privilege the voice that is the only authority in the teaching profession: the teacher' (1996, pp. 25–6). We are particularly keen to capture the thoughts, insights, reflections, and challenges of teachers in training—our co-researchers in this study. Part of this data is anecdotal evidence provided by the pre-service teachers through their field-diaries, and through their PowerPoint presentations. As co-researchers in this project they were asked to record their observations, reflections, interactions, conversations, situational details, and thoughts during the ArtBlast process in a diary in the form of field notes. The diaries open up spaces in this research where understanding can take shape, with the process of writing encouraging reflection both in-action and on-action, and with the notes used to provide valuable comparisons with the observations, interviews, and conversations that occur during the ArtBlast experience. The PowerPoint presentations serve as a useful, valuable culmination to the project. One of the pre-service teachers, in her role as co-researcher, synthesised all the presentations and created a report of her findings.

Marnee, the co-principal researcher for this case study and the university teacher of the pre-service student teachers, shares the unfolding of the ArtBlast experience—collectively forming 'pictures of practice' (Tishman, Perkins & Jay 1995) ideal for evoking open-ended and multi-layered exploration. Extracts from journals, field diaries, and direct quotations have been used for reasons Mallan (1999, p. 82) described as 'a way of weaving the voices of the teachers into the fabric of the text'.

ArtBlast: A day in a school

Planning for the day

In the six weeks leading up to ArtBlast Day, dedicated time was given at the beginning of our two-hour weekly university workshops to plan together. We would begin around the table sharing ideas/strategies/problems and then move into our planning teams to fine-tune, prepare, and gather. Students were encouraged to use their time together to play with and explore materials for inspiration, and to try out their ideas before implementation.

> Collaborative planning was great for sharing ideas, using different strengths of individuals and different teaching methodologies (Bec, pre-service teacher).

> The school had given us free choice with our focus for the day, so our first session involved coming to a group consensus on a topic. Perhaps one of the strengths of ArtBlast is the space for collaborative planning with a partner, with Marnee and with the rest of the class. Planning with the rest of the class meant that there was a forum to discuss ideas and to

Robert Brown, Wes Imms, Marnee Watkins, and John O'Toole

share sources of inspiration. It was fascinating to see how every pair took the same topic (In our Backyard ...) and interpreted it completely differently (Sally/Liz, pre-service teachers).

I also valued the team-teaching experience that ArtBlast offered. This was not only represented in the implementation stage, but also in the planning stage, where the whole group was working together to achieve a common goal. Through listening to other groups in class, we were given opportunities to reflect on how a topic could be interpreted in many different ways (Qingqing, pre-service teacher).

Attention was given to developing a unit that focused on both *creating* and *making art*, and *exploring and responding to art*, with the potential for connections to be made within the visual art domain and beyond.

We want to encourage students to explore a range of art forms using a 'zooming in' approach. The beauty of such an approach is that it creates a sense of connectedness and coherence of the lessons as each artwork reflects elements of their previous art pieces (Qingqing/Andrea, pre-service teachers).

Figure 9.6   A magnifying glass helps

Collaborating in class extended to email exchanges between the working pairs, and these email conversations proved to be invaluable for keeping each other informed and up to date; for sharing spontaneous ideas, findings, and insights; and for exploring possibilities.

Email to team partner: 'Hey I like Jeannie Baker's 'Window' picture book—it has no words—but each time you look out the window—the outside world is changing—and the little boy is growing up. I was thinking that we could use this idea—and … What do you think?' (Andrea, pre-service teacher)

I believed that it was essential for the pre-service teachers to have ownership over their planning for ArtBlast, and that this project would be exponentially enriched if they were encouraged to invest their own passions, interests, repertoire of skills, and personal goals into their day.

The really exciting thing about ArtBlast is the sense of ownership (Hayley/Penny, pre-service teachers).

However, the pre-service teachers needed to be mindful of our key partners in our ArtBlast collaboration: the students, classroom teachers, and the school. Email communication with their host teachers, and becoming familiar with their groups of students, their classrooms, and the school prior to ArtBlast Day were all highly encouraged.

There was an acknowledgment within this group that by having a whole day's access to a school to teach art we were in a privileged position 'not really afforded by any other subject' (Sally/Liz), and this generated a shared goal to be excellent in every way and for all involved. This was demonstrated in the dedication the students applied to all aspects of their planning and preparation for the day. It was clear that this ArtBlast project had moved beyond being simply an assessment task, and had become something quite special for these university students in their learning to be teachers.

I look forward to this shared planning time in my teaching week and welcome the opportunity for such rich professional conversations with these creative and artistic young teachers-to-be. Thankfully, they have embraced the program and are eager to talk and share, and are open to suggestions and constructive feedback. After today's session I am very aware of how this ArtBlast experience is well placed in their four-year degree. They are more than ready for this, and our collaborative planning sessions allow opportunities to 'pull the threads' together from three years of specialised study within an authentic and richly collaborative context (Marnee, lecturer).

On the day

The day arrived and we met at the school very early to set up. I roved from class to class, in the role of support person if needed, and watched as my initially nervous 'ArtBlasters' in their team-teaching teams gradually relaxed throughout the morning and allowed themselves to go with the flow of the day and the children's creative responses and high engagement.

Robert Brown, Wes Imms, Marnee Watkins, and John O'Toole

Note to self—Don't forget to relax and enjoy yourself (Kathryn/Nadia, pre-service teachers).

This is my third year in this program and I still marvel at seeing how these young teachers in training infuse their creative energy into bringing to life the words on a page (their detailed plans for the day) through art, role-play, images, story, poetry, humour, music, dance, and reflection, and how joyfully the children embrace *all* of these ArtBlast experiences.

Figure 9.7   A proud display

Introduction to unit plan: 'What do you do when your quiet art lesson is interrupted by a lively explorer, back from a stint of adventuring, carrying an unrecognisable egg that is about to hatch at any moment? You use your art to create an environment for the new hatchling to live, of course (Sally/Liz, pre-service teachers).

Recess and lunch breaks provided small but welcome windows of time to touch base with each other and to share, problem-solve, celebrate successes, and breathe out. There is a strong sense evident of how working as a team is valued for moral and professional support, for collaborative problem-solving and to maintain the level of creative energy demanded for quality teaching.

As part of our planning, we paid particular attention to teaching as a team, collaboratively. it was great to have the different personalities teaching (Sally/Liz, pre-service teachers).

Team teaching was beneficial in terms of variety of ideas, support network, and sharing the ArtBlast experience (Hayley/Penny, pre-service teachers).

Reflections of the day

During the afternoon we set up the culminating art exhibition in the hall, and then met there at the end of the day to debrief—tired and relieved. Watching the children after school excitely walk and talk their families through our art exhibition was affirming. Our ArtBlast day had been a success with our planning, preparation, flexibility, sourcing of resources, careful and creative attention to pedagogy, and problem-solving all paying off.

> Overall, it was a fabulous day! So much creativity and art making, although it was quite exhausting, but very much worth all the extensive planning, collecting resources, and nerves!! (Kathryn/Nadia, pre-service teachers)

We talked, sharing the highs and lows of the day, and this reflection and critical analysis continued over the following weeks in the development of the PowerPoint presentations. Reflection proved to be a critical process in improving and enhancing practice.

> Our reflective practices allowed us to step back and look at ourselves: how we prepare, plan, and implement a lesson, and where improvements could be made for future teaching (Sally/Liz, pre-service teachers).

> Although I was nervous throughout the day I do feel that this experience has helped me gain some confidence in teaching art. I need to open up more and not be afraid of being adventurous, the children love it when you are in character and I think that's what engages them most. Sal was a great explorer! (Liz, pre-service teacher)

> The supervisory teacher was able to interact at a different level within the classroom and a different class environment (Hayley/Penny, pre-service teachers).

> My teacher thought the day was wonderful! She was a new teacher at the school and hadn't experienced the ArtBlast day before. ... She congratulated us several times throughout the day and was very pleased with the results. I hope Renate and I inspired her to use more art in the classroom (Kathryn, pre-service teacher).

EXEMPLAR

This project, as described in the case study, might look ambitious, but like the multiply focused theatre-in-education described in Chapter 7, case study 7.2, there are many ways in which it can be manageable in schools even without specialised teachers. This exemplar is addressed to at least three different sets of readers:

- teacher educators like us and our art or curriculum classes. (Students, you could suggest this to your lecturers as a hands-on way of combining valuable practicum

Robert Brown, Wes Imms, Marnee Watkins, and John O'Toole

experience and visual arts curriculum, providing you give them time to plan and schedule it!)

- experienced or specialist primary or junior secondary art teachers keen to help your primary colleagues expand their class-based visual art program, and who are prepared to mobilise the energy, organisational, and creative intelligence of your own students as senior peer co-teachers
- *any* upper primary teachers with even a little experience in class-based art teaching, who are similarly prepared to trust the process and your students' ability to peer-teach.

One of the greatest strengths of ArtBlast is the space for collaborative planning at all levels—among teachers, between teachers and students, and among students.

As the case study indicates, probably the major learning benefits have been to the peer teachers—the ArtBlast program provides a priceless opportunity for hands-on practicum experience in engaging activities with children without the pressures of being directly assessed. This is just as true for upper primary or secondary student peer co-teachers of course—all the research shows that there is nothing which reinforces learning like having to teach it to somebody else, and these students are learning as much as the younger children they are teaching, and helping to monitor and supervise each other as they do so! As those who have tried peer-teaching know, children have a remarkable capability to teach other children, which we usually greatly underestimate and under-utilise in normal schooling.

The project can run as a full-day program in just the way we have described above, providing:

- you have carried out the essential pre-planning—taking into account not just the logistics, but also the interpersonal and organisational dynamic of your school
- the classroom supervision and organisational arrangements are clearly set out and followed through.

Pre-planning

First, identify your two sets of students. The first of these we will call the key class—those who take the role of the teacher education students in the case study: the peer co-teachers, who will probably be your own students. The second will be the class or classes that the key class will be leading in the activities—we'll call those the focus class(es). In calculating whether there should be one or more focus classes, remember that the key class will be working in pairs, with smallish groups of focus class students. Obviously, the more classes who can be involved, the bigger the Blast and the more impact in the school, but don't give yourself or the key class more than you can comfortably handle. The other essential prerequisite for the focus classes is that their teachers must be comfortable with the arts experience and the notion of peer teaching, and as keen as you are: if the focus class teachers are uneasy, it will transfer itself to their children. They need to be ready to welcome the key class students into their room as teaching allies, not as intruders, and in fact, to give the key class students the space to display their own expertise, without constant intervention and correction.

Next, let the school administration know what you are intending to do, get them onside, and even invite them into the planning process. If it's really going to be an ArtBlast, the whole school will need to know about it, and be ready to support it at the least by coming along enthusiastically to the exhibition. Part of this planning will involve costing the project; it is not expensive, but it will require art material resources—and if a tertiary class is involved, probably travel.

Now, sit down with the focus class teacher(s) and work out the best day for it, how it will fit into the key class and focus class curriculum, and what topic will form the skeleton on which you will hang the work units to be prepared for the focus class by the key class. (You might get an idea or two about topic-based art teaching from case study 9.1). Work out for your key class and for the focus class(es) how this work can be integrated into other key learning areas, to tie in with and provide motivation; for instance for writing, reading and literature, science or studies of society—or their teacher-education course if we are talking about a tertiary student key class.

Together with the focus class teachers, identify what other resources you may be able to use, starting with the human resources, and particularly identifying willing parents. ArtBlast and other peer-teaching projects that involve parents often prove to have added benefits in giving parents a greater understanding of the importance and value of their children's artwork. And they always get drawn into the activities and end up learning with their kids! Plan too, to use the recesses and lunchtime as important time-out: to reorganise the materials and the classroom, and if necessary to meet and fine-tune the next session.

Make sure that there is time for a pre-visit by the key class to the focus class(es), if possible the day before the ArtBlast, both to help them get to know each other, and to help set up the classroom in readiness. It is important that, when the day arrives, everything is ready for an immediate start to the activities.

Art-making, exhibition, and reflection

The first step is for you to work with your key class on the topic selected, making sure they have a sufficient range of activities and the basic artistic skills themselves. You may wish to create their key class pairings during this practical work, or wait to see how they react to different kinds of activities, and pair them according to their interests and strengths. It may sometimes be necessary to choose pairs carefully, of students who can work well together, and even on occasion to give added support by creating groups of three.

Next, help them to create and plan their work units for the focus class students. Emphasise that they are working as a team, with one person at a time normally leading, and the other observing and ready to step in and help, to give assistance to needy focus

Robert Brown, Wes Imms, Marnee Watkins, and John O'Toole

class students, or to come to the rescue when necessary (that's why they are working in pairs). Each unit should be aiming to create an artwork, or part of an ongoing art-making process, which can be exhibited at the end of the day. It should be timed to be ready and in position by when the exhibition starts.

Ensure they are fully prepared—visit the focus classroom, get the materials and the classroom ready, promote the exhibition throughout the school, and so on. Work out with the students the specific timing of the day, and how the parents and ancillary staff will be deployed (involve the key class students as much as possible in all the decisions).

A-Day—the ArtBlast Landings. In all cases, the focus class teacher is still in charge of their classroom, though you should stress to them that the key class students are like visiting teachers; they should be given their head and not constantly corrected (unless there is real danger, of course). This should give you the opportunity to move from class to class and group to group, like Marnee did in the case study, monitoring and fine-tuning—and, as she stresses, *enjoying* the ArtBlast yourself as others do the hard work: engaged, excited, and concentrated. Use the recesses and lunch-break to connect with the focus class teachers, and adjust, strengthen, or modify the program where necessary. Give the students time to finish and get their artworks ready for the exhibition. When the time comes, open the exhibition, and be prepared to over-run the end of classes, for at least those who don't have school buses to catch.

Keep the exhibition open as long as necessary, for all students and parents to have the chance to see it. Mine the opportunities provided by the ArtBlast for curricular spin-offs in other areas.

Whether you are working with a key class of teacher education students or of primary or secondary students, think about the value of the kind of reflective activities carried out in the case study—observational notebooks; the use of still photographs or video footage (to provide material for reflective discussion or visual exhibition); and retrospective presentations by the key class students on their work. This kind of activity can provide useful outcomes that *are* assessable, and it is in reflection on experience that explicit knowledge and understanding comes.

Activities beyond the case studies

Class task

a)   Review the principles of visual arts education identified in the introduction to this chapter, and locate evidence of these principles in both visual arts case studies.

b)   Review the notion of learning through the aesthetic (Chapter 5) and identify and discuss examples of this from the case studies.

Workshop: Exhibition—Student teacher as artist

a) Review the notions of teacher as artist, and teacher artistry, and create a 2D or 3D artwork to express your understanding of teaching the arts (or one art form).

Questions to consider

The process of developing a visual arts program is emergent, negotiated, and dynamic. It requires ongoing reflection on practice stimulated by several perennial questions:

1 How do I value the visual arts? What experiences have shaped such values?
2 How are my values acknowledged and represented in my teaching of art?
3 How do I ensure that art experiences are engaging and relevant to children?
4 What learning and learning processes do I want to promote through visual arts experiences?
5 How can I balance open-ended learning with skills-based instruction in my visual arts teaching?

Conclusion

With reference to our opening discussion an analysis of the two case studies presented indicates programs that were stimulating and well organised; had as their central tenet the students' interests; were designed to develop critical and creative visual arts skills; and focused on student imagination, observation, and personal memories. These are all achieved through purposeful planning, skilful teaching, and reflective evaluation. Finally, but by no means of least importance, the teachers themselves modelled a passion for the creative process.

What were the mechanisms that allowed these teachers to so successfully engage their students in this way? How did the programs ensure the learning content responded to student interests? In ArtBlast, the pre-service teachers negotiated their project topics with their host teachers to ensure there was a logical connection with work currently being done in other areas of the curriculum, and consciously designed activities that were relevant to the students' lived experiences. In Under the Sea one child's creative illustrated story was the stimulus for a year-long project that encouraged students to research and develop personal responses.

In ArtBlast, one room was over-laden with recycled materials covering every horizontal space; the effect on the students one of unbridled joy as their imagination took them from a classroom to a materials-rich playground. In Under the Sea the teacher, students, and parents all contributed to the transformation of the art studio into a fantastic and aesthetically vibrant sea-like environment.

Robert Brown, Wes Imms, Marnee Watkins, and John O'Toole

Both case studies intertwined art making and responding, and in doing so developed a sophisticated visual language through discussion and modelling by the teachers. In ArtBlast this often occurred informally as the pre-service teachers, empowered by the non-judgmental format of the program, felt confident to explore and discuss their understandings with students making their 'thinking visible'. In ArtBlast, the pre-service teachers were encouraged to participate in a research-orientated and inquiry-based approach to teaching and learning that required them to pause often, in order to reflect and consider. This experience in reflective practice had, as many commented, a reflexive component that compelled the pre-service teachers to respond, act on their feet, and make changes during the day. In Under the Sea, Jeanette's story tells of an experienced reflective practitioner informed by deeply felt personal and professional beliefs. Framed by her experience as a designer and community artist, she naturally engages her students as 'co-researchers' in a journey of discovery where thinking skills are paramount.

Art projects that allow for in-depth *immersion* facilitate greater teacher and student engagement with the creative, imaginative, and problem-solving aspects of art making. In ArtBlast, the students were involved in myriad activities, spanning a whole day, in order to approach a single topic from multiple perspectives. In Under the Sea, students and the teacher were immersed literally in an art studio environment that served as both a space for creation and reflection.

As argued by Miller and Seller (1990), if the curriculum adopts a transactional or even trans-formational approach, students move from being passive recipients to active partners of curriculum. This was clear in ArtBlast, where the traditional 'educator' (the classroom teacher) moved their role from directing and supervising the actions of the sub-educator (the pre-service teacher) to being a *partner* in the process. The classroom teacher assisted in the planning phases of the lessons, but literally and figuratively learned alongside the students and pre-service teacher. Arguably, all three parties developed skills and knowledge concurrently. Likewise in Under the Sea, teaching and learning were reciprocal with the teacher and students working together as co-learners. Jeanette's thorough research provided a clear basis from which to pre-plan a 'success-orientated' art program that promoted both individual expression and skill acquisition.

The Under the Sea case study tells a story of a long-term visual arts-centred project through the words of an experienced art teacher and artist. ArtBlast tells a different story with the focus on a group of pre-service teachers who worked in teams to present, on a single day, a kaleidoscope of visual arts experiences throughout an entire primary school. Both case studies have explored practices and issues central to engaging and challenging children to make and communicate personal meaning through the visual arts.

Key references

Bresler, L. & Marm, C. (eds) (2002) *The Arts In Children's Lives: Context, Culture, and Curriculum*, Kluwer Academic, Boston.

Connelly, F.M. & Clandinin, D.J. (1996) 'Teachers' Professional Knowledge Landscapes: Teacher Stories: Stories of Teachers—School Stories—Stories of Schools', *Educational Researcher*, 25(3), 24–30.

Efland, A. (1990) *A History of Art Education*, Teachers College Press, New York.

Emery, L. (1996) 'Heuristic Inquiry: Intensifying Subjectivity in Art Education Research', *Australian Art Education*, 19(3), 23–30.

Gardner, H. (1983) *Frames of Mind*, Basic Books, Inc., New York.

Golomb, C. (1992) *The Child's Creation of a Pictorial World*, University of California Press, Oxford, England.

Lowenfeld, V. (1947) *Creative and Mental Growth*, Macmillan, New York.

Mallan, K. (1999) *In the Picture: Perspectives on Picture Book Art and Artists*, Centre for Information Studies, Charles Sturt University, Wagga Wagga, NSW.

Miller, J. & Seller, W. (1990) *Curriculum: Perspectives and Practices*, Copp Clark Pitman, Toronto.

Tishman, S., Perkins, D.N., & Jay, E. (1995) *The Thinking Classroom: Learning and Teaching in a Culture of Thinking*, Allyn and Bacon, Boston.

Weiss, G. (1992) 'From Skills to Expression: The Arts in the Early Years of School 1880–1970', *Australian Art Education*, 16(2), 32–8.

Wright, S. (ed.) (2003) *Children, Meaning-making and the Arts*, Pearson/Prentice Hall, NSW, Australia.

10

Art Embodied and Disembodied: Expression, Representation, and Reflection

Jan Deans, John O'Toole, Jo Raphael, and Sarah Young

In this chapter a group of writers from very diverse academic backgrounds deal with the embodied and disembodied arts—from an exploration of dance with preschool children to the use of the webblog for eleven and twelve year olds to reflect on the creation of a group performance about how to change the world. The Deans & Young case study takes the reader into the world of the preschooler and the delicate craft of the dance and drama teachers who guide their small dancers through myriad choreographic and conceptual tasks in their pursuit of kinaesthetic learning. Jo Raphael allows the young bloggers to speak for themselves in her case study, How to Change the World. Through the voices of the Year 6 students, Jo raises the critical question of how to build meaningful reflection into the arts-making process, and suggests that for the current generation of 'cyber-natives', the digital world offers many great possibilities. Theory concerning forms of expression and representation in the embodied and digital world is also discussed.

Introduction

In one sense all art is the embodiment of experience shaped into something else. We sing, dance, act, draw, paint, story-tell, and in all senses play out our experience of the world, making new meanings for ourselves and others. Traditionally, our 'media' are our bodies, our voices, and the physical materials we find around us. Long long ago, all art was embodied, and the physicality, the viscerality, was an important part of not only each individual's, but especially the social and communal—the total—experience. We not only hear, but we feel and see the drums as we dance and sing. We see our decorated bodies and the masks. The painted drums both absorb and express the rhythm and the singing, connecting us to the group and the earth and the space around, as the well-known story unfolds. That was long ago, but fortunately we have not lost this capacity to embody! Every component of the picture above might describe equally a traditional Indigenous dance of welcome, a dance party or moshpit, and a gospel church service.

On the other hand, we have also been gradually evolving ways of *dis*-embodying the artistic experience, of separating out the artist or maker, the artwork or representation, and the responder or receiver of what the artwork communicates. The invention of writing broke the necessary connection between the storyteller, the story, and the audience; the invention of printing broke the connection between the artist, the medium, and the viewer. However, in doing so, both gave us new ways to make, represent, and communicate art—the storybook and the picture book, which allowed us to use our imaginative engagement to replace and extend the first-hand sensual experience—the vision, sound, and touch. Since the electronic age began, the photograph, telephone, gramophone, film, radio, television, and now the computer with its emanations from the internet to iPod have all been playing fast and loose with our five senses, giving us untold virtual possibilities that are further and further away from real-time and real-space, more and more negotiable. We can and must help our students to make the most of their bodies and of cyberspace, to make meaning with both.

Shaping expression and representation

This chapter presents case studies in drama and dance, both art forms that involve kinaesthetic knowing. All people have a kinaesthetic or muscle sense that can be described as nerve endings sending messages to the brain telling individuals how to move. Drama and dance stimulate kinaesthetic awareness and have the potential to allow participants to move out from the everyday response to experience embodiment. The process revolves around a progression that includes moving the body, sensing the body, and finally involving feelings with the individual bringing their emotions into play. What is achieved is a connection between the body, the emotions, and the mind where the participants learn about themselves and their worlds through the creative expression of their ideas and thoughts.

Jan Deans, John O'Toole, Jo Raphael, and Sarah Young

In the lasting words of Hanna (1979) 'to dance is human' and from the beginning of life the urge to move and to explore the world through the body is a natural behaviour. Everyday movements are connected to our feelings: we jump for joy, clench fists in anger, and greet with open arms. Young children run, skip, jump, twirl, and fall, and these natural locomotor movements are practised and refined through their play. The human movement vocabulary is extensive and it is this repertoire that provides the starting point for dance education.

Participants come to the dance class with their bodies, their minds, and their movements, and this is where the dance class begins (Wright 2003), with non-verbal body movement that is purposeful, intentional and rhythmic, and beyond everyday motor activity. The aim is to provide children with a wide range of opportunities for bodily exploration in an atmosphere where moving is acknowledged as having inherent creative, expressive, and aesthetic value. In this art form teachers must become familiar with the elements of dance as identified by Rudolf Laban (1971): the body (body awareness and body activities), the use of personal and shared space, and explorations in time and force.

Through dance children become acquainted with their bodies as 'instruments of expression', and over time through the practice of body part and whole body articulation they develop their unique style. Children need to achieve familiarity with a wide movement vocabulary otherwise 'creativity cannot effectively take place' (Davies 2003, p. 161), so the teacher should structure the dance class to include individual, partner, and group movement explorations that may lead to performance. There should always be a time for children to explore personal dance without being directed by the teacher, and it is during this time that children have the freedom and the time to achieve embodiment through dance. Questioning and times for verbal reflection and recording through visual representation provide additional opportunities for children to gain deeper understanding of themselves and their world.

Most things can be expressed in body movement with the world around and the world within providing a rich resource for teaching content. Teachers can also gain inspiration from children's interests, ideas, and feelings, and through the use of guided discovery (Guidici & Rinaldi 2001) they can move understandings from the simple to the more complex. It is important however that consideration be given to the movement possibilities of the selected theme, as some themes have more movement potential than others; for example, the elements of nature, earth, air, fire, and water lend themselves to extensive movement interpretation.

Inherent in the dance experience is rhythm, and rhythm is the platform from which all dance is created. It is often considered as the creative principle of movement, as it shapes the dance by providing substance to all movement exploration. Rhythm is felt internally and expressed outwardly through patterns that can range from a simple clapping beat to a more complex combination of patterns and sequences. Rhythm is an impulse, it is a beat or a swing, and can create flow and provide order for the movement patterning. Any rhythmic pattern implies repetition, but repetition does not necessarily make the movement rhythmic. Teachers need to become sensitive to the central role that rhythm plays in the dance, and out of rhythm flows music.

Music can be either recorded or performed live, and teachers need to develop skills in using both. When using recorded music, individual teachers can begin their collection with music that they enjoy and can analyse carefully for its movement potential. All teachers need to become familiar with an instrument that can be used spontaneously throughout each dance class: for beginners a tambour or a drum, and for accomplished musicians their own instruments. An instrument in the class is vital for not only establishing energy, but for accompanying improvisational dance and to provide an immediate sound to concentrate the energy of the group. The teacher's role is to help 'children focus on the music to become sensitive to the expressive potential for dance' (Wright 2003, p. 250) by drawing their attention to the differing qualities within the music and by asking open-ended questions about how it makes them feel and respond.

This overview has presented dance as a kinaesthetic learning mode; one that involves participants in open-ended bodily improvisation that leads to the development of dance skills and understandings. There is a close connection that exists between learning in dance and learning in drama. The subtle differences are of emphasis: dance focuses on meaning making using the body as the instrument of expression and drama places emphasis on meaning making using story and language. These two readily accessible art forms can work either independently or together within any arts program providing individual and holistic learning for students.

Embodiment in drama

In drama education, students experience a wide range of activities that involve their bodies. These range from simple physical exercises including stretching, ways of moving in the space, and working with others to make static shapes or scenes (freeze frames or tableaux), through to more complex physical activities including communicating through mime, gesture, and the acting out of situations. In this way of knowing, 'students are taught to use their bodies as centres of perspective, insight, reflection, motivation, and agency. Students, therefore, are taught both to listen to, and to be "in" their bodies, in order for them to express and be able to go "out" of them (Wright & Rasmussen 2001, p. 227). Experience in drama helps to extend the ways participants use their bodies, but also draws participants' conscious attention to the gestures, actions, and movements of the body that may be automatic or involuntary, so that they may be aware and better able to take account of them for both their art making and for life.

When students are invited to work in groups to create a dramatic performance on a specific theme or topic there are many decisions they need to make as art-makers as they endeavour to shape their artistic expression in order to make meaning. They need to decide

Jan Deans, John O'Toole, Jo Raphael, and Sarah Young

what it is they want to say and then go about finding an effective way to say it. They are not only thinking about the content and perhaps a narrative, but their audience, dramatic styles, dramatic elements such as developing tension, focus, use of sound, space, stagecraft elements, and so on.

It is highly likely our 'digital native' students will also want to draw upon the wide range of recent technologies that they engage with on a daily basis, such as video, CD, DVD, and the internet, for their performance making. While traditionally drama and theatre has been distinguished by physical embodiment and live performance, new technologies now allow for drama and theatre—cyberdrama—to take place in a digital world. Many of the young people we teach already experience a kind of dramatic role-play within web-based worlds and play out their theatre on a digital stage (Carroll & Cameron 2003, Davis 2006). This is a field that offers great potential for performing arts educators to explore, and it is imperative that we do, lest we lose 'our young students/audiences as they seek relevant performance forms in the mediatised world they have been born into' (Carroll, Anderson, & Cameron 2006, p. xvi).

Shaping, reflecting, and responding

The full benefits of an arts education experience are not achieved without building in opportunities to reflect on the processes along the way. The experience of creating can be rich and absorbing with the participants' bodies and minds very much engaged and in the 'flow'. In the performing arts of drama and dance the final performance takes place and then it is finished. Pausing to reflect on and think openly and critically both during the creating and after the performance can help sustain the normally short-lived and transient performing arts experience. What is going on in this process? What is my purpose? What is working? What is not and why? What else could we do? These are just some of the questions we can reflect on to better understand the artistic process, learn from the experience, and allow it to inform future performance making. At some point, therefore, it is necessary to find time and distance to take a look at what is happening in the artistic process.

Finding distance can involve some *disembodying* of the experience. For the youngest children involved in creative kinaesthetic improvisation, this disembodiment might involve them in the process of drawing an illustration of something that they have remembered from their improvisation. In order to draw they have to think about what has happened in the creative experience. They might also reflect on and draw ideas, thoughts or feelings that have arisen out of the experience. The teacher might then ask them to tell the story of their drawing, thereby providing a bridge from the kinaesthetic embodied experience through to visual, verbal, and written language.

Of our current generation of young people, the so-called 'digital natives', it is often lamented that in the twitch-speed world they inhabit, they do not take sufficient time to stop and reflect (Prensky 2001). A challenge that we face as educators is to find appropriate, exciting, and even digital ways to engage the digital natives in reflection. Online journals such as blogs are one such means. The performance that young people create and present has an audience, and so does the blog, as well as a mechanism for that audience to feed back to the blog writer. Through words and images, students can reflect on ideas, thoughts, or feelings that arise out of the arts experience. Blogs provide a way to reflect on the performance-making process that extends and reaches, in time and place, beyond the workshop or class. Their public nature encourages the students to think about the connection and impact of their art-making in the wider world.

Shaping pedagogy

There are various roles that teachers can take when engaging children in creative art-making. The case studies in this chapter provide examples of some of these roles.

Teacher as facilitator

As the facilitator in the creative process the teacher usually provides the starting point or stimulus. The area of exploration might, for example, be negotiated with the students, emerge from earlier work, or be a predetermined part of the curriculum. The teacher's role is to focus this area of exploration and then provide a catalyst to fire up the creative process. There are numerous forms that this could take such as an idea, a text, an image, music, teacher-in-role, an artefact, or a question. Once begun, the teacher trusts the students to continue to come up with ideas and gives them responsibility for this. As facilitator, the teacher also needs to provide the structures that will support the students in the creative process.

Teacher as questioner

The questioning role of the teacher is important both within the creative process and at the conclusion of it. A simple well-timed question can have an enormous effect on the creative experience by disrupting ordinary and familiar responses. This questioning is particularly powerful within the arts. As Maxine Greene reminds us, the arts are able 'to prod us beyond acquiescence. They may, now and then, move us into spaces where we can create visions of other ways of being and ponder what it might signify to realise them' (1992, p. 6). Asking the right sorts of open-ended questions can help develop critical and deeper creative thinking. The teacher can ask the questions that will not only encourage thinking about the art-making, but thinking about the thinking.

In the role of questioner, the teacher will also be asking the questions that will encourage the all-important reflection in and on his or her own practice, and perhaps also create visions of other ways and better ways of working:

> To be an arts educator is to be a reflective practitioner. Both give birth to ideas; both search
> for a medium to express and honour their vision (Taylor 2000, p. 85).

Jan Deans, John O'Toole, Jo Raphael, and Sarah Young

Teacher as participant and sharer

The arts very often involve students in collaborative learning in which the teacher can share. By taking a role as participant or co-creator, the teacher can play a part in the creative process. Part of this creativity is the teacher's role in responding to the ideas and interests that emerge from the class in the creative process and help shape the learning experience. The role of participant challenges the usual teacher–student relationship and provides an opportunity for the teacher to be co-creator of knowledge in an atmosphere of mutual respect. Teachers as co-learners in a community of learners are particularly relevant when they are working alongside digital native students who may have a more intuitive and masterful approach to the new technologies and much to teach the teacher.

The case studies

This chapter takes a look at two of the simplest and most immediately accessible forms of art-making for the children of an age where experience for these digital natives is equally embodied and disembodied: *dance*, and *drama* involving reflection through internet *blogging*. The two case studies not only highlight the differences and contrasts for the arts teacher, but show how they share common principles of both art and pedagogy.

I want to dance, let's do it again

Jan Deans and Sarah Young

> The children burst into the room, with lots of laughter and animated conversation. 'Take your shoes and socks off and come and join me on the mat.' The children lined their shoes up against the wall and gathered together with a sense of excited expectation on a colourful piece of material designated as the group meeting place. Jan played the humdrum and called the children by name to enter the space and make a starting shape. The dance class had begun.

Within an educational context, dance offers children an opportunity to learn by involving the whole body in kinaesthetic exploration, cognitive processing, and social engagement. Participation in dance education involves exploring and learning dance skills, improvising and creating dance, performing and appreciating dance, responding to and reflecting on the dance of others, and recording the dance experience through drawing and story creation. Dance differs from other forms of physical activity in that it does not focus on movement purely to achieve a concrete end or result, but rather the attention is directed towards movement as an expressive and creative form.

Figure 10.1   I want to dance, let's do it again

The dance program described in this chapter aimed to engage the children and teachers in a co-creation of thinking and learning through dance. The focus was on the emerging interests and ideas of children and their interpretation through creative kinaesthetic improvisation. The teachers had identified a number of questions including:

- What opportunities does dance provide for children to engage in collaborative problem-solving and decision-making?
- How does the teacher include the children's ideas and interests in the dance curriculum content?
- How does reflection through drawing extend children's understandings of the dance experience?
- How is the co-creation of knowledge explored through dance?

About the research

This study investigated a dance program at an inner city preschool where two specialist teachers with a group of 20 four-year-old children met together, weekly for one hour, and decided to research our own practice as a reflective practitioner case study. We, the two teachers Jan and Sarah, co-planned the class content with one teacher leading the group and the other teacher recording the flow of the lesson and the children's and teacher's comments. Classes were conducted over one term and the following vignettes record the salient 'lived experience' of the program.

Jan Deans, John O'Toole, Jo Raphael, and Sarah Young

Multiple forms of data were collected:

- Class lesson plans provided an overview of the teachers' anticipated program.
- The teachers' journals included weekly evaluative reflections, children's comments and verbal responses, and the thoughts and feelings experienced by the teachers during the class.
- Transcripts of class observations also provided additional data.
- Children's drawings and photographs recorded individual reflections and responses.

Jan is the director and the specialist dance teacher, and Sarah is the specialist dance and drama teacher at the preschool. Both have extensive experience as arts educators and are committed to creative and experiential learning for young children. Our combined philosophical platform encompasses the notion that teachers and children are co-creators in learning with the teacher/child partnership and with the teacher/teacher partnership playing an important role in supporting the learning journey. We work together in a responsive environment where leading and following are interchangeable, and ideas freely flow to stimulate the co-construction of knowledge.

The frog dance

The first class saw participants getting to know each other and learning about how to work together as a group. Jan used the humdrum to invite each child into the space. The children naturally sought each other out and formed a long line together. Jan commented, 'That's interesting, look at the picture we are making', and the children responded with various ideas and suggestions about what the line could represent including snakes, the letter 's', and trains.

At this point in the lesson the pre-planned warm-up content and up-tempo music was introduced with explorations of body part identification, moving and stillness, wide shapes, spiky shapes, round shapes, and general whole body movement—preparing the body physically for what was to follow. A bodily kinaesthetic connection between the teacher and the children started to develop, and a sense of playfulness and joy was evident with lots of individual ideas being forwarded as material for further exploration.

As the class content unfolded, Jan picked up on these ideas paying close attention to the children's verbal descriptions and physical representations. One child initiated a frog movement and within seconds the dance space was filled with jumping frogs. This topic had been explored over previous weeks in the classroom, and naturally led to body interpretation including moving heads from side to side, winking, squat jumps, fly catching with tongues, and jumping from lily pad to lily pad. Jan gave the children a chance to explore all of these movements separately. She then introduced the sequencing of the movements and the children enthusiastically repeated them, refining and embellishing to create a dance. Throughout this time the tambour was used to keep the rhythm and

Figure 10.2   The dance space was filled with jumping frogs

provide focus, and the sequencing of movement became the content for a whole group improvisation with one child commenting, 'I want to dance, let's do it again'. In response, Jan gathered the children together on the mat, providing quiet time for verbal sharing about what had just transpired. This strategy was used as punctuation in the lesson; a time to catch the breath and to lead the children into the next stage of the class, and to give the teacher a chance to think about how emerging interests could be incorporated.

The child-initiated content generated earlier in the class, moving heads from side to side, winking, and jumping, was re-visited, but this time children were asked to join with a friend to create partner dances. A musical score of sounds of a billabong was played, setting the scene for a frog dance where all of the children frog jumped from lily pad to lily pad, finding their partners to mirror heads moving from side to side, winking and tongue fly catching. Still frog shapes were then formed and the teacher called several partner groups to move through and around the still partner shapes. All of the children participated in moving and being still.

This dance reached its natural conclusion and Jan called the children to gather on the meeting mat. A small group of children was then asked to enter the dance space for 'free dance', which is the time when children have the opportunity to improvise freely. The other children formed an audience, participating as active observers, waiting for their turn to dance. 'Find your starting shape'—the room was dotted with sculptural forms and the humdrum responded to the emerging dances. At times the music followed high-energy output and at other times it picked up on stillness and pauses in the dance. A

Jan Deans, John O'Toole, Jo Raphael, and Sarah Young

reciprocal relationship between the performers and the music was established, and a strong connection created between children and teachers.

The class concluded with a reflective drawing activity that involved the whole group. Relaxing music was played as the teachers asked the children to find their own space on the floor and 'draw something that you remember from the dance today'. As they enthusiastically settled into the task of drawing their most vivid memories or thoughts, we then moved around the room. As the drawings were completed we recorded verbatim the children's stories on their paper.

The grouping dance

During the warm-up of a following session the children were encouraged to make shapes and pull faces to upbeat rhythmic music. Jan kept repeating 'change your shape, change your face' and they responded energetically. A surprising theme emerged with the children seeking out same-gender groups. Boys huddled together against the wall and Harry was heard to say 'I'm in the boy group. This is a boy group', and the majority of the girls congregated in small groups in the middle of the space. One girl separated herself from the rest of the group by returning to the meeting mat, making it quite obvious that she was not interested in participating. Jan quickly summed up the situation and made the decision to use 'groupings' as content for dance choreography. She said, 'Move around the room and find a group to sit with'. This instruction was repeated several times over and within a few minutes the children gained the confidence to connect beyond their same-gender groups. 'There's a group of three, over there I see five dancers, and oh my goodness there is just one dancer.' This response excited the children, including the child who separated herself out, and within a few repeats of the instruction the space was filled with forming and re-forming dance groups. Pathways emerged with some children spontaneously taking up the lead and others choosing to follow. Jan drew the children's attention to their curving patterns in the space, and the dance finished with still and silent curving body shapes.

The curving dance

The next session began with a re-cap on the previous week's curving dance.

The intent was to stimulate the children's memory of the previous week's content. Jan demonstrated curving through the space and said, 'Do you remember this dance?' A few children replied, 'That's the curving dance' and so the class began. Curving was explored on many levels and groupings. Hands became the focus with palms together leading the bodies forward. Movement was punctuated with stillness and the children formed a series of shapes held and released; pairs of children connecting through their outstretched arms.

Figure 10.3 'This is when we were doing the curving. This is the humdrum. This is the dance mat—me and Melissa.'

Another child released her shape to the floor and this immediately created a ripple effect through the class. Jan added falling to the dance.

Slow music was played and Jan suggested a new dance of rising, curving, and falling. As the children were rising they were encouraged to stretch up high and balance on any part of their body. As they were curving they were asked to travel across the floor using a variety of levels. In the final movement of the sequence, Jan suggested that the children try to fall by softly spiralling down with arms wide open. This was followed by Jan splitting the group; half of the children became the dancers while the other half sat on the mat as

Figure 10.4 'That's me doing the dance, the curving dance'

Jan Deans, John O'Toole, Jo Raphael, and Sarah Young

the audience, a strategy that provided opportunity for the children to enjoy a larger space, practise their skills, observe their peers, and reflect on their own dances. The roles were swapped after five minutes, and during the transition Jan led a discussion about what had been observed with individuals commenting about what they had seen:

> I can see some people sitting and others in a straight line.

> Emily looks like a starfish.

> I was a tree.

> Henry looks like a rag doll.

The web dance

Reflecting on the child-initiated class content of the previous weeks we picked up on the connection of outstretched arms that had occurred in the curving dance, seeing the potential of this movement fitting well with the children's strong interest in Spiderman. A decision was made to base the class on web making, with the emphasis on creating dances that incorporated body part connections between individuals and among the whole group.

We had observed the children using the Spiderman web-making hand gesture in their play. When questioned about the use of this Ted replied, 'This is the Spiderman's web-slinging hand, Spiderman uses this to make his webs'. This hand gesture became the signature movement of the session's warm-up and set the scene for the dance. Sarah asked the children to 'bring your arms close to your body, fists tight. Now, move your arms out from

Figure 10.5   'That's me in a shape with a web'

your body and open your hands wide. Imagine long thin, sticky threads leaving your hands and as they do there is a shhhhhh sound.' All of the children in the group responded to this imagery with powerful, forceful gestures of the arms and enthusiastically accompanied these with vocalisations. Natural body stances evolved, the legs became splayed, and strength was evident throughout the children's musculature. The sequence was repeated several times with the children moving through the space finding places to stop, making strong body shapes, and creating their webs and sounds.

A group of children formed connections with their arms, leading the way open for Sarah to develop the group dance. Once again the teacher's capacity to observe what was happening around her supported child-initiated content. One child suggested that there was a spider in the web and this image was immediately incorporated into the group dance. Suddenly the room was filled with creeping spiders; bodies were crawling on 'tippee toes' and fingertips, and a scurrying energy dominated the room. It was clear that the children had moved on from Spiderman, and their focus was now on imagery of spiders and webs.

Calling on principles of problem-based learning, Sarah set a group task that required one group to work out how to connect members' bodies in a still web-like shape. This exercise provided opportunities for the children to discuss, listen to each other's views, try out different ways of connecting together, and work as a team to find the solution. This collaborative activity took a few minutes with the teachers affirming the children's decision-making and suggesting additional ways to solve the problem. Finally, the children

Figure 10.6 Group dance

Jan Deans, John O'Toole, Jo Raphael, and Sarah Young

were satisfied with their solution and they arrived at the point of stillness. Sarah said, 'Hold that group shape there, the spiders are coming'.

Music from *Paris Texas* by Ry Cooder created a slow sustained background for the second group of children to individually enter into the web dance, maintaining the energy by transforming into spiders that invaded the still web with their moving bodies. Some children began jumping from place to place and others were creeping on the floor. The atmosphere in the room was intense as the 20 four-year-old children cooperated together to a create unique dance choreography. The dance lasted for approximately 3–4 minutes. Sarah helped the children to complete it by saying, 'Find a finishing shape: spiders be still'. After a few seconds of stillness, where the children maintained their presence as co-creators of dance, there was a spontaneous release and several children said that they wanted to 'do it again'. The groups were changed over and the entire experience was repeated.

After such a successful group dance all of the children were eager to share their thoughts and feelings about what had occurred:

It was good when me and Josh were holding hands with each other and dancing around.

While we were dancing we were jumping like spiders.

I was jumping, I was creeping on the ground.

I was spreading my arms up in the air and I was feeling good.

The learning journey

These descriptions provide insight into how teachers can create an environment where children are encouraged to explore and refine dance skills, improvise and create dance, and perform and reflect on their own dance and the dance of others. Through a combination of guided discovery and directed teaching, the children's ideas and interests became central to the development of the dance curriculum, and provided meaningful content for authentic and aesthetic learning through the co-creation of dance choreography.

There were many observable outcomes, including children displaying well-developed body awareness and confidence, and an understanding that their bodies could express their ideas and feelings. There was also evidence that over time the children's spatial awareness developed, enabling them to work cooperatively in a large space with their peers. Other outcomes were the ability to incorporate a variety of dynamic variations through expressive movement. The development of these skills was enhanced by opportunities that were given to them to make personal decisions and to engage in problem-solving tasks using the body.

Over the term the teachers' journal provided a rich source of data, especially in the form of children's voices, which became the inspiration and starting point for each class. The systematic documentation of the children's ideas and interests built a strong connection between the dance curriculum and the children's generalist play-based program. As teachers, we were prepared to spontaneously adapt class content to emerging interests and link these to the elements of dance. The journal also uncovered many examples of children moving beyond basic movement exploration to a point of transformation where creative processing resulted in expressive dance making.

An analysis of two hundred children's drawings showed that drawing after dance played an important role in enabling children to record their involvement in, and response to, the dance content. This activity provided an opportunity for the children to capture the transient nature of dance, and gave the teachers insights into each child's involvement and their thinking. With the drawing being undertaken at the conclusion of each class the children tackled the task with focused energy, and there were many examples of detailed reflection. Several themes emerged from the analysis of the drawings:

Figure 10.7 'There's the spider and he was on the web—he spinned the web'

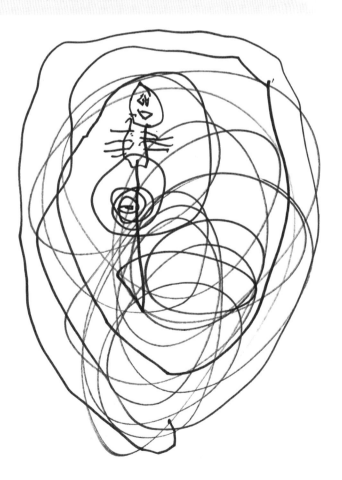

Jan Deans, John O'Toole, Jo Raphael, and Sarah Young

- an affirmation of the self with body shapes, body parts, and body activities being central to the images
- the recognition of dance as a social activity with friends and teachers being regularly represented
- the physical aspects of the space including the meeting mat, the lights, and the musical instruments
- a representational record of the stories that unfolded during the dance.

The vignettes that have emerged from this case study, informed by multiple forms of data, provide significant insight into dance teaching methodology and practice. The resultant understandings have affirmed the importance of teachers and children as co-creators of knowledge in an atmosphere of mutual respect and reciprocal sharing.

EXEMPLAR

Whatever the stimulus for dance may be, whether it is initiated from the teachers or the children, the chosen content must have the potential for interpretation through move-ment. A dance class can be simply planned by becoming familiar with the elements of dance, namely:

- **The body**—locomotor (running, walking, skipping, sliding, creeping, rolling, and so on); non-locomotor (twisting, wriggling, stretching, shaking, and so on); shapes—still or moving (pointy, curved, twisted)
- **Time**—fast, sudden, slow, gradual, accelerated
- **Force**—powerful, strong, light, gentle, soft
- **Flow**—unrestrained, ongoing, free, bound, tight, controlled
- **Space**—levels (high, medium, low); directions (forward, backwards, sideways, up, down, diagonal); pathways (zigzag, straight, curved, circular); size (big, small, medium).

The dance class can be divided into four clearly defined sections that are described below.

Step 1: Warm-up—preparing the body

At the start of the class the warm-up is designed to prepare the body for the activity to follow. Children enjoy vigorous movement to up-tempo music and the teacher can guide body part articulation using basic body movements.

Teachers must observe the children's contributions closely and try to pick up on new movement material to include in the warm-up. Children are always very keen to offer material for dance, and with the teacher's guidance the content can move from individual exploration to moving two body parts at the same time and then whole body involvement.

Guiding questions

Does anyone have another way of moving?

What does it feel like to shake your whole body?

Can you shake your body without moving your feet?

Can you find three different ways to move your body?

Can you shake your heads and hands? Can you swing your arms? Can you stamp your feet and turn your body around?

Step 2: Building a dance: creating and making

After the warm-up the main content is introduced, and this can be either emergent or offered by the teacher. The teacher needs to be thoughtful of what the dancers will be doing, how the dancers will be moving, where in the space the dancers will be moving, and who the dancers will move with. The idea is to provide improvisational opportunities for individual, partner, small group, and whole group dance experience with the emphasis placed on refining and practising skills. Movement explorations need to occur on the spot, from place to place, and a balance between high and low energy needs to be included. Stillness is an important part of every class. It can be used by the teacher as a control strategy and provide the space for thinking about where to move next.

Guiding questions

What sort of shapes are we making together?

How can you join with another person to make a shape?

How can we all join together to make a shape?

How can you move through the space without using your feet?

How can we all move through the space connected to each other?

Jan Deans, John O'Toole, Jo Raphael, and Sarah Young

Step 3: Free dance: exploring and responding

During 'free dance' the teacher provides musical accompaniment with percussion instruments. Small groups of dancers are given the opportunity to dance freely in the space ('Dance any way you like!'), and the other children in the group become the audience with roles changing so that all children have a chance to enjoy performing for their peers and to observe the dance of others. Both roles are interdependent and are seen as active and creative; for the dancers individual improvisation calls on the creative process to be ignited, and for the audience the task is to observe closely and to learn from the dance of others.

Guiding questions

What did you see in that dance?

How did you feel when you were dancing?

How did the music make you feel?

What did you like about your dance?

Step 4: Dance drawings: reflecting and recording

At the end of the class the children are immediately involved in a reflective drawing activity that is designed to record individual thoughts and feelings about the content of the class. The combination of children's drawings and the verbatim recording of the children's stories provide a rich description of the dance experience. These drawings can be used for portfolio assessment purposes, to provide feedback to parents as well as to inform the teacher's future planning.

Questions for students to consider

1   What do you remember about the dance class today?
2   Can you remember how you moved and who you danced with?
3   Can you tell me about your drawing?

How to change the world

Jo Raphael

A blog says 'I am here and I've done this!'

Toby's drama blog

This year in drama we are learning how to change the world. We are using a book called *How to Change the World*. It's a really interesting book. There is 'put your chewing gum in the bin, install at least one energy saving light bulb in your house …' The main point of this book is how the world could be a much better place if we follow these rules. I think this book is fantastic and I recommend it to everybody. We have to do plays in drama class and I am extremely fascinated by it. In my group I have Nadia, Jacinta, Louise, and myself. It is extraordinary. I'm having a great time doing the plays. Our play is about planting a tree and how it can change the world. Did you know that if you plant a tree it will give two people oxygen for the rest of their lives? … I never would have realised this if it wasn't for the experience. In our performance someone is reading a news report saying all the information that is in the book. We thoroughly listened to the report and decided to plant a beautiful tree. It sprouted and it looked great (even though it was me). This is Toby.

This case study was designed to discover some of the things young people think about and reflect on as they engage in the process of creating a performance. It explores the ways young people consider themselves as art-makers and their purpose for creating performance. The study involved a class of Year 6 students who have a drama session once a week with a specialist performing arts teacher. Along with the other three Year 6 classes in their large outer suburban school, they undertook a project in which they worked in small groups to create short performances and reflect on their processes by writing a journal entry in the form of a class web log or blog. Their classroom teachers provided time in class for the students to write their blog posts as soon as practicable after each drama session.

The study sought to understand something about the role that writing, reading, and commenting on blogs may play in encouraging reflection on the performance-making process and in building a sense of connection among students as a community of art-makers. Research questions included:

*   How might we encourage and promote a sense of students as art-makers?
*   How does drama teaching and learning change when blogs are introduced?
*   How does reflection on art making processes through blogs affect reflective thinking and performance making?

Jan Deans, John O'Toole, Jo Raphael, and Sarah Young

- In which ways do blogs within a multi-user blogging environment[1] allow students to see themselves as part of a wide virtual community of art-makers?

The data collected included:

- the blog entries written by the students during the project
- semi-formal interviews with three groups of Year 6 students
- interviews with the performing arts teacher and classroom teacher
- notes of observation, including the students' performances of their plays at an assembly
- notes of observations by university students of drama education who were invited to read and post comments to the students' blogs.

Context

The teacher chose as the stimulus *Fifty Ways to Change the World*,[2] a colourfully set out book with each double-page spread involving images and text suggesting a simple action that anyone could do to make a difference in the world. The suggestions range from environmental awareness and actions for conservation to encouraging positive human relationships and attitudes.

The students worked on this project during their weekly drama lesson over the term. The drama teacher asked each group to choose one idea from the book and to find a way to meaningfully communicate the idea through performance to an audience that would include the whole school community at a school assembly. She provided a series of activities in class to help them begin to creatively interpret ideas from the book. They began by creating freeze frames depicting ideas from different pages of the text. After finally choosing one idea to follow, each group was asked to consider the idea presented in the book as the resolution and to develop the complication that precedes the resolution. They then continued to develop their ideas for performance.

At the beginning of each weekly session the teacher would discuss with the students what they should hope to achieve by the end of the session. She encouraged students to consider particular dramatic elements to enhance their performance including tension, sound, and focus. While students rehearsed their performances the teacher roamed around each group to observe their progress, and when necessary provided suggestions and feedback. Each class included 'share time' when groups showed each other their work in progress. Classmates provided feedback so that the performances were peer-directed and not just teacher-directed. Students were asked to note opportunities for improvement (they called them OFIs), which they could then consider when next rehearsing their scenes. When the scenes were completed the class discussed ways to link all the scenes together. Volunteers were invited to write a basic narrative to link the scenes and introduce the performance. By Week 8 the class was ready to perform *How to Change the World* for the whole school assembly.

The teacher also discussed with the students the importance of reflecting on their processes as they created theatre. She asked them to consider their group work and their performance making, providing them with questions for reflection:

- What is going well?
- What needs improvement?
- What questions do you have?
- What are the issues?

They were introduced to the practice of blogging and instructions were also posted on their class blogs. The drama teacher had also briefed the classroom teachers in the project and blogging process, and they agreed to provide time for blogging in class after the drama session. The classroom teachers were to focus on the students' reflective writing and thinking strategies during this time. Laptop computers with wireless internet access were available for students to use in class. The students were encouraged to read the blogs of other groups and post comments.

Reflecting and the blog medium

Pausing to reflect provides an opportunity for sustaining the moment in the normally ephemeral and short-lived drama experience. Writing a journal or a blog creates a more tangible record. Students need to reflect on their processes and thinking in order to learn from their experiences and this can positively influence the way they approach tasks in the future. In this project the students were artists creating performance, and so needed to be aware of the artistic elements that they have to work with and the artistic choices they can make. Finding time for reflection was as important and challenging as providing the means, according to the classroom teacher interviewed for this project.

> In general we don't do enough reflecting in schools because we try to fit so much into one day that you don't spend time just reflecting upon and evaluating what you have done. We are trying to do more of that in Years 5 and 6 anyway so the blog fits in perfectly.

The blogging process provided the Year 6 students with time, space, and a purpose to reflect as they posted their reflections into cyberspace for the world to read. The first blog postings tended to be short, simple statements of what was done:

> In our drama session we had to get into a group of four or five, and act out something from a book called how to change the world. I think we are doing really well, we are nearly finished our first scene. See ya.

Jan Deans, John O'Toole, Jo Raphael, and Sarah Young

Some students did not move beyond simple statements, while others wrote blogs that increased in complexity. They reflected not only on what was done, but what was yet to be done. They considered the dramatic elements and the theme of the performance, and the ways they were endeavouring to communicate their message to their audience. They reflected on their group work and processes, and what was working and what was not, and the factors that inhibited the progress of the performance making.

> Last week was a pretty productive session for our group, beginning the development of our first scene … We organised parts and who is going to bring in sound effects. Myself and James are going to be loggers, while Mark, Carla, and Megan are kind of like environmentalists but not as serious, they just argue against logging and explain the benefits of trees. But it was a shame last week because a group member was away. Moving on to this week, today, we had all of our group members here! Woohoo! We started on development of the second scene and James brought in some chainsaw sound effects and noises of trees falling. Again, we had a discussion with all of the group members and clarified parts. We basically have our whole act thought of, but it needs a *lot* of rehearsing next week … Our group has to work on our freeze frames (which are really sloppy), voice projection, and blockage of other group members. Thats about all that i have to say for this week so i hope to talk to you soon (Adam, who thinks drama is awesome!!).

These Year 6 students, like so many students of drama, had been used to writing reflective drama journals, typically in five or ten minutes at the end of their drama class. Students can resent the loss of drama time when it is expected that they stop the practical work and start writing. With the agreement of classroom teachers, students were provided with the opportunity to do their writing back in their regular classrooms, either in the class time immediately following a drama session or a day or two later, depending on the availability of a computer and internet access. The drama teacher described the challenge of getting students to write during drama and how this changed with the blog writing:

> When they come to drama they want to be active. They don't want to sit and they don't want to write, and I have struggled with this ever since I have taught drama. Finally kids are doing written reflection in their own time, not in their fifty-minute session, and they are keen to do it.

Several of the students preferred to write their blog posts at home. Their classroom teacher explained that all students in the class had internet access at home and commented on the readiness of students to write:

> You would never get kids saying 'Oh I took my learning journal home from drama and wrote a couple of paragraphs'. The engagement is huge when you have got kids writing at home.

I haven't set it as homework at all, but they are doing it anyway. The kids are engaged and motivated to write and to reflect—you can't beat that!

When asked whether they preferred the paper journal or the blog, all students interviewed agreed that writing the blogs was better. There were many different reasons given by the students. Novelty was one:

I found that really cool because it's a new way.

Many appreciated the convenience of blogging and saw a distinct advantage in having more time and personal space to think about what they'd write. This was not something they cared to rush and just get done:

You have more time. You can really think about it.

It is easier because you can type.

With the journals you were a bit rushed, but with the blog you could do it at home and spend ages on it.

It felt better to blog because you don't have like all your friends around you, so you don't feel embarrassed to write up your true feelings and opinions. Just being by yourself when you are writing it feels a lot better.

Some students commented on the ability to be more creative in the blog, and the sense of a wider audience was a significant factor in this. Knowing that the blog would be read by others provided a greater sense of purpose and a motivation to write. According to the students, this sense of audience encouraged them to carefully consider the quality of their writing and reflection.

Blogging makes you put more depth in it because you know other people are going to read it.

It is better because you feel like you are writing to everyone. Everyone can read it ... if you do it in your book no one can see it, but if you do it on the internet everyone can see it.

I thought maybe we could actually be seen, and I thought maybe it could help someone else not just me.

The blogs also provided a sense of importance and credibility to the students' work.

People actually take you seriously. When we're not adults people don't take you seriously, but having our thoughts and people actually wanting to read our blogs is amazing. It feels like you are actually recognised for something that you've done.

Jan Deans, John O'Toole, Jo Raphael, and Sarah Young

Posting comments

One of the benefits of a blog is the ability for others to post comments on the individual blog entries. Comments allow an opportunity for a conversation to take place around the performance making. Interestingly, the students did not post many comments to each other, perhaps because they were able to speak to each other in person. Outsiders who knew about the project were able to comment, including a few parents, this researcher, university students of drama education, and even the president of the state drama education association. These comments tended to be encouraging notes and observations, or sometimes questions to seek more information or simply to provoke thought. Comments were highly anticipated by the students and getting comments proved to be very exciting. The classroom teacher explained:

> They were thrilled when a couple got comments that first time. They were buzzing, they loved it! One of them must have checked overnight I reckon because in the morning they said, 'We got comments!' Then we just put it up on our interactive whiteboard and looked at the comments that were there. They just got a real thrill out of it. That just motivated them to write more and hope that they would then get another comment.

Students also felt that receiving comments provided more incentive to write:

> If you got comments its encouraging and you think, 'Wow, maybe I might get another one' so you write more.

> When you got comments it sort of boosted your confidence.

The downside to this is when students anticipating comments don't get any posted on their blogs. With every student in four classes of Year 6s posting blog entries, it is inevitable that some will not receive a comment. One student explained her disappointment:

> Not a lot of people would comment and that got me down a bit. I wrote every week, but no one would comment. Some did get comments.

In some instances the students shared the excitement of comments. One student received a comment from his uncle in Canada; word quickly spread and it caused a considerable wave of excitement at the realisation of their potential international audience: an uncle in Canada had a small window into an arts education experience of his nephew on the other side of the world.

A community of art-makers

Students were asked how writing the blogs helped them with their group performance making. For many, being able to read each others blogs gave them insights into how others were going about their performance making. The blogs created a community of learners, providing an opportunity for students to learn from each other. This happened when students elaborated on assessment criteria and defined the dramatic elements that they were considering in their performance making as in this blog post:

> The criteria say that we have to have tension. Tension is where your audience is very interested in your acting, like when the hairs on your back of your neck stand up and when you don't know what is going to happen.

One student explained that the blog was good for simply 'Freeing your mind and just getting all the ideas in your head out there'. Others found the blog a valuable aid for remembering:

> I think because you are recording what you did, you can remember the things you did right and wrong, and the stuff you can improve.

Their teacher had asked them to focus on the positives in their blog posts and to avoid making criticisms of others. One student explained the reasoning behind this:

> Ms B wanted us to keep it to the positive because it just helps you stay up. If you sort of said, 'Oh so and so was just mucking around and we didn't get anything done at all!', then you sort of put yourself off as well.

Another student felt that this was one of the limitations of the blogs.

> I felt like it was and wasn't helpful. Like I felt like if I was a bit annoyed in our group because we didn't get much done then we couldn't really like let out our negative emotions because we knew that other people would be reading it.

The students felt that unlike earlier work in drama, this project provided them with an opportunity to create performances that were not only interesting and entertaining, but also had the potential to have a positive impact on their world.

> In the other drama plays we had like five minutes to come up with something, but this has more effort and thought in it. Even though it is short, it is better quality, better thought up.

> It is more fun performing it instead of us just getting up there to say it. Putting it into a fun act is a lot better.

> It captures people's attention. Like seeing those preps faces ... at first we didn't think they'd understand any of it until we actually did our performance and saw their faces. We were amazed. Like you hear adults talking about things all the time, but when we do it ourselves and you think we could be those adults talking about it. Maybe we could make a change. Seeing those faces was so cute because they were so enthusiastic about it.

Jan Deans, John O'Toole, Jo Raphael, and Sarah Young

Untapped potential

For the teachers and students involved in this project the reflection through blogs is a relatively new experience. None of the students had written a blog before this and the classroom teacher was new to it too. He explained the shared learning that was taking place.

> I've been learning with the kids. They were teaching me as much as I was teaching them how to do it.

In interview, all of the students believed that after several weeks of blogging they knew more about it than their teachers. They revealed that they did not realise the full potential of the blogs. Few, if any, had considered the possibilities of uploading images and photos, making links to other blogs or web sites, uploading documents such as scripts, including podcasts, adding pages, and so on. When these possibilities were mentioned the students were very interested and expressed their enthusiasm to put some of this into action in future blogging.

Other areas that were known about, but not used to full potential, mainly due to a stated lack of time, included commenting on blogs of other classes; blogs by other groups of students; the posting of comments from others including the school principal, parents, other teachers, particularly those who had taught these students in previous years; and students in other schools or classes such as the Year 5 students.

For the drama teacher this was the second attempt to engage students in reflection through blogs. She had trialled blogs within drama in a small way the previous year. Engaging the classroom teachers in the blogging process was the key to making this attempt so much more successful. She had created a portal that allowed others to see the processes and thinking that normally took place in the confines of the drama room, and to expose ways that drama processes contribute to the essential learning of the student.[3]

> Another positive is that drama is being seen by all staff, not just as a specialist subject …
> You know it's pretty unique that the arts program was the first to trial this new ICT way of the world. It has changed people's perceptions of the arts and of drama … Drama won't be seen as just another specialist subject any more. That really makes me feel fantastic.

The synergy

There was a powerful synergy at work between the theme of the performance and the blogging of the process. Both were seen as ways of changing or impacting upon the world and having a reach beyond the normal range. The theatre has impact through its capacity to engage an audience and communicate a message, and the blogs have an impact through the power of written communication and the internet with its potential to reach an even broader audience. Both the blog posts and the student interviews showed that the students felt trusted with an important job. They accepted the responsibility involved in the performance making, performing, and the writing about it. The theme they felt was critical:

> Every other generation before us has said, 'Oh well, the next generation will fix it!' and it just keeps going. And now it's time and it will be too little too late if we leave it too long so we've got to try our best.

While the performance had a reach limited to the school assembly audience, writing about the performance on the internet offered students an opportunity to perceive the broadest possible audience for their thoughts, ideas, and suggestions for making the world a better place.

> Writing on the internet is more interesting, and people from all over the world can read it—not just our peers. You feel like it can have an influence on people everywhere in the world that everyone can read it and I am helping to change the world.

The performance itself proved to be potent and empowering, and through this experience these young people came to understand the potential of their theatre to impact on the ways other people think about and act on an issue.

> I felt really enthusiastic and I thought I could change the way people think. To be able to do that makes you feel really amazing and just seeing all these faces while you are performing it kind of said to us well we did that and ... yeah, it can help change the world.

EXEMPLAR

Performance-making, reflecting, and responding for students in the middle years

This performance-making project, suitable for students across the middle years of education, assumes a drama class of around one and a half hours per week, but would work well if done more intensively, say with an hour or two a day over two weeks.

Preparation

At the outset, decide on the theme or topic for the performance. This may be decided by the class, be connected to broader curriculum studies or other learning areas the school wishes to focus on. At the same time the intended audience for the performance needs to be considered. The performance-making, presenting, and reflecting processes are integral to the project and run concurrently throughout. In the case study a specialist drama teacher collaborated with the students' regular classroom teacher so that learning

Jan Deans, John O'Toole, Jo Raphael, and Sarah Young

outcomes across curriculum areas could be maximised. The classroom teacher extended the opportunities for reflective thinking in the blogs. While this is seen as an effective way to work, it is also possible for just one teacher to manage the project.

Table 10.1   A programming map

Performance-making and presenting	Reflecting
Session 1 The performance theme or topic is introduced. This may involve some stimulus materials: a text, newspaper articles, images, song, documentary, news report, artefacts, and so on. This session is for creatively exploring the possibilities of the theme through drama. This may include role-play, teacher-in-role, tableaux, movement, and so on. Students further research the theme or topic.	Emerging thoughts and ideas generated by the class are recorded.
Session 2 Different aspects of the theme or topic are identified by the class. Students are divided into groups* with each to focus on one of these aspects. The groups create a tableau to depict an idea from the aspect of the theme or topic they are working on. These are created to get the performance making started and are shared the with whole class for feedback and discussion. * Consider the most effective way to create the groups according to the class context—friendship groups, random groups, teacher-selected groups, or groups based on interest.	Either the teacher can create a class blog or each group of students creates their own group blog. Good free blogs for students and teacher are available at http://www.edublogs.org If there are multiple blogs, links should be made to all the blogs involved in the project. Students are invited to post their individual reflections on the process on the blogs. Reflect on: • the theme of the performance • early ideas for the performance Opportunity for blogging may be provided in English/literacy time. Students can also blog outside of school.

Table 10.1 (continued)

Performance-making and presenting	Reflecting
Session 3 Groups continue to explore their aspect of the theme or topic. They create a scene or series of scenes that will meaningfully communicate their ideas. Parameters of the group performance are set (for example, each group's performance should be no more than five minutes in length).	Reflection on blogs in group work and performance ideas: • What is going well? • What needs improvement? • What questions do you have? • What are the issues? Encourage students to record any research on the topic or theme, and make links on their blogs to relevant websites. Students could also consider the possibilities of uploading images, making links to other blogs, uploading documents such as scripts, including podcasts, adding pages, and so on.
Session 4–6 Classes begin with some whole class exercises to introduce or remind students of the dramatic elements such as tension, sound, space, and focus. Groups continue to work on their scenes, remembering to take these dramatic elements into consideration. A share time is provided during each class for each group to present their work in progress and provide for teacher and peer feedback. The class and teacher work together to decide the assessment criteria for their group performances. They are asked, 'What do you think it is important for students at your level to be able to achieve in this performance-making project?'	Reflection in blogs continues as above. Students are also encouraged to post comments and questions to other groups through the blogs. The assessment criteria decided on by the teacher and class is uploaded to the blogs. Other interested outsiders are also provided with details of the blogs and encouraged to read them and post comments and questions to the students. This may include other teachers in the school, students in other classes, and parents.

Jan Deans, John O'Toole, Jo Raphael, and Sarah Young

Table 10.1   (continued)

Performance-making and presenting	Reflecting
Session 7 The class discusses ideas for linking the scenes together for performance. This might involve writing a basic narrative to link the scenes and/or the use of movement, sound, music, or song. Volunteers are invited to work on the linking device.	Student reflection on process and thinking continues to be recorded in the blogs. Different creative thinking strategies could be introduced to encourage reflection such as De Bono's coloured hats.
Session 8–9 Rehearsal of scenes continues, including a whole class run through of performance with linking.	Reflection of final rehearsal and thoughts leading up to the performance.
Session 10 Performance for an audience that may include other classes or the whole school assembly.	Reflection on the performance in blogs. Interested outsiders are also encouraged to blog their comments on the performance.

Challenge

Create a partnership with a teacher and class of the same or similar level in another school. This could be a school nearby or in another part of the world entirely. Work together on a similar project, and read and comment on each other's blogs. If the other school is local it may be possible to get together for a combined performance. If this is not possible the classes could exchange video recordings of the performance and feedback can be provided through the blogs.

Activities beyond the case studies

Planning activity: develop a movement-based workshop exploring the natural world for upper primary students.

Sharing: bring a sample activity to conduct with peers for in-class sharing.

Reflective activities: brainstorm and develop a range of reflective media and tasks for application in primary school settings.

Questions for students to consider

1   How can we best encourage students to reflect on their practice as art-makers?
2   What questions can be posed?
3   What are the conditions that can be established and what tools may be drawn on to facilitate this reflection?
4   What are some of the questions that arts educators can ask of themselves when reflecting on their practice?
5   There are various roles that teachers can take when working with students in creative art-making. What are some of these roles and what are the likely effects of these different roles for the students and the creative process?
6   What are some of the challenges and opportunities presented to arts educators when educating the digital native generation?
7   What are some ways that we can engage our digital native students in artistic processes?

Conclusion

The nature of the experience of dance and drama as a formed and performed art has been explored in this chapter. Through an exploration that has taken the reader from preschool dance to middle school blogging, teachers are given the opportunity to learn about the art forms and how they are interpreted in educational settings. These case studies present evidence that creative expressive body activity provides teachers and students with a form that lends itself readily to exploration, appreciation, representation, and reflection. Many educational outcomes have emerged as meaningful, including the development of creative thinking and problem-solving skills, with students being given the opportunity to take risks and take responsibility for shaping their learning through art-making.

The co-creation of knowledge between teachers, students, and sometimes families who join together as partners in learning, presents a framework where the teacher is not only the leader but also a participant and sharer in the learning process. The overarching peda-gogical construct that supports this framework is the development of reciprocal and positive learning relationships where teachers establish quality learning dialogues through sharing their knowledge, and modelling their passion and enthusiasm for learning through the arts.

Key references

Carroll, J., Anderson, M., & Cameron, D. (2006) *Real Players? Drama, Technology and Education*, Trentham Books, London.

Jan Deans, John O'Toole, Jo Raphael, and Sarah Young

Carroll, J. & Cameron, D. (2003) 'To the Spice Islands: Interactive Process Drama', *Fine Art Forum*, 17(8).

Davies, M. (2003) *Movement and Dance in Early Childhood* (2nd edn), Sage Publications, Thousand Oaks, California.

Davis, S. (2006) 'Cyberdrama and Potential for Youth Engagement', *Applied Theatre Research*, Number 7, 2006 retrieved 24 April 2008 http://www.griffith.edu.au/__data/assets/pdf_file/0005/52907/davis.pdf.

Greene, M. (1992) 'Texts and Margins', *Harvard Educational Review*, 61(1), 1–18.

Guidici, C. & Rinaldi, C. (2001) *Making Learning Visible: Children as Individual and Group Learners*, Project Zero, Harvard Graduate School of Education, Cambridge, Mass.

Hanna, J. (1979) *To Dance is Human: A Theory of Non-verbal Communication*, University of Texas Press, Austin.

Laban, R. (1971) *The Mastery of Movement*, Plays, Boston MA.

Prensky, M. (2001) 'Digital Natives, Digital Immigrants, Part II: Do They Really Think Differently?', *On the Horizon*, 9(6).

Taylor, P. (2000) *The Drama Classroom: Action, Reflection, Transformation*, Routledge/Falmer, London.

Wright, S. (2003) *The Arts: Young Children, and Learning*, Pearson Education, Boston, MA.

Wright, P. & Rasmussen, B. (2001) 'Children and Drama: Knowing Differently', in M. Robertson & R. Gerber (eds), *Children's Ways of Knowing: Learning Through Experience*, ACER Press, Melbourne.

Notes

1   A multi-user blogging environment—http://vineblogs.net was set up as part of the VINE Project by Drama Australia, the national association for drama and theatre in education, to provide an opportunity for the sharing of performance-making processes among drama and theatre students through the writing of blogs.

2   First published in Great Britain in 2004 as *Change the World for a Fiver* by Short Books Ltd, London. This edition was published in Australia by Pilot Australia in 2005, and it was produced for distribution to students with the support of the Victorian government.

3   The Victorian Essential Learning Standards offers a whole school curriculum-planning framework through three core interrelated strands of physical, personal, and social learning; discipline-based learning, and interdisciplinary learning that includes ICT and thinking processes.

PART THREE

Integrating and Learning Through the Arts

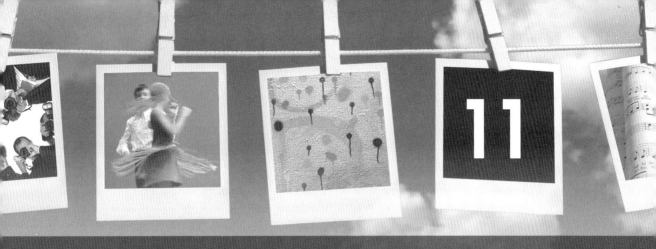

Integrating the Arts: A *Warm Bed* for Student Learning

Chris Sinclair, Neryl Jeanneret, Andrew Swainston, and Marnee Watkins

Chapters 11 and 12 deal with ways in which the arts can be differently situated in the curriculum. In Chapter 11, the two case studies provide a wide-angled and a close-up view in contrasting examples of arts-based work that bring together a number of arts disciplines. In the Frida case study, Chris Sinclair and Neryl Jeanneret each take an active participant's view of a multi-arts workshop for pre-service primary education based on an arts-rich picture book about Frida Kahlo. Sinclair and Jeanneret present the case study as an open-ended invitation to primary educators to consider the use of challenging and rich materials for multi-arts collaborations in their schools. The second case study re-introduces the readers to Julia Reid and her Year 3 and 4 students. They welcome a large cohort of university students, enrolled in an 'Integrated Arts' subject, into a school–university partnership focused on the creation of an arts festival in which all participants explore a range of artforms in the production of an event for a public audience. The chapter is bookended with a discussion about the principles that inform arts education across disciplines, and a consideration of the question of what can be gained when a number of artforms are brought together in a primary school context.

Introduction

Chris Sinclair

> An integrated arts project offers an opportunity for collaborative group work and
> problem-solving. It is a warm bed for developing effective communication skills; valuable
> and essential in our professional lives. So how do we involve individuals like the boy with
> the mask, capable on his own, running ahead of everybody else, or Evelyn, struggling on
> her own, running behind and wishing she were part of a group? I think in our planning
> and implementation, we as teachers need to notice this as well, and try to create lots of
> opportunities and entry points for all individuals to be involved with each other. What is
> a parade without people, without lots of people working together and enjoying it? (Sue
> Wong, integrated arts student)

The nature and practice of integrated arts raises many questions. Surprisingly, the
least contentious may be the question of definition. Certainly, there are differences in
approach to the terminology. In the US many of the leaders in the so-called integrated
arts movement, for example the Chicago Arts Partnerships in Education and the Arts
Education Partnership, focus on the integration of the arts within the broader 'academic'
curriculum [we've addressed this approach to integration in Chapter 2]. At the other end
of the 'integrated arts' spectrum, in Britain and Australia there is the growing practice of
integrating the arts, not only into other areas of the curriculum, but also across a number
of arts disciplines. In the UK the practice of integrating the arts in schools with the wider
community has become more prevalent through government-initiated, locally managed
creative partnerships programs. Between these two polarities there is a diversity of practice
and a wide spectrum of interpretations of the term 'integrated arts'.

One important 'definition' of arts integration identifies the making of an 'authentic
connection' between two or more disciplines as a key characteristic.

> 'Interdisciplinary education' is defined as education that enables students to identify
> and apply authentic connections between two or more disciplines and/or to understand
> essential concepts that transcend individual disciplines. 'Arts integration' is subsumed
> under this term and definition (AEP 2003, p. 5).

Madeleine Grumet also draws attention to the notion of the whole being greater than the
sum of the parts. 'Integration', says Grumet, 'comes from the Latin word *integrare*, meaning to
make something whole' (Grumet 2004, p. 50). Grumet also reminds us that: 'Arts integration
is an approach to teaching and learning that lives in lessons and the curriculum'.

The purpose of this introduction is to examine some of the key principles that
underpin the use of this term, integrated arts. These principles are based on the centrality
of arts pedagogy and arts practice in integrating the arts and the impact of this approach to
teaching and learning on both learners and teachers and the broader learning community.

Arts-based practice and pedagogy

Some researchers have identified a connection between students undertaking authentic intellectual work, their level of engagement in schoolwork, and their success in standardised academic testing. According to Arnold Aprill of the Chicago Arts Partnership:

> The arts meet those criteria for authentic work in spades, and become an exemplar for the rest of the curriculum … Making art requires students to develop deep understanding in order to represent their ideas to others through the art. Since real audiences will see the work, not just teachers, students are prompted to internalize high standards. And the work itself is an original application. You can't just copy the turkey, because that ain't art. It's just copying the turkey (quoted in Rabkin & Redmund 2004, p. 25).

Many arts educators stress the importance of discipline-based skills in integrated arts practice. With the emphasis comes three questions—just which arts skills need to be developed, how can they be applied across a number of artforms, and who should be responsible for developing those skills? Arts partnerships, where professional artists are brought in to work with teachers and children in school contexts, provide one possible answer to that third question—who provides the skills?

Taylor and Andrews (1993) suggest that the professional artist working with the child provides models of artistic form through which the child can understand and express his or her experiences of the world, and in turn can also demonstrate a growing understanding of art forms.

> The artist … in seeking the form of the creative work, not only attempts to give shape to what rises spontaneously, but in doing so also draws upon a whole range of examples known to that artist through the history of the art form, and indeed of other art forms. *This applies to the innovative artist as well as to more traditional exponents.* David Best … argues that what might appear to rise spontaneously is, in fact, actually determined and only made possible because of our awareness of the art form itself (p. 28).

Peter Abbs also provides a useful framework for the ways in which children engage with arts practice, across art forms, in the school setting. He proposes the 'four phase model of *making, presenting, responding* and *evaluating*' (quoted in Taylor & Andrews 1993, p. 14). Variations of these key phases, with slightly different emphases, appear in many arts curriculum documents in Australia and internationally. In the case studies to follow we identify the two key domains *making* and *responding*, as terms that can apply across all art forms. We have then drawn from a range of curriculum models to create some sub-groups. Within *making*, we have identified the processes of *exploring* and *creating*, and within *responding*, the processes of reflecting and evaluating. *Presenting* is a category that relates strongly to the performing arts and media, but less so to the visual arts. We include it here where appropriate.

Chris Sinclair, Neryl Jeanneret, Andrew Swainston, and Marnee Watkins

Rationale—why integrate the arts in schools?

The arguments for integrating the arts in the primary school cover a wide spectrum of approaches to teaching and learning. For example, an approach to learning based on integrating the arts invites children into a process of learning that involves the senses, the imagination, and personal experience (Taylor & Andrews 1993, p. 10).

Another way at looking at the rise of integrated arts practice is to see both the arts and schooling within a contemporary twenty-first century context. With an era of postmodernist relativism and artistic and cultural eclecticism comes the emergence of the hybrid form as mainstream practice. For many new and emerging artists (both professional and in the primary classroom) the blurring of boundaries between arts disciplines and the deliberate fusion of disparate arts practices occurs naturally. The ready availability of materials, images, and examples provided by internet, CD-Rom, DVD, cable, and free-to-air television is matched by the access to, and facility with, technological devices for contemporary hybrid art making. Haseman (2002, citing Owens, p. 124) describes hybridisation as the 'combination of materials, genres, period references to produce highly eclectic constructions, both in content and form'. Within such a context, it is not only logical that children have the opportunity to engage with integrated arts practice within their primary school education, it is possible that these young artists would naturally gravitate towards an integration of art forms in their own practice anyway.

When the curriculum dictates a single 'arts' strand (as it does in Victoria through the Victorian Essential Learning Standards) in the primary education sector, schools with limited resources often make a pragmatic decision to provide an 'integrated arts program', sometimes without regard to adequate timetabling or the provision of appropriate studio space or access to specialist skills.

Discussion of key principles

Symbolic languages

Each arts discipline employs its own symbolic language—visual, aural, spatial—and these languages are constructed from signs within the art forms' particular code. Some of these symbolic systems cross over into the everyday, and can be easily read and interpreted (for example, use of gesture or facial expression) regardless of any deliberate training in the specific artform. However, like spoken language, the symbolic languages of the arts are culturally specific, can be nuanced or ambiguous.

One of the tasks of the arts teacher in the school is to provide students with an understanding of the particular symbolic languages they wish to work in and provide them with a *vocabulary* that enables them to talk about what they are doing and to collaborate with others in shared artistic endeavours. This vocabulary need not necessarily be only in words—images, sounds, and experiences may also be important. This establishment of a shared vocabulary of practice is especially important in the integrated arts, when students, teachers, and sometimes visiting artists are working across a number of art forms. This may well be the first task in a new integrated arts program or project: to gather and define the artistic vocabulary (both verbal and symbolic) that is shared by all participants. This is particularly important when we consider that some discipline-specific words have very different meanings in different art forms. For example, when music teachers use 'tension' and 'rhythm' in relation to composition, they are referring to very different concepts to a teacher in a drama lesson, looking for 'tension' or 'rhythm' in a performance. Some words do not translate at all; for example, visual artists don't refer to the notion of 'symbolic languages' in the same way that musicians or drama practitioners do.

Moving from the known to the unknown

The collective nature of integrated arts practice is a 'warm bed' for growth as individuals and groups move from the known to the unknown, attempting to learn through a combination of new and existing skills and models of practice while solving the artistic and practical problems. Aprill talks of the 'creative frustration' of collaboration, and suggests that when artists and teachers work together in classrooms, 'they can both grow beyond their comfort zones' (quoted in Rabkin & Redmund 2004, p. 19). Of course, students also encounter the 'creative frustration' associated with working with others in the arts, and they too experience that move from the known to the unknown. Students and teachers learn to tolerate uncertainty and ambiguity as they bring new artistic, practical, and personal elements to bear in unique ways for each new project.

Artistry and learning: skills, craft, and knowledge

Many researchers report on a perceptual shift that happens for the learner, when the arts become a serious pursuit in their schooling rather than a momentary diversion. Notions of 'creativity' or 'critical thinking' are frequently identified in accounts of young people working through the arts. Aprill proposes a useful set of tangible behavioural characteristics and cognitive qualities that are associated with art making:

> The things that artists do all the time are things that kids need to be able to do—forming alternative solutions to a problem with other people, being persistent, adjusting something after you've made a choice, taking responsibility for [a] decision, looking at options (quoted in Rabkin & Redmund 2004, p. 24).

Creativity and imagination

When the UK National Advisory Committee on Creative and Cultural Education Report, entitled *All Our Futures: Creativity, Culture and Education* was conducted, they gave careful

:ration to the concept of creativity, how it might be defined, and what its place might

lucation in the future. They speculated that creativity could be identified by four key characteristics: *thinking or behaving imaginatively; engaging in activity that is purposeful (that is, directed to achieving an objective); generating something original; and generating an outcome of value in relation to the objective.* The Committee argued strongly for the role that the arts could play in the reconfiguring of an entire education system centred on creative and cultural education.

While imaginative acts are not confined to integrated arts activities, the characteristics of the imagination as defined in *All Our Futures* draw together a number of significant threads that have been discussed in this introduction. The Report defines imaginative activity as a process of 'generating something original, an alternative to the expected, the conventional, or the routine' (p. 32). Processes of thinking underpin this. Imaginative activity, the Report suggests, 'is a form of mental play—serious play directed towards some creative purpose'. Note how the following quote can be linked to the earlier discussion of the potential impact of bringing different skill sets, from differing arts disciplines together in an integrated arts project:

> Creative insights often occur when existing ideas are combined or reinterpreted in unexpected
> ways or when they are applied in areas with which they are not normally associated. Often
> this arises by making unusual connections, seeing analogies and relationships between ideas
> or objects that have not previously been related (Robinson 1999, p. 32).

Outcomes and audience: temporary communities of purpose and practice

A public art-based outcome is often associated with integrated arts practice in schools—a production, a festival, an interactive exhibition. The public nature of an outcome requires participants (students, teachers, and possibly visiting artists) to temporarily become art-makers. In order to satisfy the artistic, education, and personal purposes of this outcome, these participant artists need to be mindful of the aesthetic and practical considerations associated with the process of *art-making*, including the selection and refinement of appropriate art materials and art forms, in the context of a future audience.

A public outcome also creates an opportunity for the school community to broaden its boundaries—of classrooms, year levels, and school grounds—to include an audience of peers, other year levels, other teachers, family, and friends to be part of the temporary *arts community* (Gulbenkian Report 1982, p. 157).

About the case studies

This chapter offers two ways in which the 'integrated arts' can occur—in a whole school art-based project, incorporating and integrating the arts, or in a specific workshop where three different art forms are deliberately introduced and are co-taught (ideally by practitioners from each of the disciplines). There are many other configurations of integrated arts practice, particularly when integrating the arts with other 'academic' disciplines. There are many very useful case studies of this kind of interdisciplinary, integrated arts practice. See the reference list at the end of this chapter for some useful starting points.

Entering the realms of possibility: integrating the arts through an 'art-rich' picture book

Chris Sinclair and Neryl Jeanneret

About the research

This is a case study of a single workshop conducted with a group of twenty-five teaching students about to embark on the third cycle of a three-discipline arts program designed to introduce students to the practice of teaching drama, visual arts, and music in the primary school.

This workshop was designed as a multi-arts workshop based on an art-rich picture book. Students in this course are introduced to art-rich picture books as pre-texts for learning and engagement across all three components of their arts program: drama, visual arts, and music (Watkins 2005).

The purpose of this case study is to explore the integrated arts workshop as a possible way of crystallising prior learning and contextualising future learning about the arts through practice and reflection. The art-rich picture book provides the focus for this learning and the conduit. The researchers hope to discover how a workshop designed specifically to provide a range of encounters with arts experience—practice and responding—might assist students in the development of their own understanding of the principles that underpin arts practice

The workshop design had input from specialists across three art forms—drama, visual arts, and drama—and was led by the drama and music lecturers.

Letters to Frida: a practitioner's perspective

It's the beginning of the music cycle for the Bachelor of Teaching students who are doing their core arts study. The twenty-five students move somewhat tentatively into the unfamiliar space—carpeted music and drama studio, newly completed—accompanied by the sounds of the electricians and construction workers putting the finishing touches to the refurbished spaces.

This is Neryl's class. She is the music lecturer and will spend two hours each week for the next six weeks with this group. She and I have decided to diverge from previous practice with this first class, to provide a workshop that is designed to integrate music with the two art forms the students have already encountered in earlier six-week cycles: drama and visual arts.

Chris Sinclair, Neryl Jeanneret, Andrew Swainston, and Marnee Watkins

Planning

We plan to introduce the students to an art-rich picture book about the artist Frida Kahlo, and to work with them on ways of exploring and responding to this 'text' through arts processes. I am the interloper here, the drama lecturer who will lead much of this workshop. For Neryl and me, and our visual arts colleague Marnee, who introduced us to Frida, this is an important forging of practical and theoretical connections between our three disciplines. We are interested in collaborating more closely across art forms in the future.

Making

Creating

'Let's make a circle, sitting on the floor.' We begin simply and playfully. I take the students through a series of preliminary activities designed to establish some core principles for our work together today. We will work imaginatively, and draw on our imaginations to generate new work and new ideas. We will work individually and collectively, and will share through the making of transitory artworks (tableaux that come to life, generating sound, transforming and dissolving), and through reflection and discussion. We'll explore the senses and how to communicate the tangible, the tactile and the tenuous through our bodies, and sound and shape. We'll consider the emotion that attaches itself to objects that are precious and the ways in which different symbol systems are invoked to suggest these emotions to others.

In this first phase of the workshop we imagine a ball that provokes a response (emotional or visceral) and also changes shape and texture. We later find a way to create the shape and qualities of a precious object that might appear in a 'living art gallery'. The activities invite participation and experimentation, and the students respond with generosity and thoughtfulness. There is much laughter, some from embarrassment, some from delight. One group of students, lying on the floor, take the shape of a Christmas beetle; and their twenty-something peers are thrilled as they recognise the shape—a Christmas beetle, and yes, it even makes a sound! There is also silence, as the students consider the difficult questions of process and practice that the workshop raises.

'What was surprising to you, or challenging or difficult?'

I didn't know the sound a Christmas beetle made.

Shape was important, people seemed to feel like they needed to create the shape of the thing they were becoming.

Even coming up with something random that's precious to you and trying to put that into a form and then to actually physically represent that.

Through this introduction, students are creating and making, reflecting and responding. The seemingly simple tasks foreshadow some of the themes and issues present in the picture book, *Frida*. The processes and questions of this first phase lay the foundations for the later work—collaborative practice; developing a working artistic vocabulary that includes music, drama, and visual arts; and sharpening the tools of critical reflection through questions asked.

Exploring

Enter Frida

We introduce the students to the picture book, *Frida*. The image from the front cover is projected on the wall. I ask the students to look at this image and respond to three questions.

'What do you see?'

> Frida riding on a red bird

> The shape of her eyebrows are the shape of her symbolic bird.

'What else?'

> She's a painter, sitting on the bird, but she's not really copying it.

'What do you think?'

> I think the book will be really colourful.

> I think she might have a bit of a connection to the bird. She's painting on the bird and there's wind in her hair

'What do you wonder?'
> *(long pause)*

> I wonder if it's going to be a storybook about Frida and how she started painting.

> I wonder what's in the child's mind. I wonder how it is that one child can paint and another one can't?

> I wonder how she can stay on that bird.

> I wonder if she's happy.

Neryl explains how she transferred the pages of the book into PowerPoint and added music from the soundtrack of the movie about Frida Kahlo. She invites the students to 'read' from the PowerPoint display, in silence.

'I'll leave the book to speak for itself,' she says.

We move into the second phase of the workshop: exploring the story and the images; and the sensual, sensory, and emotional undertones of Frida Kahlo's artwork that are present in this picture book. Students are asked to respond to a single image from the book, in groups, through movement and tableau. Neryl adds music, a melancholy track from the film soundtrack. The students work quickly and with focus. Their work touches on the themes and on the narrative present in the image and implied by the minimalist text. This is an exercise in imagination and empathy, and in transformation. The students see the still image, and negotiate, within their group, how to select and represent an aspect of the page that they wish to respond to. They are working intuitively and having to communicate using a range of forms—words and their vocabulary of practice from visual arts, music, and drama.

The work is enormously varied. Each group has chosen a different way of seeing the text, and has focused on a different aspect of the *Frida* narrative to explore further. There are some common themes emerging, isolation and escape (through flight) for example. Different groups find different symbolic representations to express these themes. In one case it is in the stillness of the child who we recognise as *Frida*, in another, it is the same child reaching out and then turning away. As the students present their tableaux-in-motion, the music is played. I orchestrate the showing, ordering the groups and then suggesting that they let the music guide their starting moment and their finishing moment. The music brings an aesthetic quality to the presentation of the sometimes prosaic device, 'tableau'. In reflecting on this section of our work, students capture the difference in the experience that the music has brought.

> The music was emotion. The music to you is melancholia. All the different groups felt something from the music and they were all really different (Amelia, pre-service education student).

> I think the music really helps. We did tableaux in drama and they felt a bit stilted. It felt like we were doing 'classwork', like 'groupwork', and it was a bit more obtuse, whereas when the music starts you kind of get more into the rhythm, of the pulling of the hair and the wings, and the rocking of the baby, like we *were* portraying something not *trying* to portray something (Susanne, pre-service education student).

Making and presenting

Becoming artists

At the heart of the Frida workshop is the making of a piece of 'living art', drawing on any available *making* and *presenting* resources—musical instruments, props, costumes, large swathes of fabric, space, crayons, and paper—created in the studio by the workshop participants. It is both planned, orchestrated, and spontaneous. It is ephemeral, particular only to the people in the room and to the ways in which they have responded to the previous experiences in the workshop. Each exercise or task within the carefully structured workshop builds to the moment when the structure is opened up, and the teacher as artist, invites the students to co-create an artistic response to a page from *Frida* the book.

When the moment to begin working on this key component of the workshop arrives, I begin to slow down. Talking deliberately (and too much!) I create a verbal sketch of what our artwork might be. The work is 'framed' by delineating one part of the room as our 3D, living picture, cleared of furniture and other detritus. I suggest ways in which fabric can be manipulated to craft an image, and then finally I direct the students towards the different resources and invite them to play. They are remarkably decisive. Some students move towards the collection of instruments that Neryl has laid out. Others explore the tubs containing fabric and costumes placed in another part of the room. Others take up the pastels and coloured paper that Marnee has brought in from the art room. There is purposeful and noisy chaos for some minutes.

The group working on the musical instruments is asked to create an improvised score for our living painting when it comes to life. They work with confidence and surprising cohesiveness. This is their first time in this room and their first shared encounter with music. Two young women have found shawls and another a parasol. They create characters and locate themselves in the foreground of the slowly emerging 'picture'. Others find fabric that blends with the image from the book still projected on the wall. The group seems to know when it is ready to 'make' its living picture. As co-artist, I select from my repertoire of theatre-making tools and introduce some key elements that I sense will help shape our work without crushing the delicate offerings of my co-artistic creators.

'Use the music to guide you, use the sense of other people around you. This might last 30 seconds, it might last a minute, but we'll know when it's over. Perhaps the music will tell us? Choose moments of movement and stillness.'

Then I invite a young woman who has found chimes to make the first sounds to indicate the beginning of our work. For those of us in the room, this artwork is fleeting, but electric. The improvised musical score guides the art-makers who are part of the picture and who are shaping the picture with objects and fabric. There is a fluidity of movement and a heightened sense of purpose—it is an aesthetic moment. When it is over, signalled by a final resonating sounding of the chimes, there is spontaneous applause.

Responding

Quickly, students are directed to the next task, to write a letter to Frida. This is the artistic and personal response to the shared artwork, in preference to discussion, which seems less adequate to capture the range of emotional and intellectual experiences generated through making, watching, and being in an artwork.

> *Dear Frida,*
> *You created till the end, what an*
> *inspiration.*
> *You help us see*
> *Beauty.*
> *Thank you,*
> *Nikky.*

Chris Sinclair, Neryl Jeanneret, Andrew Swainston, and Marnee Watkins

Dear Frida
>   *I saw you today*
>   *In the thick of a dream*
>   *I wrote a poem so I wouldn't forget:*
>   *In the mouth of a bird*
>   *That is a cloud*
>   *Frida swims, gradually, back to herself.*
>   *The wind is lapping at*
>   *The hem of her cotton dress.*
Best wishes
Trist

Dear Frida
>   *You showed us that through*
>   *imagination we can escape our pain.*
>   *Your imagination led you to create*
>   *beautiful artwork, that in turn allowed*
>   *others to imagine – and escape.*
>   *Thank you for sharing your gift.*
Rebecca

Reflecting

Some of the students share their letters, and we talk a little about the possibilities for extensions of this work, into a theatre piece, an exhibition, or into composition. Neryl provides an important paradigm shift and takes the students through the workshop as 'lesson' (see exemplar). They move from artists to teachers, and reflect on the work just passed from the point of view of teachers of the arts. They consider how this approach to the arts could lead them into work in other curriculum areas: in SOSE, literacy, and philosophy. They reflect on how they themselves experienced the art forms within the workshop. One student suggests that it felt like it was 'all drama', another is mindful of the powerful yet manipulative effect that the music had on the work, another wonders how Frida might have felt about her work being appropriated by another artist for their own gain. The workshop concludes as it began, with warmth, laughter, and a real sense of possibility.

Conclusion

In this case study, we explored the use of a particular picture book as the core of a teaching program, and with an emphasis on integrating the arts. Using picture books, particularly those Watkins (2005) terms as 'art-rich', provides a teaching and learning context already redolent with art connections and with endless potential for connections with other learning areas. The carefully chosen picture book also provides the teacher with scope to engage children in broader concepts related to the development of a range of thinking skills and modes of engagement represented in Figure 11.1. Minimal text encourages children to use their imaginations in their interpretation of the way in which the visuals add another dimension to the written word. We chose a picture book about the Mexican artist Frida Kahlo, in consultation with Marnee Watkins (visual arts), who had used the book with her Year 2 class and developed a sequence of drama and music activities. Our intention was to take our pre-service primary generalists through a teaching experience already used (in part) with a Year 2 class that enabled us to respond to questions about young children's reactions to the book.

Figure 11.1   Integrating the arts using picture books: a diagrammatic overview of key characteristics (Neryl Jeanneret 2007)

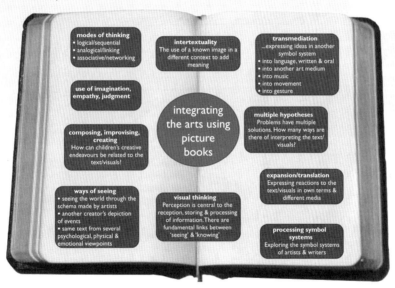

EXEMPLAR

This exemplar takes the form of a lesson outline of the Frida workshop. It is formatted as a table, with columns provided to indicate which art forms are highlighted with different activities. This provides the teacher with an easy way of checking the coverage of a range of art forms in an integrated arts workshop. There are also columns to indicate whether the activity focuses on creating (and exploring), presenting, responding, and reflecting.

(The education students who participated in the Frida workshop were provided with an incomplete version of this lesson plan and invited to complete the Art forms and Domains column themselves.)

Chris Sinclair, Neryl Jeanneret, Andrew Swainston, and Marnee Watkins

Table 11.1 Frida

Grade								
Focus	**Art form***			**Sequence of activities**	**Dimension****			**Resources/notes/links**
	D	M	VA		C & E	P	Re	R	
				Introduction to Frida Workshop					
Engaging with imagined objects	✓	✓		1. Pass the imaginary ball As you pass the ball it changes shape, texture, and quality (smell, appearance, and so on).	✓				
Communication using non-verbal expression	✓	✓		2. Imagine a very small, very precious object that you could have in your possession. Something you would love to have, to look at. Can be from nature. It doesn't have to be valuable, just precious. Now find a partner, show it and give it to them. Then they will give you theirs.	✓				
				Talk about what you shared—about colour, texture, and detail.		✓	✓		
Collaborative, artistic problem solving			✓	3. Find another pair and show them to each other. Choose one, and as a group, using all your bodies, make that object large as if someone is looking at it under a very big microscope. Add—what colour is it? If that colour had a sound, what might it be? If that object suggested a feeling, what might that be? Try to express this through the way you make the object, and the sound. What happens if the feeling changes? Transform the object/sound to reflect this change in feeling.					

*   Art form: D—Drama; M—Music; VA—Visual Arts

**   Dimensions: C & E—Creating and Exploring (Making); P—Presenting; Re—Responding; R—Reflecting

Table 11.1 (continued)

Grade									
Focus	Art form*			Sequence of activities	Dimension**				Resources/notes/links
	D	M	VA		C & E	P	Re	R	
				4. Share with others. Imagine that this is a living, breathing art gallery and when people look at the art, it is alive.					
				1. Let's read the story.					
Linking responding in the arts to critical thinking.			✓	Obviously, many of you will know that this book is about Frida Kahlo and may know a lot about her.			✓	✓	Create a visual display through data projection from the picture book.
		✓	✓	What can you tell just from the picture? What do we see? What do we think? What do we wonder?					Consider the use of music to accompany PowerPoint/or Keynote display; or the reading of the book by teacher.
	✓	✓	✓	(Record these propositions on A3 sheets; for the wall—scribe?)			✓		
				2. Complete the reading of the story—returning to the questions: see/think/wonder as we read.					
				Responding to an image from the text					

Chris Sinclair, Neryl Jeanneret, Andrew Swainston, and Marnee Watkins

Table 11.1   (continued)

Grade									
Focus	**Art form***			**Sequence of activities**	**Dimension****				**Resources/notes/links**
	D	M	VA		C & E	P	Re	R	
Exploring meaning in the visual text through embodiment—responding, through creating, making, and presenting	✓	✓	✓	Let's look at one page—for example, Lonely. Listen to the music.	✓	✓	✓		The presentational element of this task could be emphasised or de-emphasised, depending on the class. For example, parallel presentations or sequential presentations.
				In groups of three or four, can you create a response to this page, starting in movement and concluding with a frozen image—work from how the image and the music makes you feel and what other images those feelings might conjure for you					
Integrating the arts in a response to a visual text.	✓	✓	✓	Painting our own picture					
Collaborative art making				As a whole group, could we make our own response to one page or event in the story? Not to recreate the page but tell Frida how it makes us think and feel—perhaps to show her how we understand what's happening in her life?	✓		✓		Students can select the art form or art forms of their preference for this activity. They can work individually or with others, although as a culmination the whole class works together.

Table 11.1 (continued)

Grade								
Focus	**Art form***			**Sequence of activities**	**Dimension****				**Resources/notes/links**
	D	M	VA		C & E	P	Re	R	
Learning through experiencing and responding to artwork.									
Aesthetic learning				(Second image)	✓				
				Step a: Write a word that you might like to contribute to the picture we will be creating, to place around the edge or somewhere in the painting					
				Step b: Let's create a landscape for this page—let's build a frame and put objects in it. You might like to tell us what they represent, or not	✓	✓		✓	
				Step c: Find somewhere to place your word or phrase					
				Step d: Decide whether you would like to place yourself in the picture, or to give sound to the picture					
				Either:					
				By yourself or with someone else, create a sculpture using your own body, which you might put into our own page. Place yourself in the picture, look around and see if you want to modify anything you've seen that others have done.					

Chris Sinclair, Neryl Jeanneret, Andrew Swainston, and Marnee Watkins

Table 11.1 (continued)

Grade									
Focus	Art form*			Sequence of activities	Dimension**				Resources/notes/links
	D	M	VA		C & E	P	Re	R	
				Choose an instrument, or decide what sound you might like to make—share it with the others. Decide if you want to modify what you've done to fit with the image being created.					
				Bring this all together. Consider incorporating moments of movement and stillness. Be aware of the work of your co-artists, and find ways of responding to them in the art making. Use the music to announce the beginning and the end.					
				Musicians work with your co-artists, responding to the images being created, and create sound for them to respond to.					
				Letters to Frida					Students are invited to respond to the workshop through an extension, open-ended artistic or personal work
Inviting personal response—moving from the imaginative and art making to the personal and reflective.			✓	On an A4 sheet you can write a letter to Frida asking or telling her something—anything you like. You can illustrate it. You may not even use words if you don't wish to.	✓		✓		

Table 11.1 (continued)

Grade									
Focus	Art form*			Sequence of activities	Dimension**				Resources/notes/links
	D	M	VA		C & E	P	Re	R	
								✓	The workshop provides a starting point for a term's work
				Share the letters					Generate a performance or exhibition, incorporating music, drama, and art.
Generating material for further collaborative art making				Discuss the future of these letters—will they provide the beginnings of a play, an exhibition, or a musical score? An integrated arts event?					Or: Explore other curriculum areas, such as: • SOSE • Mexican culture • Spanish language • biography • media—film adaptation.

Chris Sinclair, Neryl Jeanneret, Andrew Swainston, and Marnee Watkins

The making of a festival

Chris Sinclair, Marnee Watkins, Andrew Swainston

> It is precisely the absence of a single solution to a problem that fosters and strengthens a student's critical thinking. Through the exercise of one's judgmental faculties a more adaptive and creative approach to real-life problem-solving may evolve. Few are the situations where we truly have no alternatives. It is to our advantage to own a multiplicity of perspectives; this usually open-ended nature of art provides an ideal medium for the practice of critical thinking.
>
> Constance Baumgartner 1987

In 2006, three University of Melbourne lecturers from visual arts, drama, and music, and 140 of their students from the Bachelor of Education primary subject Integrated Arts, collaborated with a local primary school to develop a three-day festival of the arts, entitled The Rhythm of Life. They worked for ten weeks, variously generating art installations and performances, making preparations for a parade, and collaborating with Year 3 and 4 students on their festival art work, multimedia displays, and performances.

About the research

During the second year of a four-year Bachelor of Education degree (at The University of Melbourne) students get to 'do' integrated arts. In the 2006 integrated arts program, the students, all training to be primary teachers, were part of a university–primary school partnership. This case study takes a close look at the 2006 program; at the way that Integrating the arts was interpreted through this subject; at the partnership; at the very particular challenges for the teaching staff and the generalist primary education students working across three art forms and two institutions; and at the direct and collateral benefits associated with this approach to teaching and learning in tertiary education. In keeping with the broad aims of this book, the case study was designed to identify principles that promote learning in and through the arts in the context of an integrated arts program.

The researchers for the case study were the three university lecturers who co-taught the subject: Chris, the drama lecturer and artistic coordinator for the project; Marnee, the visual arts lecturer and subject coordinator; and Andrew, the music lecturer who took on the role of school liaison. The performing arts teacher at the school, Julia, was pivotal to the project and the partnership, and became a co-researcher in the case study. The university students were invited to share their reflections on their integrated arts experience, and their voices resonate throughout this report.

Planning

The planning for the 2006 integrated arts project began with the reflections of the students from the previous year's project. They valued the 'authentic experience' provided through working on a project with a 'real' outcome. They reflected on risk and safety. The opportunity to take risks, to 'work beyond the known' was valuable because it was something, they said, that they would experience as teachers in a real school situation. On the other hand, some students pointed out that trust and safety were important to them. When asked to take risks, they needed to feel safe with the people with whom they were working.

The three lecturers appointed to run the 2006 integrated arts subject began meeting several months prior to the commencement of the unit. Chris's story tracks the evolution of the early days of planning.

> How did we begin? What was our starting point?
>
> Was it the long intense meetings in the uni café? Talking, drawing boxes with ideas, themes, structures, outcomes, logistics, what-ifs? What if we could create a festival of visual and performing arts, in the black box theatre on campus? What if we invited children from a nearby school to come and spend the day with us to do workshops, watch performance, create and discover art works? How could we manipulate their timetable and ours, to dare to make this dream possible?
>
> Could we base the work around the theme of 'flight'? What did that mean to us?
>
> How would we work together? What are our strengths? Do we have shared understandings of integrating the arts; of arts education; of our roles?
>
> One more meeting, this time at a nearby primary school, with the performing arts teacher, Julia, her colleague, the art teacher, and the assistant principal. Once again, pens flying over paper to capture ideas, to map logistics, to wonder about how it might be possible for 140 university students to work with 90 primary school students to make, to genuinely engage in some kind of shared venture. Gone was the theme of 'flight', and of children coming to 'a performance' at the university.
>
> There was to be a festival, and we would be going to a school. (Chris, drama lecturer)

The making of a festival: making, creating, and exploring

> Week 1 we launched our project in the gym—a large, open space, light and airy with a high ceiling and a vast timber floor; a room devoid of visual and aural stimuli, except for the usual PE apparatus (ropes, long wooden bench forms) and some simple drama, music and art props provocatively hinting to the students at what might be coming. (Marnee, visual arts lecturer)

Chris Sinclair, Neryl Jeanneret, Andrew Swainston, and Marnee Watkins

First class of the semester: the students arrived for the inevitable briefing and introductions. Formalities gave way to discussion and workshop activities: practical, embodied, and artistic problem-solving, the kind of collaborative processes that would underpin each stage of the project. For the students, this was both playful and daunting. Chris asked students to work in groups to respond through sound and body to selected quotes about the arts in education. Marnee asked, 'What do you already know about integrated arts?' *Think, pair, share* ... Andrew talked about what it would mean to work with schoolchildren.

In Week 2 the students visited the school to meet their co-collaborators, and to see where they would be presenting their work. With the Year 3/4 students they participated in a drama-based workshop led by Chris, from the university, and Julia, from the school.

Figure 11.2   The beginnings of the praying mantis

Back at university the students were introduced to some specific art-making skills through workshops: puppetry in the art room, improvisation and storytelling in the drama room, and percussion from latin to hip-hop rhythms in the music room.

All went well until the delivery of the brief—the task outline students would be asked to respond to through their integrated arts work. The brief was a very open document. There were multiple entry points for the students. They could choose to work in small groups in one of the many different art-making tasks, on a technical task or a documentary task, or they could work as co-artists with the primary schoolchildren. The brief also provided for many possibilities of collaborative art-making across three art forms (and multimedia), but described no clearly defined outcomes beyond a 'sculpture' for the parade and a scene from inside the human body, facilitating a school performance.

Burgeoning confidence gave way to anxiety. The lecturers encountered the first major challenge to a project-based integrated arts program: how can you predict the outcome when it is dependent on the creativity, the artistic inventiveness of the collaborators, and their imaginative responses to the unexpected limitations along the way? The certainty that the students craved depended on work they were yet to produce. They had never seen or been in a parade or a play set inside a human body that would look like the ones they would create by themselves or with the primary school students.

Exploring

In the weeks after receiving the brief there was a flurry of activity, especially in visual arts, which was the area where the students seemed to feel most comfortable. It was a 'constructive space', with tangible materials. Groups threw themselves into the making of large puppets, props for the parade, and colourful backdrops. Practical difficulties emerged along the way—how would the very large puppet move? How might it see? Would the 'larger-than-life' characters have a purpose, a story to tell? How would the students link to the theme provided by the school, the rhythm of life? Some students thrived on this precipice of artistic risk and challenge, while some grew to meet the challenges.

> My initial feelings when I entered the school were feelings of excitement and apprehension. Excitement because I felt we were embarking on a big project, and apprehension for the same reason. How are we going to direct the students so that we have a polished production in such a short period of time? The students are so excited and motivated though, so it should be quite an enjoyable experience. (Christy, Integrated Arts student)

Creating

As the date for the dress rehearsal and the festival loomed, the frenzied activity in the art room hit fever pitch. The drama and music studios were also available. They remained largely unused, unless students needed a quiet place to talk or plan. Many of the students felt most comfortable working in the visual arts, of all the art forms. It was the least 'embodied' form and therefore the least confronting to the relative novice. In art, they were introduced to a range of art-making techniques and processes that they could succeed at and directly translate into use for the integrated arts project (and into their future teaching), and they themselves were not on display. Both drama and music required commitment 'in the body'. In this project, the students seemed to find it more difficult to translate the skills and techniques that they had encountered in music and drama directly into their work for the festival.

Chris Sinclair, Neryl Jeanneret, Andrew Swainston, and Marnee Watkins

Figure 11.3 The organised chaos of creating

Figure 11.4 The dragon

In the final weeks of the project, groups committed to realising their ideas in many different ways. They negotiated within their groups and with the lecturers to translate their concepts into artistic product. At the school, the students were confronted with the additional demands of working within the school's timetable, juggling the needs of their assigned groups of children with the practicalities of limited resources and available expertise. Andrew, the music lecturer, spent countless hours beyond the designated project time generating and supporting multimedia resources for the school groups. Students working at the school followed his lead, shaping student composition and images into ComicLife presentations to incorporate into performances, extending their own expertise in the process.

One group's journey to performance reflected the potential for paradigm shift. A small group of students had chosen arts and science as their entry point. They planned an interactive laboratory with larger-than-life scientific experiments for children to try out. The initial idea of students creating exhibitions and installations morphed into artistic constructions for the parade. The group then focused on the idea of a scientist seeking the 'Rhythm of Life'. They embarked on the making of a giant scientist, a two-metre high puppet creature who conducts experiments, and ultimately finds the Rhythm of Life at the primary school on the day of the festival. With this conception, the group had inadvertently solved one of the major artistic questions of the parade—how would it begin and who would lead it? The scientist would lead it, as she pursued her quest for the Rhythm of Life. Would this group of shy young women be prepared to take a prominent role in the parade, generating a small performance to kick off the event, and then lead all the participants through the streets surrounding the school? They were shocked to be asked—they had invented the scientist as a protective device, because they were reluctant performers. With some additional coaching and lots of encouragement (and some persuasion) they agreed, and their extraordinary scientist and her team led the parade.

As the *creating* phase came to an end, students encountered new questions and priorities. They began to consider the real prospect of audience and they discovered the importance of refining their aesthetic—through rehearsal, responding to feedback, and solving practical problems artistically and resourcefully. In performance and presentation, students began to understand the experience of the festival through the eyes of others— the children, the teachers, and the parents—other stakeholders in the arts event. Just as the university students were finding their place, the children at the school, also collaborators in the Rhythm of Life Festival, began to find theirs:

> The whole time everything, everyone, was incredibly busy. The classrooms were filled with energy and purpose and the joy of children engaged in a journey of adventure and learning. Each child had found their niche in the project, and when they needed support or encouragement: the student teachers were there.

Chris Sinclair, Neryl Jeanneret, Andrew Swainston, and Marnee Watkins

Figure 11.5   Our magnificent mantis

Some built props, some sang songs while others painted, sculpted and danced. Others worked quietly at computers creating music, movies, and designing flyers for the festival. It really was the Rhythm of Life. (Andrew, music lecturer)

Presenting the festival

A student story

Beautiful day, lots of excitement, somewhat chaotic but lots of fun. That's how I would describe the Lee Street Arts Festival. I was supposed to be marshalling the Year 3/4s, but once the parade got started it was so full on and there were so many people that I found it hard to work out who I was supposed to be guiding. But that's just what the parade was like, unpredictable but enjoyable. So I just attempted to keep as many people together as I could.

The performers all looked fantastic and did a great job. I think a special mention needs to go to the group of scientists who led the parade the whole way through. They did their best to keep it together and connect each performance, often improvising and always in character …

It was a great experience and I think I'd like to try my hand at organising an event like this in the future. (Ebony, Integrated Arts student)

Figure 11.6   Let the parade begin …

With so many different entry points into this project, the students experienced the festival in many different ways. Each student found their meaning for it through the lens of their own contribution, and their own developing understanding of the arts in a community setting, and of themselves as artists and teachers. The progression from experience to understanding was scaffolded through the process of critical reflection.

Reflecting

Critical reflection was embedded in all of the phases of the project, but also provided the conclusion to it. Initially, the focus was on the personal, with the students considering what they had to bring to the project in terms of skills, interests, and past experiences. As the work progressed and students became collaborators and art-makers, critical reflection targeted *meta-cognition*, thinking about what and how each person might be learning and how they could apply this in later contexts. This was a deliberate and powerful strategy designed to support the practical learning through the arts that was taking place each week. The lecturers framed tasks in terms of questions and provocations, and frequently responded to questions or problems with further questions. There were questions such as:

Chris Sinclair, Neryl Jeanneret, Andrew Swainston, and Marnee Watkins

what do you need to know or what do you need to be able to do, in order to transform this concept into a reality? How can you adapt this learning to your future teaching? What might you do differently next time? What questions does this experience raise for you?

Concluding thoughts: a reflection on the Integrated Arts subject by the lecturers

It's often hard to predict just how a particular experience during an undergraduate teaching experience might influence or inform later practice. Sometimes, the students don't even realise themselves just how a particular experience will impact later. So when we undertake a project like this collaboration with a local primary school, it's an act of faith for both lecturers and students. We attempt to offer a wide range of opportunities for them to engage as learners and future teachers (and artists), hoping that they will find something that connects either in the present or later, and we ask them to trust us that this daunting and sometimes unwieldy or confusing experience, will translate into useful learning at some time—and often, to their surprise, it does.

Figure 11.7   Carlton has a street parade

THE EXEMPLAR

Based on the experiences of designing and implementing the above integrated arts subject and the project at its centre, the following proposes a broad structure and a set of steps that could guide the development and implementation of an integrated arts project at the university or primary school level.

Pre-planning

The design and shape of the arts project

a   *Identify* the core team who will work on developing the program.

b   *Decide* on the project. Clarify the outcome. Identify who will take part and how will the work unfold—in class, through the curriculum, with visiting specialists, and so on? Decide who the audience for the work will be and what their involvement might be during the project.

c   *Consider* what art, what experiences, and what learning are at the heart of the project. Be guided by your available resources, the interest and experience of your team (and your participants), and what learning you think is most needed for your students and within your curriculum requirements.

d   *Conduct* a space and resource audit: What resources are available and possible (can be sourced, made, invented, and so on)? What are our spaces—literal, figurative, imaginative, artistic—for working in, learning through, reflection and cognition, collaborating, sharing, and completing the artistic 'contract'?

e   *Responsibilities*—if there is a team working on the project, allocate them, based on skills, experience, interest, and willingness. Key roles include: artistic director, project manager, resource manager, partner liaison, and teacher/artist.

This preplanning phase may take place some months prior to the project, especially if there are staffing, resource, and curriculum considerations.

Step 1: Making (exploring)

a   An artistic brief for the project
The brief performs a number of key functions. It can ensure that the project team are all 'on the same page'. It can be used to communicate what the project is about to visiting artists, potential partners, or key stakeholders. It may also be used to inform the participants and to invite them into the project. For primary school students, this may not be necessary—depending on the level of autonomy and responsibility you are aiming for with the students.

Chris Sinclair, Neryl Jeanneret, Andrew Swainston, and Marnee Watkins

b   Groups

If the students are to work in small groups, now is the time to allocate them. Give careful thought to how this will be done (for example, random selection, student-selected friendship groups, teacher-selected groups, or student self-selection through interest in a topic, task, or skill).

c   Aesthetic experiences

Provide students with a range of aesthetic experiences to induct them into the artistic possibilities of the project. This could involve arts-based workshops that provide new skills or new insights into the themes or concepts, plus examples from film, video, artwork, or live performance. Introduce principles of symbolic languages of the artforms, and begin to build a shared vocabulary of practice.

d   Relationships

Begin to build collaborative relationships. Ensure that students know each other and are beginning to learn to work together through collaborative arts making and reflecting on group processes.

Step 2: Making (creating)

Encourage and support playfulness and experimentation, leading towards arts making, in the following ways:

a   Look out for strengths and weaknesses in the groups. Encourage leadership and individual and group initiatives.

b   Ensure that students have the appropriate skills, knowledge, and understanding to be able to work with the brief. Find ways to introduce new skills and information through the students' collaborative practices.

c   Find a balance between time and space for imaginative exploration and structured time during this phase. Provide students with set goals to achieve at the end of a period of time, or schedule reporting back time at the end of a session. Provide checklists to help the students to structure their time.

d   Make sure that the working space reflects the students' needs and provides a range of sites of exploration.

e   Consider any modifications and adaptations to the brief based on any new information—about the students and their capacities and interests, about the audience and the exhibition/performance context.

f   Provide time and opportunities for critical reflection.

Step 3: Making and presenting

In this phase, there is a process of synthesis, as students move from exploring and generating ideas to committing to the outcomes, to taking responsibility for their own work as individuals and within their group. The work moves from being inward looking—what can we make and how can we make it?—to what will this look like to others, how will this be received, and are we communicating our ideas and purpose clearly? Does our work reflect our intentions? Are we ready? What more do we need to do to be ready?

Some strategies/activities to promote problem-solving and aesthetic engagement during this phase:

a   *'Dress rehearsal'*—enacting as many components of the event as possible, working through both the *practical/logistic* elements and the *performative/exhibition* elements (for example, practising assembly and disassembly, changeover between small groups, working with props, costumes, technical elements—DVD, data projection, audio).

b   *Becoming the audience*—inviting students to act as the audience for their peers, to provide feedback, support, and questions; inviting students to stand in the shoes of the audience to view their own work.

c   *Planning for the day*—groups to prepare a readiness checklist for their work on the day, including timeline, task allocation, and things to remember—props, costumes, and so on.

d   *Teacher feedback*—tangible and constructive feedback to groups and individuals (personally, via email, or notes)—with sufficient time for them to respond if last-minute changes are required.

Step 4: Responding (reflecting)

For the arts project to engender the skills of critical reflection the teacher needs to incorporate activities or strategies within each of the phases of the project so that children experience, develop, and practise acts of critical reflection.

a   Key questions used throughout the project.

The teacher challenges students with questions to prompt reflection on their own work and the progress of the project:

–   What do you know?

–   What are your experiences at this point?

–   What have we done—what has been the purpose of our work in the past week(s)?

–   What have we achieved?

Chris Sinclair, Neryl Jeanneret, Andrew Swainston, and Marnee Watkins

> – What needs to be done next?
> – What are your questions at this point?

b   Key questions for the conclusion of the project.

While critical reflection is embedded in the process, there is a moment at the conclusion of a project where time can be taken, by teachers and students, to re-consider and review just what it was that they created; what meanings it generated for themselves and for their audiences; and what they could learn from it for themselves as people, as art-makers—and in our case, as future teachers of the arts. Generating the time and space for this guided reflection represents a critical opportunity for learning and for new meanings to be constructed for both students and teachers.

Marnee's last questions

Through this project the students were provoked to imagine new ways of teaching by showing them learning spaces quite different from those to which they're accustomed. We hoped they came to the realisation that teaching and learning don't go on only in specialised spaces.

The project also raised some questions for me as the teacher of these soon-to-be teachers:

- Exceptional teaching can occur in any space. However, the way in which these spaces are managed can enhance and encourage the learning or hinder its effectiveness. How do we best manage the range of teaching and learning spaces for optimum learning in the arts?
- How do teachers (we) meet the challenges of space (for example, finding space in the curriculum/busy week for the arts)?
- How do we use space to imagine new ways of teaching?

Activities beyond the case studies

Curriculum development—form a small group drawn from a range of art-form interests or specialisations.

- Design a unit of work that:
  - begins with an art-rich picture book
  - has three possible directions (learning or outcome) and explore each of them.

- Design a project plan that:
  - begins with an art-rich picture book
  - is used across all year levels
  - links to a curriculum standard document (for example, VELS, New Basics)
  - has a public, multi-arts outcome.

Questions for students to consider

1   What arts-based skills (and what level of skills) do primary age students need in order to practise arts meaningfully?
2   How do they come to understand the context and the traditions to which they belong?

Conclusion

In both integrated arts case studies, learning through the practice of making art is central, as is a creative, collaborative process and shared outcomes for the work. Students and teachers develop a shared vocabulary of practice, based on the art forms they are working in and the contexts they find themselves in. Both students and teachers develop proficiencies at navigating a range of symbolic languages, determined by their interests, aptitudes, the needs of the project they have embarked upon, and driven by the need to communicate with fellow collaborators. The facility with a range of symbolic languages is enhanced by experience. The experience informs the symbolic languages. In this way the art-making process becomes a medium for communication—students learn to communicate about their artworks and through them. Meanings are conveyed verbally and symbolically. In reinforcing this point, Swanwick (1988, p. 48) states, 'The arts as ways of knowing are as potentially powerful as any other form of human discourse and they are just as capable of contributing to the development of the mind on a conceptual level'.

An integrated arts project or workshop initiates an intricate web of artistic and practical problem-solving. In the *Rhythm of Life Arts Festival*, students worked beyond the known, with some embracing risk-taking and personal growth. In their artistic work, students identified and refined existing skills and developed new skills to support a variety of art-making or technical processes. Students were also encouraged to solve practical problems through artistic means and collaborative processes. In the *Frida* workshop, the main activity was an open-ended response to the experience of reading and exploring the picture book. Students discovered ways of responding to a new art experience through a range of art forms, individually and collaboratively. In addition, by offering opinions about Frida's life beyond what is presented in the book, the students as a group formed multiple hypotheses based on the evidence at hand—another example of thinking beyond the known.

Moving from the known to the unknown is not without its difficulties, particularly in project-based work. Individuals can experience frustration with others in their group, with the project, with the teachers, and with themselves. In the arts festival case study, the most effective resolutions to frustration emerged when groups and individual students deliberately and constructively chose to engage with the processes of critical reflection.

Artistry and learning: skills, craft, and knowledge

Questions of aesthetics have an important place in an integrated arts program. For teachers and artists, the balance between maximising student input and ownership, and building the necessary skills to achieve both a collaborative and aesthetic outcome can be very challenging. The availability of resources is also a factor. Time devoted to skills building and the acquisition of craft knowledge is time that may otherwise be spent in creating artworks and polishing performance. Accessing expertise across a number of artforms may not be possible. In the *Frida* workshop, students worked with a drama professional and a music professional. The final outcome of the workshop concentrated on dramatic and musical responses, and included a less structured and less informed approach to the visual arts, dance, or multimedia.

Despite this potential limitation, the *Frida* workshop revealed a number of ways in which students engage in aesthetic learning in an integrated arts workshop. They were able to explore the art-rich picture book through the arts, and ultimately they were able to construct a number of aesthetic responses to the text, which in turn generated a whole group aesthetic learning experience.

Outcomes and audience: temporary communities of purpose and practice

'Real' and aesthetic outcomes

While it is by no means essential that integrated arts work focuses on a public outcome with an audience of interested 'stakeholders', it was the cornerstone of the approach taken in the second case study. Such a structure implies individual and collective problem-solving, both practically and artistically, and, in a corollary to this, individual and collective responsibility for fellow participants and for the outcome. While there are some shortcomings in creating a very open structure with multiple entry points, this framework is a catalyst for student ownership of the work, and, subsequently, for shared responsibility between students and teachers or lecturers as they form temporary communities of purpose and practice.

A consideration of time and space

The use of space figures prominently in these case studies. The nature of the literal space can impact on the work in very practical ways but also subconsciously. Working in an inappropriate space, or one in which students feel 'exposed' or vulnerable, can impede progress. In the *Rhythm of Life Festival* project, students sought out the 'safe space' of the visual arts studio which they associated with a clarity of purpose and the opportunity to apply oneself to literal, hands-on tasks. The drama room or the gym was an open space, and as such offered the exploration of infinite possibility, especially in guided workshops run by lecturers, but an unstructured and unsupported space when students were invited to work there independently.

Students had to redefine their understanding of their artworks and their performances when moving from indoor space to outdoor. The location demanded a paradigm shift, and both aesthetic and practical problem-solving. In the Frida workshop, students entered a new music/drama space. They were surrounded by musical instruments and had access to technology of sound and vision. However, the space did not quite lend itself to the artwork the students were invited to do. The lecturers referred to making visual responses to the work, but provided only crayons, coloured paper, and the occasional glue stick and string. They wanted students to engage across three artforms, but didn't want paint spilt in their new carpeted space!

Providing space (and by implication, time) to allow for the exercise of the imagination can be critical in project-oriented work. Students need to carve out time and space for the imaginative exploration of possibilities. It's the task of lecturers or teachers to identify when this was appropriate, and to generate the literal and the imaginative space to become art-makers and collaborators.

Key references

Arts Education Partnership (AEP) (2003) *Creating Quality Integrated and Interdisciplinary Arts Programs: Report of the Arts Education Partnership National Forum, September 2002*, Washington, DC.

Baumgartner, C. (1987*)* 'Arts in Education', in *Teachon: Quotes*, retrieved from http://www.teachon.com/zizi/quotes/subjects/arts/pages/arts.htm.

Grumet, M. (2004) 'No One Learns Alone', in N. Rabkin & R. Redmond (eds), *Putting the Arts in the Picture: Reframing Education in the 21st Century*, Columbia College, Chicago.

Gulbenkian Report (1982) *The Arts in Schools: Principles, Practice and Provision*, Gulbenkian Institute, London.

Haseman, B. (2002) 'The "Creative Industry" of Designing a Contemporary Drama Curriculum', *Melbourne Studies in Education*, 43(2), 119–29.

Chris Sinclair, Neryl Jeanneret, Andrew Swainston, and Marnee Watkins

Rabkin, N. & Redmond, R. (eds.) (2004) *Putting the Arts in the Picture: Reframing Education in the 21st Century*, Columbia College, Chicago.

Robinson, K. (1999) *All Our Futures: Creativity, Culture and Education: The Report of the NAACE Committee*, National Advisory Committee on Creative and Cultural Education, London.

Swanwick, K. (1988) *Music, Mind, and Education*, Routledge, London.

Taylor, R. & Andrews, G. (1993) *The Arts in the Primary School*, Falmer Press, London.

Watkins, M. (2005) 'Magical encounters with "art rich" picturebooks', *ARTicle, 7*(3), 15–19.

Winter, J. & Juan, A. (2002) *Frida*, Arthur Levine Books, New York.

Teaching Through the Arts

Robert Brown, John O'Toole, Pam Macintyre, and Richard Sallis

In this chapter the visual arts, drama, and children's literature specialists are brought together by a visual artist, a child's literature specialist and two drama educators. Together they consider through the theoretical introduction and the case studies, how the arts can provide a vehicle for learning in other areas of the curriculum. Robert Brown and Pam Macintyre's case study revisits the Early Learning Centre (the site of the dance case study from Chapter 10) and unfolds stories from a language-rich interdisciplinary project led by a number of discipline-based specialists employed by the centre. Richard Sallis's case study looks at young children, from ages 5 to 7, and the work of the specialist drama teacher engaged to link the drama program to the broader school curriculum. Dinosaurs, magic, and weather suggest the range of possibilities of this approach to teaching through the arts.

Introduction

Robert Brown and John O'Toole

The arts are a rich way to teach, or help in teaching, right across the curriculum. You will probably have realised this by now from the earlier case studies, and particularly from Chapter 4. If you can teach right across the multiple literacies, you can teach anything! This ranges from as little as providing a way into another key learning area, or some extra engagement and motivation, right through to a virtually complete pedagogy. Something between these has already be demonstrated in the Under the Sea case study in Chapter 9, where the teacher explicitly uses visual arts to teach numeracy and maths, literacy, science, and technology.

In Chapter 1 we demonstrated how the arts naturally motivate students to learn, because they are closely connected to both creativity and play, both of which are naturally pleasurable and satisfying, so if you can tie your curriculum content into some artistic activity, you are tying it in to pleasure and satisfaction for the students and therefore yourself! However, there is much more to it than that.

The arts are primal ways in which we organise our experience. As soon as we are born we experience the world—everything, through our senses. Primarily, that means all the sense data that we receive has to be organised and ordered into some kind of meaning, so that we can cope with it and know how to respond. This we do naturally in a holistic fashion, with our cognition, our emotions, and all our bodily functions working together to make sense out of the sensory data. We have suggested that the arts are in fact symbolic languages. Sounds and utterances we shape into words and sentences, as a way of naming, ordering, and using specific kinds of sensory data—and we call it language. Physical, tactile, and kinaesthetic data too, as well as sound and words, can be further harmonised into patterns and sequences that have usefulness and meaning for us, and are also pleasurable and stimulating. We call these the arts. Like all symbol systems, they can also be communicated to others, still embodying some of the emotions and some of the sensory stimuli:

- sounds and the things we make sounds with—we shape into music
- movement and our bodies—we shape into dance
- the images we see, and the media we use to make them—we shape into visual, plastic, and media arts
- words, and utterances we use for the most basic and functional message-giving that we call language—we shape into stories and poetry
- words and gestures, and the extraordinary capacity we have to imagine something there that is not there (pretend or fiction)—we shape into drama and theatre
- the multiple senses we often call on—we shape our experience into integrated arts or use multiple media.

Communicating through the arts, then, is generating types of knowledge that are not new, but experienced viscerally and holistically, through the senses, intellect, and emotions rather than just words and logical ideation. This is sometimes called non-propositional knowledge, because you can't make it wholly explicit through words or numbers. Schools and education systems traditionally have focused almost all their attention on propositional knowledge: cognition in its most disembodied form—the ideas expressed in written language and numeration. They have often actively sought to obliterate the sensory, kinaesthetic, and emotional, and replace them with propositional knowledge cut up into blocks called subjects. It was not always thus. When learning comprised the passing on of received wisdom, much of that learning was passed on through the embodied arts, equally in Western Europe, classical Asian, African and American cultures, and Aboriginal Australia—through singing, poetry, and painting and physical ritual or dance. Then science took over from received wisdom as the basis of acceptable knowledge. The patterns of thought that accorded with abstract logic and logical sequences of thoughts, words, and numbers were privileged, and only those taught. Now in our postmodern, post-scientific age, as we grapple with new understanding about even science itself—relativity and chaos, quantum physics and fuzzy logic—we know we must help our young people to reclaim their holistic ways of knowing, that everything they learn must be given context, relevance, and meaning. This is the deep reason why we invite you to incorporate the arts into much more of your curriculum and practice than the hours they appear on your timetable.

So, we can use the arts as pedagogy for the deepest of reasons (as holistic knowing) or for the shallowest (they are a lot of fun). If you turn back to Chapter 4, you will find many concepts and suggestions that relate right across the school curriculum, and we hope they will give you ideas for using the arts to teach. Here we offer a couple of rather fuller and more specific case studies.

Navigating Symbols: an interdisciplinary arts and language program in an early learning setting

Robert Brown and Pam Macintyre
Teachers: Suzana Zaper, Sarah Young, Louise Saxton and Victoria Ryle

About the research

In the early years, children engage readily with arts and language experiences through playful activities that stimulate imagination, and actively explore the world around them. This case study provides a detailed description of an emergent, interdisciplinary curriculum project that involved twenty four-year-old children and four teachers, who undertook an imaginative journey through a world of pirates, treasure maps, and magic keys over six weeks. The mapping through a responsive, child-centred pedagogy of the rich symbiotic relationship between language and arts experiences reveals that relationships, engagement, teacher knowledge, an ability to listen to, and imagine with, children are fundamental to this exploration of how learning can be co-constructed through topics that emerge out of children's interests.

The case study is set in an early learning centre (ELC) located in an inner metropolitan city, which provides an arts-centred program for 150 children aged three to five years. Children participate in language-rich, interdisciplinary projects that are supported by one-hour weekly specialist-taught classes in drama, music and visual arts, and book making. The participants are the 'home-room' teacher Suzana Zaper, the drama teacher Sarah Young, the visual arts teacher Louise Saxton, and Victoria Ryle, who has expertise in child-created books.

We collected a variety of research data including:

- dyadic observations of 3 x 1 hour sessions (drama, visual arts, book-creation)
- records of individual interviews with four teachers (4 x 30 minutes)
- photographic records
- teacher journal notes
- artefacts and outcomes of the activities and workshops: reflective artwork, child-created books, and narratives generated in response to the program.

Descriptions of practice, and reflective commentary constructed from the teachers' voices, tell a story of a dynamic and mutually supportive group of practitioners who share a common passion in the power of arts-centred, interdisciplinary teaching and learning.

Beginnings

Navigating Symbols grew out of one child's fascination with the image of 'Jack Sparrow' from a promotional poster for *Pirates of the Caribbean*. From this interest the child constructed a Lego pirate ship and later drew it.

The home-room teacher, Suzana, observed a growing interest in this topic's potential for multi-symbolic representation. Over a period of several days (continuing into weeks), individual children related the theme of pirates to unicorns, islands, maps, messages in a bottle, Captain Hook, and sea monsters. Throughout this time, teachers exchanged ideas and brainstormed how best to develop an interdisciplinary series of sessions that would extend the children's creative expression and culminate in the production of a whole group, illustrated book.

Thus began a journey of imagination rich in language about pirates, such as 'treasure chest', 'anchor', navigate', 'parchment', and barnacles'. Books and videos like Herge's *Tin Tin—The Red Rackham Treasure* and *The Secret of the Unicorn* (1974), the picture books *Tough Boris* by Mem Fox (1994), *Blackbeard* by Victor Ambrus (1982), Margaret Mahy's *The Man whose Mother was a Pirate* (1985), and Pamela Allen's *I Wish I had a Pirate Suit* (1989) were read and discussed, prompting vivid language. 'Obstacles', 'mermaids', 'forests', 'tangled roots', 'gold', 'silver', 'metal', and the idea of keys as symbols of discovery became part of the children's everyday language.

Figure 12.1   Ship drawing

Suzana Zaper's commentary

Suzana recalls being influenced and mentored by a teacher from her beginning teaching years. 'My teacher was a bit of a poet and we have kept in contact. She would email me with the advice: "Be five again and you will know"; that is, you need to be able to transfer yourself back and see the world as always new'.

Suzana typically begins themed sessions with the sharing of verse and rich texts employing complex language. 'Whatever theme we are going to explore I begin with a poem. I might focus on one particular word or expression and go from there.' She notes that the children enjoy such language and use it in their speech. 'It's the beauty and aesthetics of the words that trigger the child to explore language.' She labels herself and the children as 'word detectives' who enjoy new knowledge and share a 'love of words'.

In the Navigating Symbols unit, favourite terms from the stories read to the children were 'parchment', 'navigate', 'hundreds and thousands of blistering barnacles', and 'practically impossible'. Suzana was delighted when a child used 'navigating' as 'navigating music'.

Robert Brown, John O'Toole, Pam Macintyre, and Richard Sallis

Figure 12.2   Music map

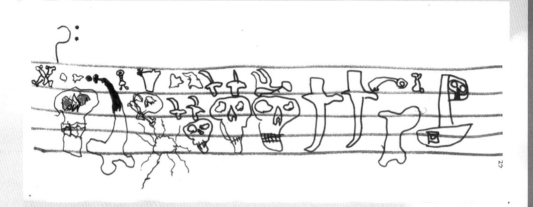

Descriptive language is transferred to other contexts, with the children constantly using and reinforcing new words. For instance, keys are widely used in the homeroom, and Suzana heard one child say, 'use your brain key', and another 'this is the key to the sky door'. Important to the children's development is the opportunity for dialogue: 'We sit down and reflect on what happened during the last hour, or during the day. I say to the children "Let's visualise. Let's meditate on it."' Suzana notes that the teacher needs to 'listen carefully' and notice 'invisible things'. Teachers must 'grab the sparks of interest' and channel them the right way. Drama, visual art, and everyday explorations link language and the arts 'into one, with a strong accent on aesthetics. It works well because children feel things more than see, and the way they say things expresses the depth of their feelings.'

Working with families and co-workers is crucial, as is reflecting every day with the children to reinforce what has been happening and to 'give them a thought to take home, to keep the flame burning'.

Grappling hooks and an empty treasure chest

Pirates and maps had captured the children's interests, so in the drama session Sarah used the group treasure map as the starting point for an embodied and imaginative co-constructed journey.

> Sarah enters the room in character, talking to herself: 'My mother, a pirate, has left, so I don't know what to do. She said I have to be a pirate, but I don't know anything about being a pirate. I've got a problem. I wonder who can help me.'
>
> 'We can. We can help', the children respond animatedly.
>
> 'She left me this', says Sarah, unwrapping a golden treasure box.
>
> 'Open the treasure box!' the children insist.

Sarah draws out a ring of antique brass keys. 'Here is the key to the treasure chest. I'm going to need some pirate helpers. Who wants to come with me?'

'Me. Me. Me.'

Sarah and the children set out on an adventure, deciding what to take, how to travel and survive sea monsters, quicksand, and a sinking ship—challenges that are solved by catching a tram to the docks, using grappling hooks, tightrope walking over shark-infested waters, and befriending the sea monsters. After the adventure of travelling through quicksand and across jagged rocks, the children and Sarah find and dig up the treasure chest. What is inside? Children suggest 'gold coins', 'strawberries', 'a skull', and a 'wrapped up mummy'. To everyone's surprise the chest is empty! Reacting to Sarah's disappointment, one child says, 'I'll give you some of my strawberries'. A spate of offers follows as children present their imaginary treasures to Sarah. Sarah then ponders: 'Why do you think my Mum gave me an empty treasure chest? Maybe she gave it to me so that my pirate friends could share their treasure with me.'

Once the story has come to an end, the children and Sarah return to kindergarten via a 'magical unicorn', a large piece of red fabric on which children are playfully pulled across the floor. Sarah leaves and returns as herself to reflect with the children. 'I want you to think of that story.' A child responds: 'You could dream about that story'. Another says: 'You could do the story at home'. And a third: 'You could make a map of this story'.

In the afternoon session following the drama, the children shared their feelings about the story:

I felt ashamed because my treasure box was full of beautiful things and hers was empty.

I felt like flying on the unicorn, and it was a flame-looking unicorn, as soft as the softest fabric.

I almost wanted to fall into the sea when I was walking along the thin rope across the bridge, because I knew the sea monsters would catch me and be friendly with me.

Stimulated by the drama, the children drew metaphorical keys, such as a 'key to a drawing box'; 'a key that opens people's hearts'; 'a key that opens a castle'.

Sarah Young's commentary

After training as a primary school teacher, Sarah worked in theatre and children's theatre, and now also teaches preschool children. It was the nature of the 'open curriculum' with its focus on the arts and story, rather than performance, that drew Sarah to working at the ELC.

Sarah believes that children learn best through doing and through play. Drama is part of children's play, so Sarah says what she does is to 'harness and put a framework around it'. She believes that the arts are important for offering different ways of seeing the world, for providing for children who may not have the language to express themselves verbally,

Robert Brown, John O'Toole, Pam Macintyre, and Richard Sallis

to communicate through image, movement, and dance. Sarah sees her role as a guide. 'I give them a starting place from where something could go, allow them to go out with huge ideas, and bring them into make a narrative, a story.' Sarah wants the children to 'experience' rather than 'learn', and believes that 'their ideas matter and that there is more than one way of seeing something'. At the core of her drama is language, both body language and verbal language. In Navigating Symbols, all children were able to go on the journey. Children who couldn't verbalise participated with their bodies: 'Physically they were in the boat, and crossed the bridge delicately to avoid the sea monsters'.

Sarah begins the preparation for her sessions with a written story. This planning is vital and involves talking to Suzana and connecting with what the children are learning elsewhere in the program. Sarah took the idea of the pirate and interpreted it as a metaphor for the child. 'Children are risk-takers, adventurers, problem-solvers. So the story is about going on an adventure. I wanted a girl to be a pirate, and an idea about finding treasure evolved.' The girl pirate being on her own positioned the children as the experts in deciding what she should do and where the story might go. The idea of the treasure box came from Sarah's reading of the children's poetry about treasure. The brass keys used in the drama session were an important visual stimulus, but the end of the journey was a surprise to Sarah:

> I certainly didn't know that there would be no treasure in the box. Originally, I was going to have a parrot in the box. The idea of it being empty came from their responses to my question 'What is treasure for you?' Because the answers were materialistic I thought I would challenge that perspective. At the end of the imaginative journey it is important to come back to kinder because emotionally the children are in the imagined world.

Sarah retells the story to quieten the children, who usually draw something they have remembered as a representation of what is important to them. The images and stories are composed into small books and used as a reference in other sessions.

Cartographers, natural treasures, and hidden symbols

Prior to the visual arts session the children knew that they would be making treasure maps for a book. As inspiration for the session, Suzana and Louise collected gum leaves of all shapes and colours for use by the children in a map collage. Louise prepared 'olde worlde' materials by creating tea-stained pages, complemented by gold and silver Chinese Joss paper, coloured pencils, food dyes, and fine brushes. The physical learning environment was also aesthetically stimulating with sensitivity given to colour, texture and light through display of a map of the world, Chinese writing on a scroll, a treasure map under-lit on a light box, an olde worlde globe, an embossed treasure box, children's art work of a large pirate ship, and a book of drawings of keys.

At the beginning of the session, Suzana and Louise led a group discussion in which every child spoke to previously created maps and stories. Louise also shared with the children a map of the Galapagos Islands made by an eight-year-old boy, to introduce the idea that 'we will be cartographers'. Throughout this time, the children sustained a deep interest in their own work and that of others.

Following this, the children created pencil map drawings on tea-stained paper that were later built up with gold and silver paper and gum leaf collage. They were encouraged to verbalise their stories, and to describe their thinking in creating the artworks. Children used words like 'path', 'journey', 'message in a bottle', and 'navigating'. They were also invited to 'hide words and objects' in the drawing and in the binding section of each page, which deepened their imaginative and embodied story making. Alphabetic letters as visual symbols, such as NSEW, became important, and in a drawing of a compass, one child wrote the letter N for the first time. Once the children had finished their precious map drawings, sheets of transparent paper were overlaid for them to trace their map contours. Following the visual art session, Suzana recorded each child's story in preparation for the final book.

Figure 12.3   Map display

Louise Saxton's commentary

Louise is a practising artist who has worked as a teacher assistant, and now undertakes visual art sessions with children from the ELC. Her passions are creating art—'working with young children from the perspective of an artist'—and sharing with them the 'joy of exploring art materials and aesthetic concepts'. She says 'you can be a good artist, but

Robert Brown, John O'Toole, Pam Macintyre, and Richard Sallis

that doesn't necessarily make you a good teacher', and that she is learning from children and other teachers. She sees her role as inspiring the children and also as sharing her ideas, techniques, and the works of artists.

In relation to the Navigating Symbols project Louise drew attention to the significant collaboration among teachers that inspired and made actual an emergent, child-centred curriculum design that built on existing child knowledge of stories, songs, and the world.

Louise believes that 'children learn best when they are interested in something—if it engages them creatively and intellectually'. Louise also notes that 'Children really respond to what other children do', and she believes that children relate well to personal stories from adults and children that make art-making relevant, real, and purposeful.

In relation to language she believes that visual art experiences support the development of 'spoken, material, and conceptual languages of self-expression'. Through art, children explore a specific 'art language' and many become more comfortable to communicate with others. Asking children to tell others about their artworks generates language as does book making centred on storytelling. 'It's amazing how some children create an unrecognisable drawing—what some people call a scribble—but give an elaborate story about a rocket ship blasting off to the moon.'

Book making

A week later, Victoria led a session on book making. This revisited the children's stories centred on the earlier map images and stories created in the visual arts session.

> The children come together in a circle with their precious map drawings carefully wrapped, tied, and placed in the centre. Suzana says, 'Put your hand on your hearts, take a deep breath, relax, and imagine that we are sitting in the sand at the beach. Today we are going to do a book about maps.' Victoria, adapting the classic children's chant, 'We're going on a bear hunt', says playfully, 'We're going on a treasure hunt; we want to find lots of treasure. I'm not scared.' The children slap their hands on their legs in rhythmic reply. At regular intervals, Victoria pauses to invite each child to talk about their map drawings, and to incorporate their responses in the treasure hunt chant.
>
> Children: 'We're going on a treasure hunt.'
>
> Victoria: 'What's this? (With reference to the child's map.) Lots of water! We can't get over it. We can't go under it. We can't go around it. We have to go through it. We have to swim through it! Show me how to swim.'
>
> Children act swimming and breathing.
>
> Suzana: 'This looks like swamp! We can't get over it. We can't go under it. We can't go around it. What shall we do?'

Figure 12.4   Treasure map—mountains (drawing with writing overlay)

Figure 12.5   Treasure map—rainbow (drawing with writing overlay)

Robert Brown, John O'Toole, Pam Macintyre, and Richard Sallis

Children: 'Swim …'

The child who created the map says 'No! There is a big trap door and a spider. But he's just sleeping.'

Suzana: 'Oooh, we must be quiet then.'

Children and teachers act creeping silently through a dark tunnel so as not to wake the spider.

The children continue a map-inspired journey on hot air balloons, through forests, around a giant octopus, trip trapping over a bridge, flying over an angel's garden, before running, climbing, rolling down, and tiptoeing all the way home. Suzana settles them: 'Let's close our eyes and remember the magic.'

Victoria: 'Today we are going to finish our special book together.' She explains that the tasks are to draw obstacles such as trees, bridges, and swamps on to the transparent overlays on their map drawings, and to design and produce the front and back covers of the book. The children readily select which activity they want to do and move to the tables.

At the writing table the children choose the title, *The Treasure Map Book*. They create decorative letters on small pieces of gold and silver paper, with Victoria modelling how to write 'fat letters' and upper and lower case letters. The children are encouraged to visualise letters, and share their knowledge with each other. Victoria encourages children to 'have a go' even when the letter is difficult to form correctly. In such cases she scaffolds letter formation by drawing the child's attention to its composition as a series of shapes. While this is happening, Suzana writes the children's stories on the transparent overlays following their map contours.

Victoria Ryle's commentary

Victoria, an experienced primary school teacher, has specific expertise in literacy and child-created books. For her, book making is 'a natural way to build awareness of books, focus on creativity and the language children bring to the book. It provides a natural way to talk about features of language without children thinking they are being taught.' There is, though, 'a danger' associated with creating books with children if teachers see the reasons for the task as satisfying a narrow interpretation of literacy as only reading and writing. The main aim for Victoria is to engage children in a process that 'reflects their world back to them' through books based on everyday experiences as part of a 'community of readers and writers'. Collaborative books support class identity and have several layers including 'the children's immediate responses, plus the narrative that they have shaped collaboratively over time … It is a powerful language experience on lots of levels.' The process of book making is described simply and playfully by Victoria. 'Let's bake a book!

Here are our ingredients: we have some words, pictures, and backgrounds, and we now have to work out how to put it all together.' Throughout this process she explains that the children learn much from each other through observation and discussion that stems from interests in letters and/or visual images.

In relation to the Navigating Symbols session, Victoria notes how important it was to begin with a game based on child-created 'poetic maps' to re-motivate and involve the children. She states:

> In the rhyme I was trying to pick up on their language, trying to tread a balance between keeping the shape of structure of the rhyme and pattern, and letting them take charge of it. I tried to echo what the children said rather than follow a formula ... I think young children respond to patterned language. The richer the pattern, the easier for young children to remember, and that's why songs are so powerful. Rhyme is very closely tied to song, and children respond strongly to drama and movement when they are linked to story.

To Victoria, the act of creating pictures also stimulates oral language by providing children with 'the space and time for language to spontaneously arise from activities that make sense to them'.

This case study illustrates how children's language, imagination, and creative expression are supported and extended through a variety of linked arts experiences culminating in the production of a whole group illustrated book. It articulates a flexible and emergent child-centred curriculum design made possible by the knowledge, skills, and commitment of a group of experienced teachers who collaborated in a co-creative learning journey. It provides a reference for other practitioners wanting to explore a topic through a series of interconnected teaching sessions. The fundamental elements of this journey include: responsive and collaborative planning and reflection, and engaging practice and learning environment design.

EXEMPLAR

Promoting language through interdisciplinary arts
Step 1: Topics with rich, 'non-everyday' language

Identify topics of interest to the children that have the potential to extend their language. What type of rich language would invite the children to use it, experiment with it in new contexts, play with it, and represent it symbolically and metaphorically in visual art, drama, storytelling, and book making? What words and phrases might capture their imaginations, stimulate their creativity?

Robert Brown, John O'Toole, Pam Macintyre, and Richard Sallis

Step 2: Stimulus texts with evocative language

Once the topic is selected, set about making the environment 'print-rich'. Choose poems, rhymes, chants, and songs that pattern the language and give it resonance. Let the children hear the language, so read it well with intonation and rhythm, talk about it—how do the words make them feel? Do the words make them want to *do* something? Use favourite words and phrases yourself in new, everyday contexts—play with the language. Picture books and narrative texts are wonderful supports to stimulate language, so choose a range to share.

Step 3: The arts as ways of learning

Now that the topic is chosen and the children are immersed in its language, how can the arts—music, visual arts, drama, storytelling, and book making—best be integrated to help the children learn deeply and meaningfully? You might like to identify how each provides a different way into the topic and method of articulating engagement and learning for the children. For instance, in Navigating Symbols, the children created maps, acted the story, drew symbols, and told their stories to be written down, to represent the elements of the pirate story and the treasure hunt that were meaningful to them individually and then collectively through the book making.

Step 4: Multimodal teaching and learning strategies

Select and integrate various ways into the story created around the chosen topic. Telling and retelling, incorporating all the children's points of view (for example, using the children's maps for the chant that preceded the book-making session in Navigating Symbols) deepen the story. Children experience the world best in different ways and need multiple entry points to express their understandings—through their bodies, words, images, symbols, movement, song, and rhythm and rhyme.

Step 5: Create a classroom environment with objects related to the theme

Immerse the children in the atmosphere of the topic with thoughtfully chosen, actual and symbolic objects to be placed appropriately in the classroom. These serve as props and reminders for revisiting the topic, and as stimulus for story making. In Navigating Symbols, an old map, a globe, Chinese writing on a scroll, a treasure map on a light box, and an embossed treasure box were displayed, with children's art work being added during the project.

Step 6: Time for reflection

During the course of the exploration of the topic, provide time for discussion, reflection, and sharing of what the children have learned and enjoyed—as Suzana said, 'to keep the flame burning'.

Magic carpets, dinosaurs, and dragons: teaching other curriculum areas through drama

Richard Sallis

In pairs, the Year 1 students sit on their magic carpets. Anita, their drama teacher, is in role as the leader of an expedition to outer space. She says, 'Now hang on to your flying carpet because we are going to be travelling a long way. Get ready. Here we go!' She plays music suitable for the journey, and she and the students sing 'Twinkle, twinkle little star, magic carpet take me far'. Using a piece of blue material, she wafts each of the flying carpets. 'Magic carpets need wind,' she calls out. The children scream with excitement as they pretend to fly into outer space. 'And land!' says Anita. The students mime coming down to earth with a thud. Anita holds a stick up to her mouth and says, 'I am speaking to you with my special outer space microphone. We are on the planet Neptune. We need to collect rocks and other samples. We also need to take notes of the surrounding area to find out if humans could live here. You need to make all the right tests to find that out. Remember, we are a long way from the sun, so it might be very cold here and there is a very big storm approaching.' Some of the students begin to shudder.

Introduction

This case study reports on three drama programs taught by specialist drama teacher Anita, and her Prep (preparatory year) and Year 1 classes. Her pedagogy is based on *dramatic play* and *process drama*. All three units use drama to integrate other arts areas (music, visual arts, and dance), as well as one or more other key learning areas. There was one unit for Prep, Abracadabra, which taught English, and two units for Year 1, Dinosaurs (History and Science) and Weather (Geography and Science).

The data collection included:

- participant observation of Anita's Year 1 and Prep classes
- interviews with Anita and some of her students
- analysis of publicly available documents circulated by the school

Robert Brown, John O'Toole, Pam Macintyre, and Richard Sallis

- curriculum documentation prepared by Anita for these units. Anita's unit plans form the basis of the 'exemplar' linked to this case study.

Anita is one of two drama teachers at the junior campus of an independent school in a middle-class beachside suburb, attended by students from Prep through to Year 9. Having been a single-sex boys' school for over one hundred years, in recent years it has been transformed into 'parallel education'. From Year 5 the male and female students are taught in single-sex classes. However, in years Prep to Year 4, boys and girls are placed in the same classes to 'discover the world together' (according to the school's publicity brochure).

Anita began her teaching career as a generalist primary teacher. After a few years she completed a graduate diploma in secondary teaching, with a method in drama, and a fourth year of primary training focusing on children's literature. From this background and experience she has formed the opinion 'that primary drama is such an important area and has such potential for learning in and beyond the arts'. As one of the arts 'specialists' she does not teach one particular class. Once a week for fifty minutes, each Prep and Year 1 class comes to Anita for a drama lesson. Anita also teaches secondary drama to years 7 and 8. Her classes take place in the purpose-built drama studio, or in one of two other spaces at the school designated for drama teaching. The students also attend weekly classes in music and visual arts. In years 5 and 6 they have four fifty-minute lessons a week spread across two of the arts areas, offered on a rotational basis. Beyond primary school drama is a core subject up until the end of Year 9. From years 10 to 12 it is an elective subject along with other arts subjects including music, visual arts, and dance. Anita's school encourages its staff to periodically plan 'rich tasks', integrated units of work planned and taught by a number of teachers. Anita also constructs and teaches units of work that integrate the arts and other key learning area(s) as part of her regular classroom drama program. These units often draw on the students' knowledge from other areas of the curriculum. Anita finds it to be 'incredibly successful to use what the students are doing in their other classes as a starting point for drama. The students come with a wealth of knowledge about (the topic) and this deepens the drama experience.' Additionally, by taking part in the drama unit, Anita believes that her students gain an enhanced understanding of the topic, which in turn, they take back and feed into other classes.

Teaching Prep and Year 1, Anita sees her role as 'taking the students on a journey; using drama as the means to do that'. At the Prep and Year 1 levels Anita's classes are usually based on dramatic play and process drama—spontaneous role-plays and improvisations without audience or rehearsed performance. In a typical lesson students may take on a variety of roles and visit many imaginary worlds. For this reason, Anita believes that when it comes to the use of props and costumes in her drama teaching, 'Less is more: I am very much about using what is at hand for the students to use to create. Giving them specific items that have an obvious use can limit their imagination. I think it is better for them to use what's there and to transform it.' One of Anita's main drama teaching 'essentials' is a tub in the Drama Studio containing coloured material of various lengths. The material is used virtually every lesson by the students to create costume items, props, and sometimes sets and backdrops. In the Dinosaurs unit the Year 1 students created a prehistoric jungle for their drama by draping material over objects in the room.

Through dramatic play and process drama, Anita provides opportunities for her students 'to become immersed in the drama experience and to be creative and make decisions (about) what to bring to the drama'. Two specific process drama techniques that Anita regularly uses are 'Teacher in Role (TiR)' and 'mantle of the expert'. She finds that using these techniques 'encourage the students to bring so many good ideas to the drama, through the roles we all take on'.

Anita believes that integrating other arts areas is essential for the teaching and learning that takes place in her drama classes. This approach is consistent with the teaching of drama in many comparable primary programs (for example, Drama Australia 2006). She explains, 'I tend to integrate the arts in my drama program in organic ways; when I talk about the arts I mean music, dance, and visual art'. Visual artworks, such as photographs, illustrations, or paintings are a regular stimulus for class activity, and sometimes students create their own visual artworks within the drama. Anita recalls that, 'in Abracadabra I got the students to design and sketch modifications to the witch's house from *Hansel and Gretel*. So the visual art was used as a way that the students could respond *within* the drama'. As part of this unit, I helped the students make rod puppets out of cardboard and icy-pole sticks, which they used to portray their dragon characters in a drama activity.

Anita integrates music into most of her drama classes, as a way of enhancing the atmosphere in which the drama is taking place. For instance in the Weather drama various pieces of music denoted each of the environments that the students 'visited'. Her intention was to 'create the mood of the place and help the students get into the experience of being there'. For Anita, using music in this way, 'deepens the meaning and enhances the content of the drama. The music works with the drama to become a whole experience for the students.'

Dinosaurs

When devising a unit that integrates the arts and other aspects of the school curriculum, Anita starts by deciding on a topic that she considers will hold the students' interest over a number of lessons and has dramatic potential. She views such integrated units as being 'a two-way street' with drama and other subject areas 'coming together to enhance the students' experience and deepen the meaning'. Dinosaurs was taught in drama at the same time the students were studying this topic with their regular classroom teacher. Within the drama unit the students engaged in a range of activities that required them to share that knowledge and develop it within the activities. On one occasion, Anita gave each student a white lab coat, and told them that they were scientists. They entered a time machine and went back to Jurassic times to observe, make notes, and collect samples. Then Anita provided opportunities for the students to share their knowledge of dinosaur behaviours, eating habits and sleeping patterns, the Jurassic period, and archaeological techniques and processes. According to Anita the students' interaction 'with the whole imaginary experience was strong, complex, and richer because they had acquired knowledge to feed into it from what they had learnt in their regular classes'.

Abracadabra

Anita planned the unit Abracadabra for Prep on fantasy, myths, and legends to draw on and enhance the students' literacy skills. According to Australian drama educator Robin Pascoe, each art form has its own intrinsic language that students develop and apply to their artworks. Additionally, in schools the arts also 'contribute to the general literacy of students' because they provide them with 'language rich opportunities for developing their own language and for making and communicating meaning' (2003, pp. 28–9).

In her teaching Anita frequently uses the language of drama and reinforces its use by the students.

> Like with Year 1 I will say to them, 'find a different level to work on' or 'I want you to now move a different body part'. Or I will ask the students, like, 'who can remember what "character" means?' And by doing this I feel like I am reinforcing that vocabulary. I had a class a couple of weeks ago and I did an improvisation with them and they knew what an 'improvisation' was when I mentioned it. I was so impressed because considering they only do drama once a week it was very gratifying to see that they had an understanding of that concept.

Abracadabra contained a number of literary sources and references, and required students to use a variety of literacy and oracy skills. Anita read her students a variety of texts such as a picture book, *The Discovery of Dragons* by Graeme Base, stories and folk tales (for example, *Peter Pan* and *The Three Billy Goats Gruff*). The students learnt songs such as pirate chanteys, nursery rhymes, and ritual chants. They studied and used literature-based artefacts such as a treasure map and a witches' spell book, incorporated into the unit as stimuli for the drama. Through their exposure to the literature, the unit also taught them some of the principles or oral and written storytelling.

Weather—reflecting on planning and implementation

While I was visiting the school, Anita was teaching a Year 1 unit using drama and other arts areas to teach geographical and scientific knowledge about the weather. It was ultimately a most successful program; however, it highlighted for her some of the difficulties associated with teaching other curricula through the arts. Quite early on, she 'found it a struggle because the students were not as engaged and motivated as they had been with previous (integrated) units'. Through reflective practice Anita isolated the concerns she had with this unit and planned ways to solve them.

Anita initially thought she would tap into and enhance the students' geographical and scientific knowledge of the topic attained elsewhere in the school's curriculum, based on the belief that, 'everybody knows at least something about the weather'. She decided that she would draw on this knowledge by placing them in the role of 'mantle of the expert'. She would impart additional information on the topic through a variety of drama techniques including TiR. However, the students soon lost interest.

> I thought that because the topic was something that everybody has got experience of, it would appeal to the students. But what I found was that they did not respond to it as I had expected them to. I knew it wasn't working and so I had to work out why. Dinosaurs was a topic the students obviously enjoyed and they were doing lots of work on it at the same time in their other classes. With the Weather program they soon seemed to struggle with it and their drama work seemed limited. They just weren't bringing a lot to the drama that they were producing. I realised that this was mainly because I had expected them to have more knowledge of the topic than they had and they soon exhausted what they knew. I also thought that perhaps the fact that the topic was so ordinary was also a problem; it didn't come across as exciting.

Anita came to a further realisation—even though the unit 'tapped into work they had been doing in Geography', unlike Dinosaurs, their work on the weather was not linked to work they were *currently* undertaking outside the Drama program. For Anita this was significant because it highlighted that when teaching other curriculum areas through the arts, context is most important. From this experience Anita realised that arts units that integrate other key learning areas may work more effectively when students are concurrently studying the same topic in other areas of the school curriculum.

Anita decided to amend the unit, to provide more opportunities for the students to draw on their own experiences of the weather, along with more resources about the topic. On further reflection, Anita reasoned that what her unit lacked was a suitable 'hook' (O'Toole & Dunn 2002, p. 13), something that would draw the students into the drama. Anita decided from past experience that what might appeal to them was travelling to different places and experiencing the weather in each location.

When teaching any of her integrated units Anita ensures that 'everything in the classes is linked in some way to the topic'; 'by thoroughly immersing' the students in the topic they would 'find it more meaningful and be more engaged in it'. This was particularly important for this unit. The subject matter became integral to warm-ups, the main body of the lesson, and the reflection activities.

Anita began each of her classes in this unit with a warm-up. One lesson during the Weather unit began with the students walking around the room 'as silent snowflakes'.

Robert Brown, John O'Toole, Pam Macintyre, and Richard Sallis

They then had to pair up and brainstorm words and phrases about the weather. Later in the lesson they used this vocabulary to develop characters and situations. Anita told the students that they were going on an expedition to discover what the weather is like on a desert island and on the planet Neptune. She paired them up and asked them to place in an imaginary bag what they would take. As well as building up an expectation of the journey that lay ahead, this activity drew on the students' knowledge of what they had previously learnt about the two environments. After the students played at preparing for the trip, Anita sat the class in a circle and asked each pair to tell what was in their bag. This led to a lively discussion, the suggestions showing understanding of the likely weather conditions: hot and dry for the desert island and stormy for Neptune.

In her Prep and Year 1 classes, Anita teaches her students some of the foundational conventions and devices of drama such as movement, tableau, use of voice and gesture, and improvisation and character/role development, through which the students will explore the subject matter. In the main part of this particular unit, Anita took the role of leader of the expedition to Neptune and to the desert island. Each pair was given a piece of coloured material, which they were told was their magic carpet. She talked the students through their journey as they flew to each location, and in the role of geologists they collected samples from the environment. On the desert island they were required to design a dwelling to live in and build it from materials available in the room. In her role as 'expedition leader', she was able to give instructions within the drama itself, such as 'You now need to carry out tests of the planet's surface', and to drive the narrative Anita would urge, 'It is time to leave now because the big storm is almost here'.

A high level of discussion and reflection takes place in Anita's classes. She finds that posing problems for them to solve increases their involvement. On the desert island she called a 'tribal meeting' and announced that food and water were running low. The students were encouraged to suggest ways of alleviating the shortage. Anita accepted their ideas, but challenged them too when she considered the information conflicted with the body of knowledge they had previously established for the drama. When a boy suggested they could drink from the water surrounding the island, Anita replied, 'But that has salt in it and this would make us very ill. How might the salt water be useful to us?' 'For fish to eat,' was his response.

At the end of each of her classes Anita held a reflection session where she encouraged her students to draw together the various links between the thematic content and the dramatic processes they had undertaken. In one class the students developed and presented characters from different countries who explored the weather there. At the end of the lesson Anita asked her students, 'Is there anything you'd like to share about your adventures today?' Here is a representative sample of their responses:

> I really liked when we went on the magic carpet and there were all different places and weathers, and we had to act the weather like it was cold or really hot.

I liked learning about the weather in all different places and how Scotland has different weather to Egypt.

My favourite thing was when I acted as the person I was going to be and we had to talk to someone else and tell them where we came from and what our weather was like.

I liked how you got to hear where other people came from, and what (the weather) was like there.

It was good how you got to dress up like you had to if you lived in that place because of the weather.

EXEMPLAR

This exemplar is derived from Anita's Year 1 unit of work, Dinosaurs.

Step 1: Scoping the field

To begin, find out what is being taught in other areas of the school that you think might provide a suitable theme or topic for classroom drama. As Anita discovered, integrated units can work very effectively when they are conducted at the *same time* that the students are studying the subject matter elsewhere at the school. For example, Anita decided to teach her Dinosaurs drama when the students would be studying the Jurassic period in their other classes.

Step 2: Brainstorming

Once the subject matter has been determined, brainstorm ideas of what specifically you would like your drama unit to contain. You need to consider why you wish to create and teach this unit. What is it about the subject matter that interests you as a drama teacher and that is also a hook for your students? What aspects of the content might have the most effective dramatic potential—giving them problems and dilemmas to deal with? What type of roles and characters could be in the unit? Where and when will it be set? What concepts, themes, characters, and situations will be most appropriate for the cognitive level of the students? Anita decided to include different types of dinosaurs, such as the tyrannosaurus rex and the pterodactyl, the time and setting of the Jurassic period, the lifestyle of dinosaurs, the work of archaeologists, and travelling back in a time machine.

Step 3: Resourcing the unit

Now that you have a clearer idea of what you want in your unit, you need to find out what resources the students have already been given or exposed to in their other classes. Once you have this information you can then identify the gaps, if any, and seek out the resources you will need to introduce to the students. In addition to what they already knew, Anita decided to show her students excerpts from the BBC DVD, *Walking with Dinosaurs*, and the picture book *Imagine* by Alison Lester.

Step 4: Incorporating the arts elements

What arts elements would you like to include in the teaching of the unit? In Dinosaurs, Anita incorporated a range of drama devices and conventions including TiR, mantle of the expert, tableau, character development, role-play, dramatic play, and improvisation. As Anita did, you can also include the use of other arts areas. Dinosaurs contained music (pre-recorded music used as a stimulus for character development and to create a sense of place: a drum to tap out the beat for movement sequences), visual art (designing and constructing a jungle setting for the dinosaurs), and dance (a whole group movement sequence as dinosaurs in the jungle).

Step 5: Sequencing the unit

When teaching other curriculum areas through drama, it is useful to begin with activities that help to determine the students' knowledge base about the topic, such as warm-up exercises requiring the students to move around the room as a particular type of dinosaur living in its environment. Anita could ascertain what the students' already knew about dinosaurs by what they brought to their characterisation. When in role as scientists, their answers to questions determined how much understanding they had. Once it is established what the students already know, new resource material can be shared to further their knowledge. Anita often used TiR to impart new information to the students.

Step 6: Transforming the classroom

Transforming the classroom to create an inviting environment for the drama and the other curricular learning can help spark the students' imagination and enhance their engagement. Anita got her students to create a Jurassic jungle out of available objects and materials in the room. Once the jungle setting had been established the students created and played their dinosaur and scientist characters, learning the history and science through dealing with the dilemmas and problems faced in the drama.

Step 7: Reflection

Analysis or reflection sessions at the end of a lesson are important to reinforce the curricular learning. Anita's reflection sessions provided opportunities for the students to share both what they had learnt about dinosaurs and analyse the drama processes they had engaged in.

Activities beyond the case studies

Workshop activity: Draw on the principles of multi-literacies in Chapter 4, and design and implement a workshop for primary aged children, in which an art form is used to promote and develop literacy or numeracy.

Solo or group task: Create an art-rich picture book (in 3D, e-book, or PowerPoint form) and plan an accompanying workshop or arts task in another medium that would enhance the experience of children encountering your book in class.

Questions for students to consider

1   Which art forms have natural kinship with which particular subjects and content in other key learning areas of the curriculum?

2   How can we use the arts for motivating and engaging the students?

3   How can we use drama to frame any content by turning the classroom into someplace else?

4   How can we use the other arts to enrich and transform the content?

Conclusion

As it happened, both of these case studies show teaching across the curriculum in the early years. However, the same principles apply right through the years: our second case study writer is himself a secondary teacher who understands Anita's practice because he works in this way too. Other case studies throughout this book actually also demonstrate the arts pedagogy used to teach other subjects at different age levels (history and navigational science to Year 6 in Chapter 7, and Indigenous studies in Chapter 8). We chose the two case studies in this chapter to demonstrate a range of art forms and a diversity of curriculum content— science and geography, language, poetry, and history. Both of them use a combination of art forms, in order not only to teach about those arts, but to help the children to learn new knowledge from other areas of the curriculum.

In the first case study, the learning is specifically about language and about books. Throughout this unit, visual arts in particular—and the other arts too—provided enriching and complementary images, ideas, and experiences to broaden and deepen the children's understanding of language and its possibilities. The maps, building the pirate ship, the picture books, and the story drawings wove the visual images and imaginative landscapes into the children's language use, in a context that the drama, movement and music made embodied, exciting, and satisfying. At the same time, these activities were challenging

Robert Brown, John O'Toole, Pam Macintyre, and Richard Sallis

them to push their imagination and their own storytelling further and more ambitiously. Furthermore, the poetry and the child-created books gave them confidence and motivation to communicate to others, towards writing down their discoveries and excitements.

In both of the case studies, drama plays an important part. For the second, we have chosen a case study that deliberately focused on drama (though other arts make an appearance here too!), because for the purposes of this chapter, drama is different from the other arts and very special in terms of providing pedagogical tools across the whole curriculum.

All the arts provide those two special qualities we referred to in the introduction to this chapter: *motivation* and *symbolic languages*. What makes drama especially special is that it can provide a virtually complete and alternative pedagogical framework, which can remove some of the physical limitations of the classroom as a site of learning. This alternative pedagogy is built on the two most basic of dramatic acts: *making an agreement to pretend* (what the poet Coleridge called 'the voluntary suspension of disbelief') and, having done that, *putting oneself in somebody else's shoes*. And those shoes can be standing in any area of the curriculum at all.

Through drama we can actually experience, bodily and through language, any situation that is capable of being imagined, with that imagination being shared. The classroom can be suspended, and become anywhere, at any time or age, and we can *virtually* become whatever people or beings we want to explore and find out about. (Drama is in fact the first virtual reality!) The experience can have all but one of the elements of real experience. When carefully prepared and structured, the fictional dramatic context provides emotional engagement and identification, as much factual information as we can load it with, excitement and tension as we (the people or beings in the drama) try to reach our goals and protect our interests. The one real element the experience does not have is consequences in the real world—which is just as well! Through saying 'let's pretend' we are creating a living, breathing model of a real situation, as best we can with what we know. We can play with the model, experiment as we like. We can wind it back or forward in time, change locations, replay scenes to find how they might have worked—and when we have finished we just step out of the model world and put it away.

At this point we are not necessarily talking about acting out that experience for other people, for an audience—that is called theatre, and comes later. In the examples we use in this chapter, and the Chapter 7 drama case studies too, we are focusing on the embodied experience for the participants themselves. In the second case study, the teacher has fashioned the three sets of curriculum content—history and science (Dinosaurs), English (Abracadabra) and geography and science (Weather)—into more complex units called process drama, where the teacher and students create a single fictional world, which they people with themselves, playing people and beings who have tasks to complete and problems to solve. Sometimes they inhabit that world through 'experiential role-play', living through the context as the inhabitants (the scientists and space travellers); sometimes they step sideways and explore through theatrical techniques (practising dinosaur movements);

sometimes they step in and out of the drama, going off to research new knowledge to enrich the fiction.

This pedagogical platform that is laid by the drama not only makes possible the exploration through direct experience of any area of the curriculum, but it provides a natural entry point for all the other arts. Notice how Anita and Louise, and Sarah, Suzana, and Victoria seamlessly build in art and music, storytelling and poetry, and into their Jurassic expedition, their flight to Neptune and their pirate ship adventure.

You will probably also have noticed two very important pedagogical aspects of both these case studies, characteristics of good teaching not confined to the arts, but very much a necessary part of arts pedagogy. First, the teachers are all reflective practitioners, critical about their own practice and constantly seeking better ways to help the students to learn. Louise, who is not primarily a teacher, draws on her own experience as an artist as the basis of her pedagogy. Anita is self-critical and adaptable: when she realises that her first plan on teaching about weather is not working, she completely reshapes her approach through shrewd observation, listening to the students and finding a new 'hook' that will engage them.

And this is the second key characteristic of good teachers. All the teachers involved encourage and draw on the children's ideas. They do not treat curriculum as content to be 'imparted' or 'transmitted'—with the students as empty vessels waiting for all-new information or skill training. All of these teachers recognise that the students already have lots of relevant life experience on which to scaffold what is to be learned. They consciously or unconsciously anchor their teaching on Vygotskian principles, working from the 'zone of proximal development', and building on what the children already know and can do, through challenging tasks that are contextualised through the artwork, simultaneously playful and deeply serious.

Key references

Allen, P. (1989) *I Wish I Had a Pirate Suit*, Viking Kestrel, Ringwood.

Ambrus, V. (1982) *Blackbeard*, Oxford University Press, Oxford.

Base, G. (1996) *The Discovery of Dragons*, Viking, Ringwood.

BBC (1999) *Walking with Dinosaurs*, BBC Worldwide, London.

Byron, M. (1938) *Peter Pan and Wendy Retold by May Byron*, Hodder & Stoughton, London.

Drama Australia (2006) *Australian Drama Education Magazine*, Drama Australia, Brisbane.

Fox, M. (1994) *Tough Boris*, Harcourt Brace, Orlando Fl.

Hergé (1974a) *The Secret of the Unicorn*, Methuen, London.

Hergé (1974b) *Tintin—Red Rackham's Treasure*, Methuen, London.

Lester, A. (1989) *Imagine*, Allen & Unwin, Crows Nest.

Mahy, M. (1985) *The Man Whose Mother Was a Pirate*, Dent, London.

O'Toole, J. & Dunn, J. (2002) *Pretending to Learn*, Pearson Education Australia, Frenchs Forest.

Pascoe, R. (2003) 'The Language of Drama: Making and Communicating Meaning', in J. Livermore (ed.), *More Than Words Can Say, A View of Literacy through the Arts*, University of Canberra, Canberra.

Smith, J. (1986) *Three Billy Goats Gruff Retold by Judith Smith*, Methuen, North Ryde.

Art is a Place You Can Go

Chris Sinclair and Neryl Jeanneret

The arts provide a powerful means for learning and insight about ourselves, others and the world in general. We have endeavoured to show you the importance of the arts and their capacity to engage children in meaningful learning, both from a theoretical perspective and from how theory translates into practice through the case studies and exemplars.

In this chapter, we decided to leave you with a collection of quotes and comments as some of the highlights of previous chapters. There didn't seem much point in us providing you with *our* reflections—the authors have done that throughout the book. Instead, we encourage you to read the following and reflect, alone and in discussion with others.

Theatre is like a place where you can visit any world you want or any character you want.

Who sees the human face correctly: the photographer, the mirror or the painter?
(Pablo Picasso)

I thought it was going to be really stupid and boring, but it was fun …
(Year 4)

A work of art is never finished—it simply stops in interesting places.
(Julia, performing arts teacher)

Note to self—Don't forget to relax and enjoy yourself.
(Kathryn and Nadia, pre-service teachers)

He is very softly spoken in class and doesn't put himself forward to speak up, you couldn't shut him up.
(Year 4 teacher)

Music is fun. Everyone had musical ability. Even if you can't sing, you can be musical. Everyone has the ability to compose.
(Pre-service generalist primary student)

It captures people's attention. Like seeing those preps' faces … at first we didn't think they'd understand any of it until we actually did our performance and saw their faces. We were amazed. Like you hear adults talking about things all the time, but when we do it ourselves and you think we could be those adults talking about it. Maybe we could make a change. Seeing those faces was so cute because they were so enthusiastic about it. (Year 6)

I was jumping, I was creeping on the ground. I was spreading my arms up in the air and I was feeling good.
(Preschooler)

But couldn't everyone's life become a work of art?
(Michel Foucault)

It's a powerful message really to be able to go to a space and see a large mosaic developed from children's drawings. (Jeanette, visual arts teacher)

I felt like flying on the unicorn, and it was a flame-looking unicorn, as soft as the softest fabric.
(Year 1)

You would never get kids saying 'Oh I took my learning journal home from drama and wrote a couple of paragraphs'. The engagement is huge when you have got kids writing at home. I haven't set it as homework at all but they are doing it anyway. The kids are engaged and motivated to write and to reflect—you can't beat that! (Primary drama teacher)

Beautiful day, lots of excitement, somewhat chaotic but lots of fun. That's how I would describe the Lee Street Arts Festival. I was supposed to be marshalling the Grade 3/4s, but once the parade got started it was so full on and there were so many people that I found it hard to work out who I was supposed to be guiding. But that's just what the parade was like, unpredictable but enjoyable. So I just attempted to keep as many people together as I could. (Ebony, pre-service education student)

Teaching becomes a form of artistry in which it is hard to tell the dancer from the dance (Jenny Simons)

I still can't dance/ hold a tune/ act. The students know more about this stuff than me! (Primary teacher)

Mark said, 'Time is precious to me. And although I love the arts myself and the kids seem to love it, I need class time to teach the basics …'

Student: 'You help us turn our ideas into really good stuff.'

Dear Frida
I saw you today
In the thick of a dream
I wrote a poem so I wouldn't forget:
In the mouth of a bird
That is a cloud
Frida swims, gradually, back to herself.
The wind is lapping at
The hem of her cotton dress.
Best wishes
Trist

Input by everybody is a very important attribute when planning these productions. If we feel a sense of ownership in the piece then we will be more motivated. (Amy, pre-service drama education student)

It's very hard in an art room to be productive in an hour, as this gives you and the children only half an hour of time with materials. (Jeanette, visual arts teacher)

Chris Sinclair and Neryl Jeanneret

The theme of home and friends really got them. I think what happened was the simplicity of the lyric and the repeated themes of home and friendship, 'Home is where the heart is'. That was what really sunk in the end, when a real empathy began to develop, came together.
(Year 8 teacher)

It opened up a lot of opportunities for deeper learning. The workshop made me think greatly about human actions and motivations: how easily emotions can be stirred up in groups, how people can transform in a dramatic role with ease. Drama is not just about acting and poses, but it can be developed to analyse what a character is thinking. Drama can be used to explore any issue in society, whether it be big, small or controversial.

I almost wanted to fall into the sea when I was walking across the thin rope across the bridge, because I knew the sea monsters would catch me and be friendly with me.
(Year 1)

What about the Term 3 concert? How would it fit in? Where are we going to find the time?
(Primary teachers)

It compounded my belief that drama education can foster team work and interpersonal skills in children.
(Phuong)

When they come to drama they want to be active. They don't want to sit and they don't want to write, and I have struggled with this ever since I have taught drama. Finally kids are doing written reflection in their own time, not in their fifty-minute session, and they are keen to do it.
(Primary drama teacher)

'Maybe we could get louder at this part and softer at that'; 'Maybe it could get faster; I think the Tyrannosaurus Rex should be stamping its feet like this' …

By fourth term 'we've created the space, and we virtually live in this space and enjoy it for the rest of the year. I think that's really what it's about.'

I think the most important thing I learned is to just try different musical activities. It was hard before to even think of doing any of it and now I'm comfortable trying anything once.
(Pre-service generalist primary student)

Management with these kids is a pain in the neck. I just get everyone settled and listening to instructions, and someone disrupts things again and we start all over again about 'When I'm giving you instructions, you need to listen otherwise you won't know what to do… how hard is that?'. The real shock was realising this was all *my* problem now.
(Cathy, first year music teacher)

I think the arts is a thing that you have to make in your own world and do it in your own way. Art is a place you can go but I suppose you can't go deeper unless you do what you haven't done before. I tried bull riding and it is one of the best things I have done in my life and rugby—that is great. I haven't tried bungee jumping and I reckon if I tried that it would be great. They also change people—almost like an artist. (Patrick, Grade 7)

The things that artists do all the time are things that kids need to be able to do – forming alternative solutions to a problem with other people, being persistent, adjusting something after you've made a choice, taking responsibility for decision, looking at options.
(Arnie Aprill, Chicago Arts Partnerships)

Hey, I like Jeannie Baker's 'Window' picture book—it has no words—but each time you look out the window—the outside world is changing—and the little boy is growing up. I was thinking that we could use this idea—and … What do you think?'
(Andrea, pre-service teacher)

There were just no breaks in the school day for me to catch up on things. Recess and lunchtimes were spent getting ready for the next group of children. Even though it was a relatively small school, I saw every student over the two days I was there, from Preps to Year 6. It was a bit of a baptism by fire, constantly adjusting to the different year levels and the management issues. (Cathy)

Sounds and utterances we shape into words and sentences, as a way of naming, ordering, and using specific kinds of sensory data—and we call it language. Physical, tactile, and kinaesthetic data too, as well as sound and words, can be further harmonised into patterns and sequences that have usefulness and meaning for us, and are also pleasurable and stimulating. We call these the arts.
(John O'Toole, arts educator)

Let's close our eyes and remember the magic.

Chris Sinclair and Neryl Jeanneret

Glossary

aesthetics: the branch of philosophy that deals with the nature and expression of beauty, as in the fine arts, but also including the study of psychological responses to beauty and artistic experiences. It is also a conception of what is artistically beautiful or pleasing in appearance.

affective: a psychological term that refers to arousing feelings or emotions.

anklung: a musical instrument made out of two bamboo tubes loosely attached to a bamboo frame. It is shaken. Anklungs come in different sizes that produce different pitches.

ArtPlay: a centre established by the City of Melbourne in 2004 to promote the learning of creative arts for children. It provides a setting for children and their families to come and broaden their education and skills by being involved in artistic, interactive and creative projects.

art-rich picture book: a work of narrative fiction or narrative non-fiction specifically featuring art, artists and art-making.

blog (from 'web-log'): a website that displays in chronological order the postings by one or more individuals and usually has links to comments on specific postings.

building belief: see *enrolment*.

cartridge paper: a high-quality heavy paper used for drawing and painting.

ceramics: refers here to artwork made out of some form of clay that is fired in a kiln.

chaos theory: a contemporary scientific system for understanding the laws of nature, originated by meteorologist Edward Lorenz. It acknowledges the notions of unpredictability and contingency in the behaviour of objects.

Chinese joss paper: in this context, paper that has gold or silver foil attached. Traditional joss paper is burned as a religious offering in Chinese Taoist and some Buddhist ceremonies.

cognitive/cognition: a term that is used in different ways by different disciplines. In psychology, it refers to an information-processing view of an individual's psychological functions. Other interpretations of the meaning of 'cognition' link it to the development of concepts. In education it usually refers to thinking and is the process by which a person learns. It involves strategies for processing information, prior knowledge about content, and problem-solving and thinking skills.

collage: an artistic technique and style involving the assembling together of a range of different artistic media or materials, often including cloth, newspapers and found objects.

ComicLife: a computer program designed for the creation of comics, picture albums and other image-based computer-generated presentations <http://plasq.com/comiclife/>.

connoisseurship: a term coined by Elliot Eisner to describe a key attribute of the teacher who embraces the artistry of teaching. It is the capacity to see, not merely to look, and the ability to name and appreciate the different dimensions of situations and experiences and the way they relate to each other.

conscience alley: a drama convention whereby, within a dramatic activity, a character with an important decision to make or problem to solve walks down an 'alley', comprising two rows of people. As he or she does so, the people forming the alley speak aloud the inner thoughts of the character and/or offer advice for her or him to consider. Sometimes one side of the alley is asked to take an opposing view to the other side.

comprehensive musicianship: the interdisciplinary study of music, as opposed to the study of aspects of the subject as separate and distinct areas of music. The word 'comprehensive' means that students will be involved with music in school in the same ways in which people are involved with music in the outside world—that is, as composers, performers, listeners and scholars. The curriculum is based on seven basic concepts—tone, rhythm, melody, harmony, form, tonality and texture—which are presented in the form of a spiral that represents a taxonomy of musical concepts progressing from the general to the specific, and from the simple to the complex.

convergent thinking: thinking that brings together information focused on solving a problem (especially solving a problem that has a single correct solution).

creative thinking: a mental process involving the generation of new ideas or concepts, or new associations between existing ideas or concepts. It is sometimes referred to as *divergent thinking*.

cultural capital: a term coined by Pierre Bourdieu to refer to those forms of knowledge, skills, education and advantages that give a person a higher status in society

cultural toolkit: a term coined by Jerome Bruner in a discussion about schooling and children's learning. Bruner's theory focused on the idea that children come to school equipped with a 'cultural toolkit' based on their past experiences and the enculturation provided by the family and the community in which they lived. This toolkit inevitably influences how they approach learning and the school experience. According to Bruner, 'culture shapes the mind ... it provides us with the toolkit by which we construct not only our worlds but our very conception of our selves and our powers', presupposing 'that human mental activity is neither solo nor conducted unassisted, even when it goes on "inside the head"' (*The Culture of Education*, 1996).

cyber-/digital natives: young people who have grown up in the era of digital technology such as computers, the internet, mobile phones and MP3s.

divergent thinking: 'outside-the-square thinking', which moves away in diverging directions so as to involve a variety of aspects and which sometimes lead to novel ideas and solutions. Divergent thinking is associated with creativity.

drama conventions: ways of working in drama or specific activities that contribute to a drama.

dramatic elements: the basic elements of form that make up any drama or theatre, including tension, time, space, conflict, rhythm and symbols.

dramatic play: the activity that young children naturally engage in, involving pretending to be other people and things. (See also *personal play* and *projected play*.) In classroom settings, this means that a drama is played out in real time without any rehearsal and with little or no planning. This may lead to acting out, where children improvise around a topic in small groups, without being required to show what they are doing to the rest of the class.

dyadic observations: the use of pairs of observers taking notes on a single event, such as a classroom lesson.

embodiment, embodied arts: refer particularly to those art forms that use the human body as a primary artistic medium, such as drama and dance. In education, 'embodiment' can also refer to any teaching that generates expressive and tangible outcomes; this would include all the arts, including music and digital art, which are of course not physically embodied.

engagement: in an educational context, this refers to children being 'on-task', with focused and sustained concentration, evidence of motivation, active responses, heightened awareness and animation, task completion, evidence of deeper thinking strategies, and expressions of enthusiasm, optimism, curiosity and interest.

enrolment: a drama term referring to the process of building belief, empathy and identification with a role. Sometimes it just entails giving the participants a point of view and a task. If the role demands deep empathy and passion, this must be painstakingly built with preliminary 'enrolling' activities.

ethnographic, ethnography: refer to a research methodology that concentrates on the close study of groups and communities of people and how they operate.

experiential role-play: a dramatic convention whereby players are each asked to identify or empathise with a fictional person and behave naturally as that person would, or as they would in that person's situation. See also *role-play*.

forum theatre: a type of group-devised theatrical presentation developed by Augusto Boal as part of his 'Theatre of the Oppressed'. A play, usually focusing on a social or moral problem, is performed once through and then repeated. When it is repeated, the actors and the audience make suggestions to assist the characters to overcome their conflict, with audience members invited to participate in the drama.

freeze-frame: a drama convention whereby a significant moment of dramatic action is suspended and frozen so that it can be examined closely, sometimes using other conventions such as *thought-tracking* or time-jumps (moving forwards or backwards in time through a series of freeze-frames). The word *tableau* means the same.

fuzzy logic: a contemporary philosophical system acknowledging reality and causality as provisional or changing; it is now being applied to computer design and computation.

hook: a way of engaging students in a subject unknown, alien or initially uninteresting to them, by finding a connection between that subject and what *is* familiar and interesting to them and building the lesson from that.

hot-seating: a dramatic convention whereby a student or teacher takes on a fictional role and is questioned by other participants.

humdrum (also known as a 'split drum'): among the oldest instruments in the world, now widely used in music education. By cutting tongues of different lengths and widths in the top wood of the drum, various musical tones are created.

improvise, improvisation: to invent, compose or perform with little or no preparation.

kinaesthetic: describes the ability of the body to receive and respond to stimuli, knowing which part of the body is moving, where it is moving and how it is moving.

Key Learning Areas (KLAs): the subject areas identified and developed by CURASS (the Australian Education Council's Curriculum and Assessment Committee) in answer to a formal initiative to develop 'national collaborative curriculum projects'. The subject areas are The Arts, English, Health and Physical Education, Languages other than English, Mathematics, Science, Studies of Society and Environment, and Technology.

Kodaly: The Kodaly teaching method was developed in the 1940s and 50s and evolved in Hungarian schools under the inspiration and guidance of the composer Zoltan

Kodaly, who believed that music should be at the heart of the curriculum and used as the basis for all early instruction. The goals, principles and philosophy were Kodaly's, but the pedagogy was a combination of previously separate techniques in one unified approach.

LOTE: Languages other than English.

manipulative skills: refers here to the ability of students to physically manage the objects they touch, in particular art-making media.

mantle of the expert: a dramatic convention in which a student is endowed with a role that enables or empowers them to be an 'expert' on, or have specialised knowledge of, a given topic, meaning that they have some useful knowledge or an opinion that can further the drama. Often the role they are given is that of someone in the adult world.

metacognition: thinking about thinking and knowing about knowing. It refers to being aware of and controlling your own learning process.

Musica Viva: Musica Viva Australia (MVA) is a not-for-profit organisation founded in 1945, with headquarters in Sydney. It is now the world's largest and most successful entrepreneur of ensemble and chamber music. Musica Viva In Schools (MVIS) provides a variety of education programs, ensembles and musicians for primary and secondary schools in all Australian states and territories.

NRSME: *National Review of School Music Education: Augmenting the Diminished.* This document reported on the current state of music in schools at the end of 2005, and also contains a very comprehensive literature review, a series of profiles of exemplary practice and guidelines for the teaching of music.

oracy: This word is a variant of 'literacy' and refers to the skills of effective speaking and listening. As well as verbal language, it also refers to vocal tones and expression, and the non-verbal signals, or *paralanguage*, that make up how we communicate in person with each other.

Orff Schulwerk: an approach to music education developed by the Austrian composer Carl Orff, after collaboration with dancer Dorothy Gunther. Orff believed that movement and music were inseparable and that it was critical that students physically experience beat, metre, tempo and rhythm, expressing these elements in dance and through instruments. The emphasis in music education should be on *doing* rather than *learning about*, and children should be provided with opportunities to explore and create at every level.

paradigm: a pattern or model; a collection of assumptions, concepts, practices and values that constitutes a way of viewing reality, especially for an intellectual community that shares them.

paralanguage: the non-verbal cues, signals and gestures that are part of how we speak and communicate to each other in person.

pedagogy, pedagogical: the art or profession of teaching. It is also used to define particular approaches to teaching or styles of teaching.

peer teaching: students teaching other students, either individually or in groups or classes. This may be at the same level (e.g. Year 5 students teaching other Year 5 students) or older students teaching younger ones.

percipient: a highly involved or perceptive participant (for example in a drama class), one who perceives keenly.

personal play: a form of dramatic play in which the young child takes on an imagined role for himself or herself and acts on his or her own behalf in the fictional world created with or without the assistance of adults.

PETA: the Philippine Educational Theatre Association, an organisation that provides a range of emancipatory theatre activities in the Philippines and internationally, including creative arts workshops and performances to empower children who have experienced physical and emotional abuse and social deprivation.

phonics: a system of teaching children to read by helping them to connect letters and groups of letters to the sounds they represent, and then blending them to make up words.

picture book: a blend of text and illustrations in which the two elements are mutually dependent and work to produce an artistic unit stronger than either words or pictures would be alone.

picture postcard: a drama activity in which students are given a setting (e.g. the beach) or an abstract concept (e.g. loneliness) and each takes up a frozen position in response to the stimulus, contributing to the overall picture that is formed. The activity continues until all participants have taken up their position somewhere in the 'picture postcard'.

playbuilding: the development of any dramatic performance for the stage (whether or not from an existing script); more specifically, the techniques students use to create a performance work they write/devise and perform, often incorporating improvisation.

postmodernism: a philosophical stance that claims it is impossible to make grand statements—meta-narratives—about the structures of society or about the causes of historical events, because everything we perceive, interpret and express is influenced by our gender, class and culture. Knowledge is partial and situated, and no one interpretation is superior to another. Hence everything, including 'truth', is relative.

postmodern relativist paradigm: a framework of belief or practice that highlights or reflects provisional or multiple versions of an event or theme.

projected play: a form of dramatic play in which the young child projects an imagined role into or onto an object. Toys, dolls or puppets take on this imagined life, and the child gives them voice and action, within an imagined world of their creation.

preps: Preparatory—the first year of formal schooling in Victoria and the equivalent to kindergarten or reception in some other Australian states.

pre-text: a drama term referring to the basis or subject matter for drama. A pre-text can be in many forms—for example, a picture book, a photograph, a poem, a story or a real-life incident (such as a newspaper article). A notable feature of a pre-text is that it can include unanswered questions, which encourage the students to speculate and try out possible scenarios through drama.

process drama: an extended classroom drama activity based on a *pre-text*. From the pre-text the teacher creates an imaginary world in which the events take place. Through the process drama, students participate in the moment in learning, inquiry and discovery. The emphasis is on participation rather than on performance to an audience. There are a number of conventions associated with process drama, including *teacher in role* (TiR), *mantle of the expert*, *role-play* (of many kinds), *hot-seating*, *freeze-frames* and *conscience alley*.

psychomotor: of or relating to movement or muscular activity associated with mental processes. For example, playing an instrument involves both psychomotor and cognitive skills.

relativity: the scientific theory propounded by Albert Einstein at the beginning of the twentieth century. It overthrew the previously accepted Newtonian belief that matter was stable and certain, in favour of the proposition that space and time (and matter) can only be perceived or understood in terms of their movement in relation to each other.

role-play: a broad term encompassing a number of central dramatic activities, essentially where participants identify with someone other than themselves, real or fictional, and enact a situation involving that person in order to explore or depict that person's behaviour. A role-play may have no audience, and be conducted solely so the participants can experience what it would be like to be a particular person or be in a particular situation. See *experiential role-play*. In 'performance' or 'procedural' role-play, the participants enact a character or situation for an audience, in order to depict a person's expected or desired behaviour.

reflective practice, reflective practitioner: a term frequently used in educational contexts. Donald Schön introduces the term in his book *The Reflective Practitioner* (1983) and describes it as thoughtfully considering one's own experiences in applying knowledge to practice. In the school setting, the teacher engages in reflective practice through thoughtfully considering his or her teaching methods in order to better understand what is going on in the classroom and which approaches to teaching and learning might work best for the students.

scaffolding: a popular metaphor used by educators to describe a process in which teachers or adults guide children's learning in an interactive way, building on what is already known and taking the learner safely into new understandings (entering the *zone of proximal development*). For example, through scaffolding, teachers may be able to help students explore and understand academic issues beyond those they are able to understand on their own. Jerome Bruner and Lev Vygotsky were key theorists in the development of the practices underpinning this educational metaphor.

self-regulation, self-direction: terms used in an education context to describe learning that is guided by *metacognition*, strategic actions such as planning and monitoring, and motivation to learn. Self-regulated learners understand their academic strengths and weaknesses and have a series of strategies to deal with tasks.

SoSE (Studies of Society and the Environment): a school subject in the Victorian and some other state curricula, comprising history, geography and allied areas. In New South Wales it is known as HSIE (Human Society and Its Environment).

soundscape: a sound picture or sound story that depicts a mood or event.

sub-text: the meaning underlying the actual words or the explicit meaning of an utterance, an action or an object. Sub-texts of language are conveyed by the vocal or non-verbal cues, which often run counter to the explicit text.

symbolic languages: a term that reflects the way in which each art form uses symbols to represent thoughts, ideas, emotions and concepts—for example, the musical sound, the visual image, the 'stage picture', the soundscape and the abstracted movement.

tableau: see *freeze-frame*.

teacher in role (TiR): a drama convention in which the classroom teacher takes an active part in the drama, adopting a role to manage the action from within. Often their character(s) is portrayed through the simple use of a prop, costume or change of voice or physical stance.

theatre-in-education (T-I-E): coined in England, this phrase refers to plays and other dramatic experiences performed in schools, normally by visiting adults, with a specific educational objective and elements of active participation from the audience.

thought-tracking: a drama convention in which what a character is thinking or feeling at a given time is articulated for the audience. The 'thoughts' may be conveyed directly by the character or by someone else, such as a chorus or a narrator.

TiR: see *teacher in role*.

zone of proximal development: a phrase invented by the educational psychologist Lev Vygotsky, meaning 'the distance between the actual developmental level as determined by independent problem solving and the level of potential development as determined through problem solving under adult guidance, or in collaboration with more capable peers' (Vygotsky 1978, p. 86).

Bibliography

Abbs, P. (1987) *Living Powers: The Arts in Education*, Falmer, London.

Abbs, P. (1989) *The Symbolic Order*, Falmer Press, London.

Abbs, P. (1994) *The Educational Imperative: A Defence of Socratic and Aesthetic Learning*, Falmer Press, London.

Ackroyd, J. & Boulton, J. (2001) *Drama Lessons for Five to Eleven-year-olds*, David Fulton, London.

Allen, P. (1989) *I Wish I Had a Pirate Suit*, Viking Kestrel, Ringwood.

Ambrus, V. (1982) *Blackbeard*, Oxford University Press, Oxford.

Arts Education Partnership (AEP) (2003) *Creating Quality Integrated and Interdisciplinary Arts Programs: Report of the Arts Education Partnership National Forum, September 2002*, Washington, DC.

Australia Council (2000) *Arts in a Multicultural Australia (AMA)*, Australia Council, Sydney.

Australia Council (2004) *National Education and the Arts Strategy*, Australia Council, Sydney.

Bamford, A. (2006) *The WOW Factor: Global Compendium of Arts Education research*, Waxmann, New York.

Barrett, M. & Smigiel, H. (2003) 'Awakening the "Sleeping Giant"?: The Arts in the Lives of Australian Families', *International Journal of Education and the Arts*, 4(4).

Base, G. (1996) *The Discovery of Dragons*, Viking, Ringwood.

Baumgartner, C. (1987) 'Arts in Education', in *Teachon: Quotes*, retrieved from http://www.teachon.com/zizi/quotes/subjects/arts/pages/arts.htm.

BBC (1999) *Walking with Dinosaurs*, BBC Worldwide, London.

Best, D. (1992) *The Rationality of Feeling: Understanding the Arts in Education*, Falmer, London.

Bolton, G. (1998) *Acting in Classroom Drama: A Critical Analysis*, Trentham Books, Stoke on Trent, UK.

Bowell, P. & Heap, B. (2001) *Planning Process Drama*, Davis Fulton, London.

Bredin, H. & Santoro-Brienza, L. (2000) *Philosophies of Art and Beauty*, Edinburgh University Press, Edinburgh.

Bresler, L. & Marm, C. (eds) (2002) *The Arts In Children's Lives: Context, Culture, and Curriculum*, Kluwer Academic, Boston.

Bruner, J. (1990) *Acts of Meaning*, Harvard University Press, Cambridge, MA.

Byram, M. & Fleming, M. (eds), *Language Learning in Intercultural Perspective*, Cambridge University Press, UK.

Byron, M. (1938) *Peter Pan and Wendy Retold by May Byron*, Hodder & Stoughton, London.

Cameron, J. (2002) *Walking in this World: Practical Strategies for Creativity*, Random House, London.

Carroll, J., Anderson, M., & Cameron, D. (2006) *Real Players? Drama, Technology and Education*, Trentham Books, London.

Carroll, J. & Cameron, D. (2003) 'To the Spice Islands: Interactive Process Drama', *Fine Art Forum*, 17(8).

Castles, S. (1995) 'Introduction', paper presented at the Global Cultural Diversity Conference, Sydney.

Catterall, J.S. (2002) 'The Arts and the Transfer of Learning', in R. Deasy, *Critical Links: Learning in the Arts and Student Academic and Social Development*, Arts Education Partnership, Washington DC.

Cazden, C. (1996) 'A Pedagogy of Multi-literacies: Designing Social Futures', *Harvard Educational Review*, 66(1), 1–30.

Chapman, L. (2001) 'Can the Arts Win Hearts and Minds?' *Arts Education Policy Review*, 102(5), 21–3.

Christensen, C.B. (1992) 'Music Composition, Invented Notation and Reflection: Tools for Music Learning and Assessment (Composition Notation)', *Dissertations Abstracts International, DAI–A*, 53(06).

Clegg, A. (1972) *About our Schools*, Oxford, Blackwell.

Clegg, A. (1972) *The Changing Primary School—its Problems and Priorities*, Chatto & Windus, London.

Connelly, F.M. & Clandinin, D.J. (1996) 'Teachers' Professional Knowledge Landscapes: Teacher Stories: Stories of Teachers—School Stories—Stories of Schools', *Educational Researcher*, 25(3), 24–30.

Cooper-Solomon, D. (1995) 'The Arts are Essential', *School Arts*, 94(6), 29.

Csikszentmihalyi, M. (1990) 'Literacy and Intrinsic Motivation', *Daedalus*, 119(2), 119.

Davies, M. (2003) *Movement and Dance in Early Childhood* (2nd edn), Sage Publications, Thousand Oaks, California.

Davis, J.H. (2005) 'Redefining Ratso Rizzo: Learning from the Arts about Process and Reflection', *Phi Delta Kappan*, 87, 11–17.

Davis, S. (2006) 'Cyberdrama and Potential for Youth Engagement', *Applied Theatre Research*, Number 7, 2006, retrieved 24 April 2008 from http://www.griffith.edu.au/__data/assets/pdf_file/0005/52907/davis.pdf.

Davis, J. & Gardner, H. (1992) 'The Cognitive Revolution: Consequences for the Understanding and Education of the Child as Artist', in B. Reimer & R.A. Smith (eds), *The Arts, Education and Aesthetic Knowing*, University of Chicago Press, Chicago.

Deasy, R. (2002) *Critical Links: Learning in the Arts and Student Academic and Social Development*, Arts Education Partnerships, Washington.

Department of Education (2005) *National Review of School Music Education: Augmenting the diminished*, DEST & Centre for Learning, Change and Development, Murdoch University, Perth.

Dewey, J. (1934) *Art as Experience*, Minton, Balch, New York.

Donelan, K. (2002) 'Embodied Practices: Ethnography and Intercultural Drama in the Classroom', *NJ (Drama Australia Journal)*, 26(2), 35–46.

Drama Australia (2004) *Equity and Diversity Guidelines*, retrieved 22 September 2007 from http://www.dramaaustralia.org.au/guidelines.html.

Drama Australia (2006) *Australian Drama Education Magazine*, Drama Australia, Brisbane.

Dreyfuss, R. (1996) Speech at the 38th Annual Grammy Awards, 29 February 1996.

Dunbar-Hall, P. (1996) 'Designing a Teaching Model for Popular Music', in G. Spruce (ed.) *Aspects of Teaching Secondary Music: Perspectives on Practice*, Routledge (in association with the Open University), London, pp. 173–181.

Dunbar-Hall, P. (2002) 'Designing a Teaching Model for Popular Musi', in G. Spruce (ed.), *Teaching Music*, London Routledge in association with the Open University.

Dunbar-Hall, P. (2005) 'Colliding Perspectives? Music Curriculum as Cultural Studies', *Music Educators Journal*, 91(4).

Dunn, J. (2002) *Imagined Worlds in Play*, unpublished PhD thesis, Griffith University, Brisbane.

Edwards, C., Gandini, L., & Forman, G. (eds) (1998) *The Hundred Languages of Children: The Reggio Emilia Approach to Early Childhood Education*, Ablex, Westport, CT.

Efland, A. (1990) *A History of Art Education*, Teachers College Press, New York.

Eisner, E. (1976) *The Arts, Human Development, and Education*, McCutchan, Berkeley.

Eisner, E. (1982) *Cognition and Curriculum: A Basis for Deciding What to Teach*, Longman, New York.

Eisner, E. (1991) *The Enlightened Eye: Qualitative Inquiry and the Enhancement of Educational Practice*, Macmillan, New York.

Eisner, E. (2002) *The Educational Imagination: On the Design and Evaluation of School Programs*, Prentice Hall, New Jersey.

Emery, L. (1996) 'Heuristic Inquiry: Intensifying Subjectivity in Art Education Research', *Australian Art Education*, 19(3), 23–30.

Fennes, H. & Hapgood, K. (1997) *Intercultural Learning in the Classroom*, Cassell, London.

Fiske, E. (ed.) (1999) *Champions of Change: The Impact of the Arts on Learning*, Arts Education Partnership /President's Committee on the Arts and the Humanities, Washington, DC.

Fleming, M. (1998) 'Cultural Awareness and Dramatic Art Forms', in M. Byram & M. Fleming (eds), *Language Learning in Intercultural Perspective* (pp. 147–57), Cambridge University Press, Cambridge.

Flood, J., Brice Heath, S. & Lapp, D. (1997) *Handbook of Research on Teaching Literacy through the Communicative and Visual Arts*, Prentice-Hall, London.

Florida, R. (2002) *The Rise of the Creative Class and How it's Transforming Work, Leisure, Community and Everyday Life*, Basic Books, New York.

Florida, R. (2005a) *The Flight of the Creative Class*, HarperBusiness, New York.

Florida, R. (2005b) *Cities and the Creative Class*, Routledge, New York.

Fowler, C. (1994) 'Strong Arts, Strong Schools', *Educational Leadership*, 52(3).

Fox, M. (1994) *Tough Boris*, Harcourt Brace, Orlando Fl.

Gardiner, F., Fox, A., Knowles, F. & Jeffrey, D. (1996) 'Learning Improved by Arts Training', *Nature*, 381, 284.

Gardner, H. (1979) 'Development Psychology after Piaget: An Approach in Terms of Symbolization', *Human Development*, 22, 73–88.

Gardner, H. (1980) *Artful Scribbles: The Significance of Children's Drawings*, Basic Books, New York.

Gardner, H. (1983) *Frames of Mind*, Basic Books, Inc., New York.

Gardner, H. (1990) *Art Education and Human Development*, The Getty Center for Education in the Arts, Los Angeles.

Gardner, H. & Perkins, D. (1989) *Art, Mind, and Education: Research from Project Zero*, University of Illinois, Urbana.

Gee, J. (2005) *Why Video Games are Good for Your Soul: Pleasure and Learning*, Common Ground, Altona.

Golomb, C. (1992) *The Child's Creation of a Pictorial World*, University of California Press, Oxford, England.

Grady, S. (2000) *Drama and Diversity*, Heinemann, Portsmouth, NH.

Greenberg, M. (1972) 'A Preliminary Report of the Effectiveness of a Pre-school Music Curriculum with Pre-school Head Start Children', *Council for Research in Music Education Bulletin*, 29, 13–16.

Greene, M. (1992) 'Texts and Margins', *Harvard Educational Review*, 61(1), 1–18.

Greene, M. (1995) *Releasing the Imagination: Essays on Education, the Arts, and Social Change*, Jossey-Bass, San Francisco.

Grumet, M. (2004) 'No One Learns Alone', in N. Rabkin & R. Redmond (eds), *Putting the Arts in the Picture: Reframing Education in the 21st Century*, Columbia College, Chicago.

Grumet, M. (2007) 'Third Things: The Wondrous Progeny of Arts Integration', *Journal of Artistic and Creative Education*, 1(1), 115–39.

Guidici, C. & Rinaldi, C. (2001) *Making Learning Visible: Children as Individual and Group Learners*, Project Zero, Harvard Graduate School of Education, Cambridge, MA.

Gulbenkian Report (1982) *The Arts in Schools: Principles, Practice and Provision*, Gulbenkian Institute, London.

Hanna, J. (1979) *To Dance is Human: A Theory of Non-verbal Communication*, University of Texas Press, Austin.

Harker, R. (ed.) (1990) *Education and Cultural Capital*, Macmillan Press, London.

Haseman, B. (1990) 'Working Out!: A Survey of Drama in Queensland Secondary Schools', *NADIE Journal*, vol. 14, no. 2, 34–41.

Haseman, B. (2002) 'The "Creative Industry" of Designing a Contemporary Drama Curriculum, *Melbourne Studies in Education*, 43(2), 119–29.

Heathcote, D. & Bolton, G. (1995) *Drama for Learning: Dorothy Heathcote's Mantle of the Expert Approach to Education*, Heinemann, Portsmouth NH.

Hergé (1974a) *The Secret of the Unicorn*, Methuen, London.

Hergé (1974b) *Tintin—Red Rackham's Treasure*, Methuen, London.

Holt, J. (1967) *How Children Learn*, Pitman, New York.

Huizinga, J. (1970) *Homo Ludens: A Study of the Play Element in Culture*, Temple, London.

Hunter, M.A. (2005) *Education and the Arts Research Overview*, Australia Council for the Arts, Sydney.

Jeanneret, N. (2006) 'The National Review of Music in Schools and the Endless Debate about Music in Primary Schools', *Australian Journal of Music Education*, 1, 93–7.

Jeanneret, N. & Forrest, D. (in press) 'Policy and Music Education: A "New" Culture of "Creativity"?', in C.C. Leung, R.L.C. Yip, & T. Imada (eds), *Music Education Policy and Implementation: International Perspectives*, Hirosaki University Press, Japan.

Johnson, H.L. (2007) 'Aesthetic Experience and Early Language and Literacy Development', *Early Child Development and Care*, 177(3).

Laban, R. (1971) *The Mastery of Movement*, Plays, Boston MA.

Laurel, B. (1993) *Computers as Theatre*, Reading, Addison-Wesley, MA.

Leach, J. (2001) 'A Hundred Possibilities: Creativity, Community and ICT', in A. Craft, R. Jeffrey, & M. Liebling (eds), *Creativity in Education*, Continuum, New York, pp. 175–94.

Leong, S. (1999) 'The Plight of Novice Music Teachers in Australia: Initial Preparation and Workplace Expectations', *Issues in Educational Research*, 9(1).

Lester, A. (1989) *Imagine*, Allen & Unwin, Crows Nest.

Lowenfeld, V. (1947) *Creative and Mental Growth*, Macmillan, New York.

Lunenfeld, P. (1996) 'Theorizing in Real Time: Hyperaesthetics for the Technoculture', *After-Image* (Jan.–Feb.), retrieved 24 April 2008 from http://findarticles.com/p/articles/mi_m2479/is_n4_v23/ai_18339993.

Mackinlay, E. & Dunbar-Hall, P. (2003) 'Historical and Dialectical Perspectives on the Teaching of Aboriginal and Torres Strait Islander Musics in the Australian Education System, *Australian Journal Indigenous Education*, 32, pp. 27–40..

Mahy, M. (1985) *The Man Whose Mother Was a Pirate*, Dent, London.

Mallan, K. (1999) *In the Picture: Perspectives on Picture Book Art and Artists*, Centre for Information Studies, Charles Sturt University, Wagga Wagga, NSW.

Manley, A. & O'Neill, C. (eds) (1997) *Dreamseekers*, Heinemann, Portsmouth, NH.

Marshall, A. (2004) 'Singing Your Own Songlines: Approaches to Indigenous Drama', in M. Mooney & J. Nichols (eds), *Drama Journeys: Inside Drama Learning* (pp. 55–76), Currency Press, Sydney.

Matthews, J. (1999) *The Art of Childhood and Adolescence: The Construction of Meaning*, Falmer, London.

McLaren, P.L. & Giarelli, J.M. (eds) (1995) *Critical Theory and Educational Research*, State University of New York Press, Albany.

McLean, J. (1996) *An Aesthetic Framework in Drama: Issues and Implications*, NADIE Publications, Brisbane.

Miller, C. & Saxton, J. (2004) *Into the Story: Language in Action through Drama*, Heinemann, Portsmouth, NH.

Miller, J. & Seller, W. (1990) *Curriculum: Perspectives and Practices*, Copp Clark Pitman, Toronto.

Ministerial Council on Education, Employment, Training and Youth Affairs, & Council (2007) *National Education and the Arts Statement*, Cultural Ministers' Council & MCEETYA, Forrest ACT.

Morgan, N. & Saxton, J. (1989) *Teaching Drama: A Mind of Many Wonders*, Stanley Thorne, London.

Neelands, J. (2002) '11/09 The space in our hearts', *Summer 2002*, 4–10.

Neelands, J. & Dickenson, R. (2006) *Improve your Primary School through Drama*, David Fulton, London.

Nicholson, H. (1999) 'Aesthetic Values, Drama Education and the Politics of Difference', *NJ (Drama Australia Journal)*, 23(2), 81–91.

Nicholson, H. (ed.) (2000) *Teaching Drama*, Continuum, London and New York.

O'Neill, C. (1995) *Dramaworlds: A Framework for Process Drama*, Heinemann, Portsmouth, NH.

O'Toole, J. (1992) *The Process of Drama: Negotiating Art and Meaning*, Routledge, London.

O'Toole, J. & Donelan, K. (eds) (1996) *Drama, Culture and Empowerment*, IDEA Publications, Brisbane.

O'Toole, J. & Dunn, J. (2002) *Pretending to Learn*, Pearson Education Australia, Frenchs Forest.

Oreck, B. (2006) 'Artistic Choices: A Study of Teachers Who Use the Arts in the Classroom, *International Journal of Education & the Arts*, 7(8).

Parsons, B., Schaffner, M., Little, G., & Felton, H. (1984) *Drama, Language and Learning: NADIE Paper No 1*, National Association for Drama in Education, Hobart.

Pascoe, R. (2003) 'The Language of Drama: Making and Communicating Meaning', in J. Livermore (ed.), *More Than Words Can Say, A View of Literacy through the Arts*, University of Canberra, Canberra.

Perrin, S. (1994) 'Education in the Arts is an Education for Life', *Phi Delta Kappan*, 75(6), 452.

Piaget, J. (1962) *Play, Dreams and Imitation in Childhood*, Routledge & Kegan Paul, London.

Podlozny, A. (2000) 'Strengthening Verbal Skills through the Use of Classroom Drama: A Clear Link', *Journal of Aesthetic Education*, 34(3/4), 239–75.

Polanyi, M. (1967) *The Tacit Dimension*, Anchor Books, New York.

Prensky, M. (2001) 'Digital Natives, Digital Immigrants, Part II: Do They Really Think Differently?', *On the Horizon*, 9(6).

Prensky, M. (2007) *Games and Simulations in Online Learning: Research and Development Frameworks*, Information Science Publishers, Hershey PA.

QSA (2002) *The Arts: Years 1 to 10 Syllabus*, retrieved 15 April 2007 from http://www.qsa.qld.edu.au/downloads/syllabus/kla_arts_syll.pdf.

Rabkin, N. & Redmond, R. (eds.) (2004) *Putting the Arts in the Picture: Reframing Education in the 21st Century*, Columbia College, Chicago.

Read, H. (1943) *Education Through Art*, Faber and Faber, London.

Reid, L.A. (1986) '"Art" and the Arts', in M. Ross (ed.), *Assessment in the Arts*, Pergamon Press, Oxford.

Reimer, B. (1992) 'What Knowledge is of Most Worth in the Arts?', in B. Reimer & R.A. Smith (eds), *The Arts, Education and Aesthetic Knowing*, University of Chicago Press, Chicago.

Reimer, B. (2003) *A Philosophy of Music Education: Advancing the Vision*, Prentice Hall, New Jersey.

Robinson, K. (1982) *The Arts in Schools: Principles, Practice and Provision*, Gulbenkian Society, London.

Robinson, K. (1999) *All Our Futures: Creativity, Culture and Education: The Report of the NAACE Committee*, National Advisory Committee on Creative and Cultural Education, London.

Robinson, K. (2001) *Out of Our Minds: Learning to be Creative*, Capstone Books, Oxford.

Robinson, K. (2005) 'Do Schools Kill Creativity?', lecture recorded online, Technology, Ideas, Design: Ideas Worth Spreading, retrieved 24 April 2008 from http://www.ted.com/index.php/talks/view/id/66.

Rosen, H. (1999) 'Narrative in Intercultural Education', *European Journal of Intercultural Studies*, 10(3), 343–53.

Rosenholtz, S. (1989) *Teachers' Workplace: The Social Organization of Schools*, Longman, New York.

Ross, M. (1983) *The Arts, A Way of Knowing*, Pergamon, Oxford.

Runfola, M. & Rutkowski, J. (1992) 'General Music Curriculum', in R. Colwell (ed.), *Handbook of Research on Music Teaching and Learning* (pp. 697–709), Schirmer, New York.

Saldaña, J. (1995) *Drama of Color*, Heinemann, Portsmouth, NH.

Scott, K., in J. Johnson (Project Director) (1991) 'What Children Think About Talk' in *Talk and Learning 5–16: In-service Pack on Oracy for Teachers*, The Open University, Milton Keynes, UK.

Simons, J. (2000) 'Walking in Another Person's Shoes: Storytelling and Role-play', in Nicholson, H. (ed.), *Teaching Drama* (pp. 16–25). Continuum, London and New York.

Simons, J. (2002) 'Drama and the Learner', in *Melbourne Studies in Education*, 43(2), 1–11.

Slade, P. (1954) *Child Drama*, Cassell, London.

Slade, P. (1977) *Natural Dance*, Hodder and Stoughton, UK.

Smith, J. (1986) *Three Billy Goats Gruff Retold by Judith Smith*, Methuen, North Ryde.

Smith, R.A. (2001) 'The Harvard REAP Study: Inherent "Versus" Instrumental Values', *Arts Education Policy Review*, 102(5).

Snow, C.P. (1959) *The Two Cultures*, Senate House, Cambridge.

Stevens, R.S. (2000) 'Where Are We Twenty Years On? A Review of Australian Music Education Research for the Period 1978–1997', *Research Studies in Music Education*, 14, 61–75.

Stevens, R.S. (2003) *Trends in School Music Education Provision in Australia*, The Music Council of Australia in collaboration with the Australian Society for Music Education and the Australian Music Association, Sydney.

Swanwick, K. (1988) *Music, Mind, and Education*, Routledge, London.

Taylor, P. (1998) *Redcoats and Patriots: Reflective Practice in Drama and Social Studies*, Heinemann, Portsmouth, NH.

Taylor, P. (2000) *The Drama Classroom: Action, Reflection, Transformation*, Routledge/Falmer, London.

Taylor, R. & Andrews, G. (1993) *The Arts in the Primary School*, Falmer Press, London.

Tishman, S., Perkins, D.N. & Jay, E. (1995) *The Thinking Classroom: Learning and Teaching in a Culture of Thinking*, Allyn and Bacon, Boston.

Toye, N. & Prendiville, F. (2000) *Drama and Traditional Story for the Early Years*, Routledge Falmer, London.

Trinh, T.M. (1989) *Woman, Native, Other: Writing Postcoloniality and Feminism*, Indiana University Press, Bloomington.

VCAA (2007a) *Victorian Essential Learning Standards 2005–2007*, retrieved from http://vels.vcaa.vic.edu.au/.

VCAA (2007b) *Victorian Essential Learning Standards: English*, retrieved 6 November 2007 from http://vels.vcaa.vic.edu.au/essential/discipline/english/index.html.

VCAA (2007c), *Curriculum and Standards Framework II*, State Government of Victoria, Melbourne, retrieved 24 April 2008 from http://www.vcaa.vic.edu.au/prep10/csf/index.html.

Vygotsky, L. (1971) *The Psychology of Art*, MIT Press, Boston.

Vygotsky, L. (1978) *Mind and Society: The Development of Higher Psychological Processes*, Harvard University Press, Cambridge, MA.

Wagner, B.-J. (1998) *Educational Drama and Language Arts: What the Research Shows*, Heinemann, Portsmouth, NH.

Wallas, G. (1926) *The Art of Thought*, Jonathan Cape, London.

Watkins, M. (2005) 'Magical Encounters with "Art Rich" Picturebooks', *ARTicle*, 7(3), 15–19.

Weiss, G. (1992) 'From Skills to Expression: The Arts in the Early Years of School 1880–1970', *Australian Art Education*, 16(2), 32–8.

Wiggins, J. (2001) *Teaching for Musical Understanding*, McGraw-Hill Higher Education, New York.

Wild, M. & Brooks, R. (2000) *Fox*, Allen & Unwin, NSW.

Winston, J. (1998) *Drama, Narrative and Moral Education: Exploring Traditional Tales in the Primary Years*, Falmer Press, London.

Winston, J. (2000) *Drama, Literacy and Moral Education 5–11*, David Fulton, London.

Winston, J. (2004) *Drama and English at the Heart of the Curriculum*, David Fulton, London.

Winter, J. & Juan, A. (2002) *Frida*, Arthur Levine Books, New York.

Wolf, D. & Gardner, H. (1980) 'Beyond Playing or Polishing: A Development View of Artistry', in J. Houseman (ed.), *Arts and the Schools* (pp. 47–77), McGraw-Hill, New York.

Wright, P. & Rasmussen, B. (2001) 'Children and Drama: Knowing Differently', in M. Robertson & R. Gerber (eds), *Children's Ways of Knowing: Learning Through Experience*, ACER Press, Melbourne.

Wright, S. (2003) *The Arts: Young Children, and Learning*, Pearson Education, Boston, MA.

Wright, S. (ed.) (2003) *Children, Meaning-making and the Arts*, Pearson/Prentice Hall, NSW, Australia.

Young, W. (1974) 'Efficacy of a Self-help Program in Music for Disadvantaged Pre-schools, *Journal of Research in Music Education* (22), 158–169.

Index